God's
BAD BOY

James Blake and the System

To: Aunt Agnes and Cousin Lydia —

I love you beyond words!

Bessie

Dr. Bessie W. Blake 4/26/2014

Lit Lore   New York
2014

God's BAD BOY: James Blake and the System

By Dr. Bessie W. Blake

Copyright 2014

Blake, Bessie W.
God's BAD BOY: James Blake and the System
ISBN: 978-0-9835699-5-4 (casebound)
        978-0-9835699-4-7 (paper)

First printing

Cover Design: James Carter
Cover Photo: Eugene "Kwame" Gervin

Library of Congress number: 2013922569

Published by   Lit Lore
                    P. O Box 3924
                    New York, NY 10163

http: www.litlore.com
email: LL@LitLore.com

Acknowledgement

God's BAD BOY: James Blake and the System is the story of my husband's journey from Little Jimmy, the frightened boy, to the person he has become. To provide a full and candid sense of the man, I have chosen to write from his point of view rather than my own. Thus, Jimmy's voice is the "I" that you hear throughout the narrative.

Because Jimmy does not wish to open old wounds for friends and associates, he has asked me to change the real names of some and to use only first names of others who might want to mask agonizing periods in their lives. The goal in revealing personal episodes of his life is to shed light on forces that shaped him, and to do so in ways that benefit children.

While the events of this book are viewed through my husband's lens, I am grateful to his sisters Gloria, Carol, Frances and Ruth; and his aunts Carrie Mae and Constine for sharing difficult stories that triggered some of his buried memories.

Thanks to all who helped to make this healing prayer for children available to readers. Much appreciation goes to RiShana Blake for her tireless effort as editor; to Rev. Alfonso Wyatt and Dr. Robert Mendelson for their critical reads of early drafts of the manuscript; to Takbir Blake, for his poem; to John Banks for his many hours of technical assistance; to Dr. Anthony Gronowicz for his rigorous attention to the final manuscript; and finally, to Jack Estes who has had an immensurable impact on my writing.

Dr. Bessie W. Blake – January 2014

Foreword

In an effort to understand the plight of children under the supervision of social services agencies, Gil Noble's popular Black affairs talk show, *Like It Is,* profiled me on Sunday, March 21, 2004. Immediately after the broadcast on ABC's New York affiliate, Lula King, my former youth activity director, shouted into the phone, "You our leader! All the Woodycrest children watched and we agree; you are our leader."

That Monday I received an excited call from Gil, "The response has been astounding!"

"Man my phone's ringing off the hook," I said.

We were busy swapping comments from emails and phone calls that praised the broadcast when a woman in her seventies appeared at my door leaning on a cane and peering down at me.

"Can I help you with something?" I asked, hanging up the phone.

"No, I don't want to interrupt your business. I come down here just to look at you. I saw you on *Like It Is* and bad as my Arthritis is this morning, I decided to get out that bed and come on downtown to gaze on you."

"Come in and have a seat."

"No, son, I got to get these old tired bones back up to Harlem. Just wanted to thank you for having the courage to tell your story. It's my story too." She nodded, "Thank the Lord!" and hobbled away.

Ten years later I still receive calls from parents and children—their voices full of liberating hope because I spoke up. In answering the many questions about the details of my life, *God's Bad Boy* took shape. It is my fervent prayer that this book gives voice to the thousands of adults who were displaced as children; encouragement to today's abused, neglected and dejected youth, and guidance for their concerned helpers.

Gil passed in April of last year but his legacy lives on. He will be remembered for giving a voice to the voiceless; and, I personally thank him for inspiring me to get moving with this project.

Bessie, I love you for mystical and tangible reasons. I appreciate your steady hand in my affairs and I thank you for patiently listening and for marshaling your talents to bring my story to life.

James Blake – January - 2014

Dedicated

to

Gloria and Joseph - Noah and Matthew

Part One:

The shadow knows

———•———

On the morning of the worst day, a passion for helping was born. Mama cooked breakfast as usual. After feeding us, she followed Granny around the house like a small child. I was nine years old and like most boys in 1950s New York City, my mind was on Johnny Ride the Pony, Stick Ball, Skelly and other summer street games. I didn't notice Mama until she grabbed Granny around the waist, slid to her knees and moaned, "Pleeease don't go. If you go, I won't be here when you come back."

The calm on Granny's face betrayed her panic as she snapped, "Nettie stop your foolishness!"

Mama then released her hold and returned to the kitchen. "Whaaat a friend we have in Jeeeesus..." rang throughout the apartment. The hymn usually meant hot biscuits to follow but that morning she was baking a cake for my younger sister Carol's eighth birthday. Singing trailed off to humming, interrupted by soft grunts as Mama reached for a spice tin from the cabinet, then bent to check the flame, making sure the oven was the right temperature. Her melodic voice reassured me as I inhaled the sweet aroma of hot dough. Granny relaxed and went off to work. I hung around long enough to wolf down a warm piece of sampler cake before rushing out to play.

Sylvester, Billy, Henry and I played war on the empty construction site in back of my house. We ducked behind cement blocks with finger-guns cocked and thumb-triggers pumping. The scene rolled like an action-packed movie:

1

"Bang! Bang-bang!" Sylvester and I take aim at Billy and Henry who dive behind the dirt mound.

"We got you, Henry! Come on out! We got you!" I yell. Billy pops up and ducks back down.

"You dead! I got you! You dead!" Sylvester starts toward the mound then stops. "Little Jimmy, ain't that your mama?" he points at my kitchen window.

My head jerks up.

Mama stands tall, slender, black skin glistening in the afternoon sun. Her hair is wild, but her face is serene. Calmly, she steps off the second floor ledge.

My heart stops. I'm frozen in time. Then, "Thud!" Time ticks past me.

"She's running toward the bay!" It's my father's voice. "Catch her! Catch her! Nettieeee!" he takes chase. Neighbors rush to his aid and my friends join in the race while I'm glued in place.

Uncle Esau tackles Mama. Down she goes arms and legs thrashing in the weeds but quickly Daddy clutches her with his thick arms.

Abruptly, like a speeding car slamming its brakes, the action halted then crept forward in a slow-paced slideshow.

Neighbors mill in front of our house... Daddy holds tight to Mama... Strange men in white suits take Mama and Daddy away... A car with flashing lights eases down our street... The day fades to blackness.

Like Mama had sworn at breakfast, she was not there when my grandmother returned from work. Faint rays of sunset forced their way through the trees and lay across the road as Granny trudged in and out of shadows up the slope to our house at 32-49 108th Street in Corona, Queens. I ran to her shouting with high-pitched excitement, "I was playing, and out the window Mama jumped! She in the hospital!"

I can't remember Granny's immediate reaction to my news, but later that night, I overheard her say to Aunt Carrie Mae, "Lucky she didn't hurt herself today. Lucky she didn't break her leg jumping like that."

For days, Granny and Aunt Carrie Mae searched through the shattered pieces of Mama's life. They thought none of the children were listening but I hid behind the kitchen door peeping at them and straining to hear.

"There was signs," Aunt Carrie Mae sniffled on the first night of conversations. "Remember last week Nettie left them children in Flushing?"

"Yeah," Granny recalled. " *'Where your children?'* I asked. *'Oh I left them in Flushing. I'll go back and get them,'* she said without battin' uh eye."

"Thank God she found them children where she left them. We shoulda went with her. We shoulda knowed then that..."

"Lord, Carrie Mae! How we gon' know?" Granny retorted and ended the conversation.

The next time I overheard them from my hiding place behind the door, I blushed warm with embarrassment at their description of Mama.

"Nettie slipped into that favorite straight dress that hugged her body in all the right places and headed for the door," said Aunt Carrie Mae.

"Yeah, nights at the Silver Rail Bar took on new meaning when Howard's marriage failed," added Granny.

"Oh Nettie loved that man," Aunt Carrie Mae continued.

Granny nodded, "Back when she was twenty-two, and we still lived in Clear Pond, South Carolina all Nettie and Cousin Julie Mae could talk about was 'Howard and BoBo,' but Howard was no good. I saw it the minute he started breaking the house rules. I didn't care how crazy Nettie was about him, I kept a decent home. When he came calling, I said, *'Rest your hat on the hook by the door.'* It showed good manners. I kept respectable courting hours too. At nine o'clock I tapped on the wall: *'Time to git your hat!'* He'd snatch his hat off the hook and head over to Cousin Valerie's house because her mama didn't have no rules."

"Wasn't that something," Aunt Carrie Mae shook her head. "Yes we had rules, but was that a reason for him to fool around? You know Nettie would complain to me. I was only twelve or thirteen at the time but I said to her, 'Valerie got a baby! Ain't that a shame! What kind of man wants a girl with a baby instead of a nice girl like you, Nettie, with no baby?' I tried to be grown up and comfort her; but shameful or not, Howard married Valerie and it almost killed my sister."

They went on and on until their conversation broke into bits and pieces that were hard for a nine-year-old like me to understand: "...wild thoughts!" "Nettie kept all the rules." "Valerie got her man!" "Nettie worked herself into a heap of coals and lit the fire with shots of moonshine." "...showed up on their wedding night! Taunted the bride 'Might be your husband but he's mine tonight.' "Valerie

4

yelled and cried." "Howard left with Nettie. Next day, he went home to his wife."

"Now what kind of man was that?" Aunt Carrie Mae asked Granny and then added, "I told her straight up, 'Nettie, Julie Mae got her BoBo but you ain't gon' never get your Howard."

None of it made sense to my young mind. After many days of snooping, I learned that Mama's wild night with Howard, was followed by her move from Clear Pond ten miles to Bamberg, South Carolina, where she worked as a cook for a White family. Then, when she was twenty-five a man-friend paid her way to New York in 1937.

What I didn't learn was how these facts explained why my mother had jumped out of the window. Even worse, Granny and Aunt Carrie Mae couldn't stop our neighbors' gossip. They whispered: "She runs the street with him all hours of the night." "She was planning to leave her husband but the Toomer Boys drove him off." The chit-chat that had swirled out of reach soon pierced me with angry stabs.

My mother seemed helpless in the face of so many verbal attacks. I became her nine-year-old defender. Without her knowing, I ducked in and out of doorways and trailed her whenever she left the house. If mystery man Howard showed up, I was going to fight him. Of course, I wasn't aware at the time, but this early determination to protect my mother left me with compassion for needy, helpless people.

I must admit, though, my grit to stand and fight for Mama came with mixed emotions. I didn't want to believe whisperings about "another man," but the talk of threats from her brothers, known in the neighborhood as the Toomer Boys, was hard to ignore because I knew them up close.

Violent images of my uncles were fresh in my mind. Just weeks earlier, they had been sitting at the kitchen table eating, drinking, smoking and gambling when, without warning, foul words landed like bricks against the plasterboard partition that separated them from my twelve-year-old sister Gloria, my ten-year-old brother Joseph, Jr. and me. Granny must have been outside; otherwise, the argument over money wouldn't have developed into the brawl that made us children scramble to the end of the bed just in time to see a knife slice through the air. It split open Uncle Jacob's massive upper arm like a red meat watermelon. He grabbed a chair and flung it across the room at one of his brothers' head. In all the confusion, I couldn't tell whether Uncle Willie or Uncle Esau was doing the cutting, but blood was everywhere. Fist pounded against flesh. I tried to keep my eyes on the knife, but afraid someone was going to die, I squeezed my lids shut tight. The ruckus rumbled on. A small china cabinet crashed against the wall; dishes shattered on the floor; bodies thumped against one another. The room quaked until Granny appeared out of nowhere. "I brought you into the world and I'll take you out!" she shouted above the fray. The fight ended instantly.

I had decided that day never to cross my uncles. If there was such a person as Howard hanging around, he probably felt the same way. When the Toomer Boys threatened a man he usually left running. So, I believed the rumor about their sending him packing for messing with their sister. However, the murmuring did not stop with Howard's disappearance. *"Yeah, he's dead; she got the news too."*

"After that, Nettie was never the same," Granny said and began planting rumors as truth in the shadows of my young mind.

In the swirl of confusion, I stayed silent. It was Gloria who spoke up about Mama. "Something is wrong," she told Granny.

My older sister was in Miss Cornbloom's sixth grade class at Public School 143 and had gone to school with her hair uncombed and her slip hanging. Until then, she had always been impeccably neat. When the other children began teasing her, Miss Cornbloom took her aside and asked about our mother. That day Gloria came straight home to Granny.

"Something's wrong with Mama," she cried.

"Why you say that?" Granny wanted to know.

"'Cause she won't comb my hair."

"Stop it Gloria! You know your Mama do your hair."

The Toomers were hush-hush that way. Silence covered a heap of mess. While Gloria's physical appearance worsened, so did Mama's health; and, bits of information continued to drift to me when adults thought I wasn't listening. "Joe saw Nettie's doctor," Granny half-whispered to Aunt Carrie Mae. "She can't..." (or was it "*shouldn't*"?) ...have no more babies." In muted tones, jumbled facts reached my ears. Without the full picture, I assembled the fragments in my own childish way: *It's my fault Mama's sick. If I hadn't been born, she'd be fine.* In search of a truth that would prove me wrong, my eavesdropping increased, but no simple answers were found. Any number of painful upsets or strains could have triggered Mama's breakdown: too many children too fast, a love lost forever, an unruly family crowded under one roof, a domestic's job where, *she was raped by the man of the house,* someone had hissed.

I coped mostly with mystery. There was, however, one firm reality: the pressure of it all was too much for Mama.

Like the earth after a major quake, things shifted in our house. I sulked for most of the week and perked up on weekends when Mama visited from the hospital. I couldn't really see the change in her. She was still the cheerful person who delighted me. Because she knew how much I liked to play outside, whenever it rained she teased, "Seems like it's raining all the time," then followed quickly with "Rain, rain ago away, Little Jimmy wants to play." She sang to my seven-year-old sister, Carol, and me, "Carol will take the high road and Little Jimmy will take the low road and I'll be in Scotland before them." I was filled with glee whenever she included me in her songs. She was a great dancer too. We bounced around her room to blues rhythms; and, occasionally, she'd grab Joseph or Gloria and sway gently to her favorite tune, "Stormy Weather," by Lena Horne. She didn't cook as often as before, but boy she could still "burn." I loved her fried chicken and biscuits, the fruit and sweet potato pies, and her butter pound cakes.

With Mama home, everything glowed. She sang, "Little Jimmy wants to play," and I would hit the door running. I felt more carefree when I entered my world of nine and ten-year-olds chasing up and down the block.

Starting at the top of the hill, scooters—made from discarded wooden milk crates and wheels from once new skates—zipped down the street weaving between clusters of children and dodging the traffic. Except for interruptions by passing cars and short breaks for meals we played from early morning until bedtime. At nightfall everybody crowded into Glenn Miller's hallway, arranged ourselves on the stairway leading to the second floor apartment, and howled at the teenager's tall tales about how Peewee Reese got his name by peeing around the bases.

The fun of our children's world dwarfed everything else—until that frigid Saturday that Carol kept whining about the cold. I was engaged in a serious game of Johnny Ride the Pony with Billy Moore, Sylvester Moore (not brothers), Freddie Ferdinand, and my brother Joseph with their backs bent parallel to the ground. One behind the other, their arms gripped tightly around the waist of the boy ahead of him. The human chain reached out and latched onto me as I leaned against the wall of one of the houses. Interlocked in this fashion, they were the pony and I was their pillar. They thought I chose to be the pillar because I was too skinny, too weak to bear the weight of the guys from the other team, when actually, I was too smart to have a group of running, jumping, bucking boys on my back.

At nine, I had already learned caution. The previous summer, in a game of follow-the-leader, the boy ahead of me had straddled his legs wide but failed to clear the fire hydrant in a leapfrog jump. I watched him rolling on the sidewalk, holding himself and groaning. From that day, I refused to jump fire hydrants, or dart across the street in an attempt to outrun a fast-moving car in a game of chicken. Later, in my teens, I would refuse to jab a needle in my arm. If it looked painful, I wanted no part of it.

A game of Johnny Ride the Pony was no exception. I was satisfied with my job as pillar. Or, I would have been if Carol had stopped whining about the cold. Each time she came to me, I sent her right back to play with Vera Moore (Sylvester's Sister), Barbara Moore (Billy's sister) and our cousins Clara Williams and Elizabeth Blake. But, Carol was stubborn; she kept coming. Finally, I told her, "Go inside!" Then, I pressed my back against the wall to anchor the pony and warned my team, "Here comes a crazy rider." Henry landed, "Ayyeee!"

ɔur rowdy shrieks, a thud was heard the
_e Sylvester yelled, "Whoaaa! Little Jimmy
_ɑr hit your sister!"

Carol was a tiny lump lying in the middle of 108th
Street. The driver who hit her stopped, opened the door to
get out but shut it quickly and sped away when he saw all
those Black people spilling out of their houses.

"Don't move that child! Don't you touch her!"
ordered Mrs. Moore, Sylvester's mother.

"Call an ambulance," someone in the crowd
shouted.

I raced inside to tell Mama but everyone was
crowded into Granny's tiny basement apartment.

"Let me go! Let me see about my baby! Where's my
baby?" Mama wailed. Afraid the sight of Carol bleeding in
the street would be too much, my uncles held her down.

I rushed back outside to see what was happening to
Carol. Someone had run down the street to get Daddy
from the garage where he washed cars. Meanwhile, the
scene turned chaotic as voices rose against the backdrop
of screaming sirens: "The car was gray." "No it was blue."
"You get the license plate?" "Aw man, I thought you got
it." "It was a White dude; that's all I know." Not one person
in the crowd could give a detailed description of the driver.

In all the excitement, Mama's hysteria blurred. My
eyes were glued to the men in white who scooped my
sister up and carried her and my father away just like
they had done with Mama months earlier.

I moped on our stoop for hours before Daddy
returned without Carol or an explanation. He rushed past
me and reappeared almost instantly with Mama bundled
in a winter coat and flanked by two of my uncles. They
steered her into the car and hauled her back to the
hospital.

No one noticed that it was way past time for me to come in for the night. That evening, I was called inside by the raspy voice of my radio superhero asking, "Who knows what evil lurks in the hearts of men? Hee-Hee-hee! The Shadow knows."

The Shadow was a master at mental control. He entered a room unseen to protect the innocent but his shadow loomed over the bad guys to cause confusion and interrupt their evil deeds. Usually, I listened to the program on the edge of my seat but that Saturday night I was thinking how unfair it was for Mama and Carol to be in the hospital. Evil was lurking around our house and I needed a powerful force. I didn't know anything about God or saying nightly prayers; so, I tried to conjure The Shadow's spirit to protect my sister and my mother. I guess it was sort of a prayer.

Carol stayed in the hospital for weeks. Her neck was fractured, her eyes were tangled, and she was deaf in one ear. After what seemed forever she returned home and to school. Her well-meaning teacher sat her on the front row so she could hear but the gesture put her on display. Classmates teased her about her crossed eyes and I, her own brother, was the worst culprit. I cocked my eyes and mocked, "Hey Carol, how you doing? Is it two Jimmys? Ha-Ha-Ha! Two heads? Two Carols, huh?" I didn't know that she was lucky to be alive.

Over time, Carol's eyes straightened out and her tomboy ways ruled again, but permanent hearing loss in her left ear caused her to twist to the right when anyone spoke to her. In time, I discovered that I was more deeply disturbed by my sister's accident than my antics suggested.

I thought everybody had to get hit by a car and I began to stalk the traffic on our block so that I could get my accident out of the way quickly and painlessly. In an attempt at caution, I chose slow-moving cars, darted into the street and caused the drivers to jam their brakes.

Nobody explained to me that accidents are chance happenings, mistakes that are sometimes preventable. Matter of fact, adults never discussed Carol's injuries with me, nor did they speak to me about Mama's hospitalization. At nine, I was left to sort through these two monumental events by myself.

My dance with the traffic on 108th Street continued while Mama, who had stopped coming home on weekends, slipped into the shadows of my life.

Daddy **emerged** at random periods during my childhood with two distinctly different faces: one was a charging bull, the other an overripe melon dissolving into water. The fighter knocked cats out; the gardener cried at every turn. The fierce father filled me with awe but the crumbling man frightened me. However, his contradictory demeanors were not the most persistent puzzles; the big question was figuring out my father's place in our family.

I recall few instances when Daddy was inside our house. Once he squeezed my jaw open and ordered, "Swallow it! It'll keep you from getting sick," as he forced a spoonful of thick, slick castor oil down my throat. Then, he handed me a piece of rock candy to stop the gagging and erase the nasty taste.

There was also the day my friend, Henry Johnson and I got into a scuffle in the living room. The heroic dad showed up, laced boxing gloves on two hot-headed nine-year olds and commanded, "Now, fight!" We slugged it out with no apparent winner but I swelled with pride because Daddy was no chump. He staged a fight when most adults would have grabbed a belt and whipped our behinds. If his intent was to do more than teach me the joy of boxing, he failed. I walked away from that scuffle with a lifelong passion for the fight game.

The most vivid memory of Daddy under our roof had to do with Mama. I had sneaked two quarters from pants he had left lying on a kitchen chair. Carol was still asleep but Gloria, Joseph and I were slurping down spoons of cornflakes from Daffy and Donald Duck cereal bowls when our father appeared in the doorway in his underwear.

"Which one of y'all took fifty-cents from my pocket?" No one answered but I almost strangled on the icy milk sliding down my throat.

"Little Jimmy, did you take it?" he zeroed in on me.

"No, Daddy."

Water swelled in his eyes. He sputtered, "I guess... I can't go... see your mother. I was gon' use that money for gas."

"Here Daddy," I handed over the coins. The thought of robbing my mother of a visit upset me almost as much as the sight of him quaking with tears.

Except for briefs scenes, it's hard to summon memories of my father prior to my ninth year; and, those recollections contain no images of him with Mama. I never saw my parents eat at the same table, sleep in the same bed or even talk to one another. Though I now know that they were not divorced or separated, I am not sure Daddy lived with us. I thought at the time that he didn't come inside our apartment because he didn't want to be the only Blake in a house full of Toomers. So, without a sense of my parents as a couple, I developed separate lives with each of them.

My relationship with Daddy developed in semi-public and public places. In the summer of my ninth year he emerged as the pivotal person in my life.

On 108th Street, he was the farmer. Oh, Mrs. Moore was the best gardener. Brilliant flowers flourished in the boxes beneath her windows and a patch of hearty snap beans and collards grew in her backyard. Daddy, on the other hand, cultivated the lot between the garage and

Delano's social club. The space was more an open field where, between car washes, he grew tomatoes, okra, cabbages, carrots, tight sweet watermelons no bigger than cantaloupes, and towering stalks of corn with silky tasseled ears that gleamed in the sun.

A single peach tree loaded with fruit stood in the middle of Daddy's garden. My friends and I HAD to strip it! In our eagerness to reach the peaches, we trampled his prize tomatoes and knocked over stalks of corn. When Daddy walked up, sweet juice was trickling down my chin, into my palm and along my inner arm. The friends scattered and left me to face the music.

In 1952, when just about every parent believed in whipping, Daddy did not. Weeping was usually his weapon. With tears in his eyes, "Don't make me hit you. If I hit you, I will kill you," he'd scold; but that day he pulled off his belt and tore up my backside. It was the only time my father lifted his hand at me.

As much as Daddy loved gardening, boxing was his true passion. In the forties he had worked out constantly and fought with local amateurs in anticipation of a bout with Joe Louis. His excitement for boxing dated back to his arrival in Corona in 1936 when the neighborhood was gradually changing from Italian to Black and the talk of Joe Louis' battering of former heavy weight champion, Primo Carnera, lingered on everybody's lips. Following that fight, ethnic strain hung in the air like a stalled cloud. People were also upset by Joe Louis' shocking loss to Max Schmeling in Germany earlier that year.

Happily, in less than two years, neighborhood tensions had been replaced by a frenzy of enthusiasm shared between Blacks, Italians and all Americans. On June 22, 1938, Joe Louis stepped into the ring at Yankee Stadium and avenged his 1936 loss to Schmeling. Along with every Black community in America, the thrill of Louis' conquest swept Corona in a tide of jubilation. Hundreds of people flowed into the streets dancing, drinking and bragging about how "the Brown Bomber's deadly punch took that White boy out." The knockout was a sweet vindication for Louis, a symbolic victory over Nazi aggression, a flash of hope for Blacks and the spark that set my father's sights on a boxing career.

Daddy had only a third grade education. Boxing was to be his glory ticket. In the apartment building on the corner of Northern Boulevard and 108th Street, he started his bodybuilding routine in a makeshift gym next to the boiler room. To augment his workouts, he took on strenuous jobs in the neighborhood. In the winter, he hauled wood to the many homes in Corona that still had wood-burning stoves. Summers, he delivered ice to those same houses. Daddy hadn't minded carrying twenty-five, fifty, even hundred-pound blocks of ice from the 104th Street Ice House up unending narrow flights of stairs. He had heard stories of how the very same work had made Louis muscular back in Detroit before he started his boxing career.

When America entered World War II, my father's routine changed but he still got plenty of muscle-building exercise as a longshoreman on the Brooklyn waterfront. Jobs loading supplies on warships were plentiful but after the war ended Blacks were hard pressed to get assignments. While working in the hole of a merchant ship, my father got into a heated argument demanding a job. He paid dearly for that quarrel. He could not say for certain it was the man he argued with, but someone sneaked up behind him and ripped his side open with a heavy lifting fork. Daddy thought it was the Mafia's way of putting him out of commission for future assignments, because that is exactly what happened. Even worse, it destroyed any hope of his making it big in the boxing world; and, unable to pass the physical, it completely shattered the already slim-to-no chance of him, a Black man, becoming a New York City policeman.

The closest my father came to being a police officer was the security job he landed guarding construction sites of suburban subdivisions started after the war but completed in the early fifties.

To get me out of Granny's hair, many times he took me with him to Long Island in his old humpback Chevy. We'd leave before nightfall and return after daybreak the next morning.

At age nine, sleeping in the car all night was exciting. Daddy packed a feast of bologna and cheese on Italian rolls and a jelly jar of lukewarm Kool-Aid for me. We both munched on the sandwiches but he took swigs from a bottle of Gordon Gin and laid out his plans: "See them houses; gon' get me one of them, Little Jimmy."

"I don't want to live out here; it's too spooky." The area was all woods. I squinted against pitch-blackness and wondered aloud how my friends would find me.

"Naaa, they gon' light the place up before they finish," he tried to sell me on the idea but I couldn't see it. Finished or not, the place was a no-man's-land. I wanted to stay in my world, on my block, with my friends.

Once Daddy got that Gordon Gin under his belt, his talk turned to pretty girls.

"Son, get yourself a pretty girl."

Though I had not seen her in a long time, Mama popped into my head. "Yeah Daddy, I'ma get me a pretty girl," I chirped—clueless that he was talking about women other than my mother. It would be years later before I learned that pretty girls were his buffers against hopelessness. However, on those cold nights on Long Island, he was satisfied with dreams and his gin.

When the last construction site was finished, World War II veterans moved into the new homes and none of them were Black. My father plodded through a string of odd jobs. For a while he worked at Corona's Palace Theater, known by all the neighborhood kids as The Dumps. He was the strong-arm usher who bounced onto the streets wild dudes who hung out in the movies. At first, the bullies jumped Joseph and me, but the Toomer Boys soon corrected that situation. After leaving The Dumps, Daddy did light cement work, patching crumbling stoops and driveways. He eventually ended up washing cars for a living; and, though hopes of becoming a "real" policeman had faded, he volunteered to be an auxiliary policeman. It was a duty he did with pride for his community.

Though his workout routine had ceased long ago, in 1952 Daddy was still buffed up rigid as steel. My friends and I often huddled on the sidewalk in front of the garage to watch him shadow box, and to listen to his tall tales of exploits.

"See that tree over there." Our heads swung around. "I hit a man and he went sailing over the top of it."

"Wowww!" "Oh man!" Palms slapped five around the circle. "Little Jimmy, your daddy is Superman!" "Nobody better not mess with him." We were gullible ten-year-olds—too young to know that Daddy's dreams had already zoomed beyond his reach.

Throughout the week, Finocchio's fleet of bread trucks rolled into Daddy's garage to be washed. My job was to sweep from the back of the trucks crumbs that had fallen into the ridges of the floor. I worked on my knees with a small whiskbroom. "Little Jimmy, sweep them into the dust pan; don't let them hit the sidewalk," Daddy scolded, robbing me of the best part of the job. I loved grabbing the water hose and chasing the fallen crumbs from the pavement to the gutter.

Friday was the hardest work day. A stream of Packard Clippers, Oldsmobile Ninety-Eights and Cadillac Coupe de Villes belonging to upper crust Blacks from East Elmhurst lined up for three-dollar washes or the twelve-dollar compound and simonize jobs. Everybody was in a hurry. "Joe I got to be out of here by six" one man barked. "Got a hot date tonight," bragged another. Daddy worked as fast as humanly possible but the labor was backbreaking—especially the simonizing. After he washed a car, he smeared the orange compound over it; then bending to the fenders, bumpers and doors and stretching to the roof, he rubbed the dry paste off inch by inch. Once every speck of compound was removed, he waxed the car to a brilliant shine. The Brillo-scrubbed whitewall tires and compounded rims and hubcaps topped off the job. At the end of two and a half hours, a work of art glimmered in the afternoon sun.

I loved the sight of the sparkling hubcaps and the smell of the leather interiors. Often, I climbed inside one of the cars and pretended to be the owner dressed in a three-piece suit. That fantasy turned into a cruel hoax the day Mr. Uppity himself rolled into the garage with his son. I hated the humiliation Daddy suffered under the watchful gaze of my classmate. The arrogance was unmistakable as the big-shot owner of Uppity Cleaners marched back and forth. He was a man accustomed to looking for spots and was quick to point out any little smudge. "Let me look inside, Joe." He inspected the interior and failing to find anything, he combed over the exterior. "Oh, you got some water here," he nodded at the bumper of his car.

Dressed in overalls and open goulashes, and wearing a wide grin, my father ran over and wiped the bumper down like a butler. At the very least, it had taken two sweaty hours, bending, washing, waxing and buffing to produce the shiny piece of steel that stood before us, but the quality of the work was all wasted on Mr. Uppity. He strutted around his car like a proud rooster pumping himself up by belittling my father. I swelled with angry envy. I wanted to punch Mr. Uppity for treating Daddy so poorly. At the same time, I admired and respected him and men like him; they had somehow unlocked the secret access to all that Daddy and I desired.

Lucky for me I had men other than Mr. Uppity to measure my father against. Except for Billy and me, my friends' fathers lived at home. These men were mostly hardworking but also hard-living. Mr. Walters, a name I use to protect the guilty, was an auto mechanic. He had dirty nails and I never saw him without oil smeared over his clothes and up to his elbows. He drank hard liquor, puked the filthiest curses, and beat his wife and children with his fists. He taught me to detest foul language but it seems he taught his neighbors to look the other way. "He sho' provide for that big family of his," they nodded. Mother and children had a roof over their heads and food on the table, and it was enough to make an entire community ignore Mr. Walters' violence. Nobody wanted to "drag a neighbor's dirty laundry out for a public washing." Since the courts didn't intervene in domestic abuse matters like they do today, the battering continued for as long as I knew the Walters. When I saw the scars and bruises on my friend, Sparrow, I was glad Daddy didn't believe in hitting.

Then, there was the neighbor I will call Mr. Berry. He was a pudgy man with straight black hair combed back off his pale face. Like Mr. Walters, he was a boozer but the similarities ended there. Mr. Berry did not work. He dressed impeccably and simply stood on the corner of Northern and 108th Street all day long. Though I never saw him turn a bottle to his lips, his drinking was the talk of the neighborhood.

The pillar of our block was Sylvester's father, Mr. Moore. On Sundays, he dressed in a suit and tie and took his entire family to church. Though he never spoke to me outright about religion, he was the first person to make me wonder about God. He was a busy man whose job as a Pullman porter frequently took him out of town. When he was home, he made his presence felt among the young people on the block. He quietly corrected us when we were wrong and often chatted with me though he had seven children of his own. I respected him because he and his family never whispered about my mother. Sylvester and I played together and his daughters, Betty Ann and Vera, were good friends even though I was mischievous. During Vera's voice training, I would crouch beneath her window and mimic her "do-re-mi(s) and "fa-sol-la(s)" until Mrs. Moore chased me away. I don't recall Mr. Moore ever scolding me; he was truly a compassionate man. Matter of fact, he provided my first glimpse of Godly love. Though what went on behind church walls was a mystery to me, I thought it had to be good if Mr. Moore kept attending.

Rather than the likes of Mr. Uppity and other stuck-up men who frequented the garage, Mr. Moore, Mr. Berry and Mr. Walters were the yardsticks I used to measure my father. Daddy was not the best or the worst of these men. He landed somewhere in the middle; and, despite the fact that he lived outside of our home, I loved him. He had little in the way of material possessions but when he got dressed in a suit and tie, he looked every bit as good as

Mr. Uppity. He was also a good dancer and he knew how to have fun.

Like most everybody in Corona—church people, 'livery cab drivers, men and women—Daddy played the numbers. When the numbers runner came around, even my Granny reached into her bosom and pulled out the handkerchief with nickels and dimes knotted in one corner. Whenever Daddy won, I thrilled at the shout, "Hit the number today! Gon' get some gin. "Happy times! Happy times!" For me it meant a day at The Dumps, followed by black-eyed peas and ham hocks over rice, with Kool-Aid prepared by Granny. In celebration of Daddy's wins, neighbors would stop by the garage for sips of gin and a plate of peas.

Hanging out at the garage had its winning moments, but the day Daddy made me wash cars until my hands throbbed was not one of them. Just when I thought they would explode with pain, they went numb. "I can't do it," I cried.

"Little Jimmy," my father said, "there are two kinds of people in the world: them that work with their hands like me and them that work with their minds." For the first time I saw what the lack of meaningful work had done to my father. I decided right then that I would one day work with my mind.

Despite many joyful days at the garage, Daddy continued to tread along at the edge of my existence. With Mama gone and only public glimpses into his life, an undetected loneliness drifted into my life. Sometimes, I sneaked daises from Mrs. Moore's flower boxes and plucked the petals: "She loves me; she loves me not." Always, the last petal said that Mama "loved me not." I hated those daisies. They confirmed my fears. I prayed to Jesus, the friend she sang about in her favorite hymn, but

Mama didn't come home.   She didn't even answer my letters.

G ranny was no joke. She didn't have Mama's education, but she took charge of the Toomer clan. Because my mother was the oldest child—the one who brought everyone else up from South Carolina to live in our apartment—and, because she had an eighth grade education, she ran the affairs of the family before she got sick. With the help of her sister-in-law, my Aunt Constine, who had a secondary education, Mama transacted business dealings for my uncles. The two women kept track of the little money the men earned doing odd jobs, and helped them fill out job applications. They even took my uncles to their job interviews because none of them could read well enough to follow the street signs.

When Mama fell ill, all her duties went to Granny. No, my grandmother couldn't read and figure numbers. Aunt Constine continued handling the business end of things, but Granny's character and physical strength made her more than fit to shepherd the boisterous energy of her family.

At fifty-five, she was tubby, low to the ground with thick legs that spilled into brown lace-up oxfords. Because of her light skin, high cheekbones and the jet black straight hair inherited from her mother, the family bragged that Granny was one-quarter Cherokee when she was actually from West Indian stock. However, it was not Granny's bloodline that caught my ten-year-old fancy; it was the muscular arms developed from years of dragging hundred-pound cotton sacks in the sandy fields of South Carolina.

The day my friends and I raided Mr. Underwood's peach tree, I got to know Granny's strength. After work, she came straight inside, "Little Jimmy, get the belt!"

"What did I do? Ain' done nothing." I trembled at the thought of the beating she was about to lay on me.

"You stole Mr. Underwood's peaches."

How did she know that? Joseph musta told her I gave him some peaches. I'ma tell on him too. "Granny, Joseph told you about the peaches?"

"A little birdie told me."

"A little birdieeee..." Before I could get the question out, she lit into my behind and I danced, danced, danced.

A few days later I got into a fight with Billy. Again, Granny walked in demanding her belt and again it was the "little birdie."

I was mad at those birds. I went outside and threw rocks at the birds perched on the telephone wire. "Now go tell that," I yelled.

Minutes later, Granny was ordering, "Git my belt!" I begged to know my crime.

"You been throwing rocks."

Them birds can talk? I wondered.

After that third encounter with Granny's strap, I checked to see where the birds were before I got into mischief.

Years later, I discovered that Mrs. Moore was the "little birdie" who sat at her window and looked out for the children on the block. When she was well over eighty and I was in my forties she and Betty Ann met me on the streets.

"Mama, it's Little Jimmy," Betty Ann explained because her mother's sight had grown dim.

"Bad boy," Mrs. Moore mumbled and smacked me hard across the face. Betty Ann was a little embarrassed, but I smiled and remembered the fifties when she, Granny and Aunt Carrie Mae watched children play and taught us to treat others the way we wanted to be treated. It was my guiding principle for years to come.

Those old women were crafty too. Had I known it was Sylvester's mother telling on me, we would have settled the score down at the construction site away from the watchful eyes of adults. Thankfully, peace held between friends and my grandmother got much-need help with her grandchildren while she worked.

Just as Granny seemed to settle into the routine of a fulltime job, maintaining the household and cooking two meals a day for our eleven family members, Mama resumed weekend visits home. Keeping a watchful eye on my mother strained her even more. So, Aunt Carrie Mae and Uncle Esau's wife, Aunt Reather helped out with the endless chores. Many nights, after feeding her family, Aunt Reather cooked and cleaned at our house. Aunt Carrie Mae was separated from her husband, and was free to end every day sweeping floors, making beds and washing clothes for us.

One evening when I was acting out because I missed Mama, I thought Aunt Carrie Mae was going to whip me for sure but she told me a story instead:

"You got so po' in that hospital. I told Nettie that you'd never make it but she shook her head and cooed baby talk to you. *"Don't* you worry, Aunt Carrie Mae' she rocked you in her arms. 'I'm gon' grow up and have lots of babies and them gonna walk right up to you and say *Hi Aunt Carrie Mae.* You'll see; I'm gonna be a big man,' she whispered in your ear."

"I was sick?" I beamed with a wide grin, happy to hear a story about myself.

"Un-huh. Nettie spent hours at that hospital worryin' over you. You was a little ol' thing, two months old and we didn't know what was wrong. Nettie wanted to sign you out and take care of you at home but I stopped her 'cause them doctors warned her they wouldn't take you back if you got worse. When you come home, she took good care of you. Look at you now; you skinny but you a strong little fellow."

"Is that why they call me Little Jimmy?"

"No. It's because your uncle is sixteen and you only ten. He's Big Jimmy and you Little Jimmy." She patted me on the leg and chuckled, "You sho' a Mama's boy."

Aunt Carrie Mae ate a plate of Granny's roast pork and snap beans then headed home with her twins, Elizabeth and Elijah. They lived a block away where they shared an apartment with Uncle Esau, Aunt Reather, and their children, Wilbur and Gereline.

A Mama's boy: that sounded good to me. At night I missed Mama most but that evening I snuggled in bed with warm thoughts of her.

After Aunt Carrie Mae's story, whenever Mama came home, I stayed right under her. I loved the way she smelled like peppermint candy, the way she laughed nice and loud, the way she always looked me straight in the eyes and made me the center of her attention when she spoke to me, and the way she wiped my tears when I got into fights with children on the block. I even liked when she combed my hair—an ordeal that usually disrupted the entire household.

"I'm never gon' marry. I'm not leaving you Mama."

"I don't want you. When you grown, you got to go," she teased.

"No, Mama. I'm staying with you."

"You get to be a big man, you got to have your own family. Got to!" With Mama I was safe, happy.

"They don' operated on Nettie's head." Again, I stood in the shadows listening to my aunt and grandmother wrangle with an awful thing that I could not grasp.

"Say they just took a little piece off the front there. Say she won't be so mad anymore. I don' know. She can't talk; don' even know us. Me and Joe done signed them papers so she could get better," Granny moaned.

"She don't look any better," Aunt Carrie Mae whimpered. "All them bandages and her head hanging down between her legs. Lord my sister done suffered."

"Pull yourself together Carrie Mae; you don't want them children to hear you." Just above a whisper, Granny rambled on, "Them nurses was angry with Joe. They say they done told him no more babies..."

Babies! I was happy about the babies. I had gone with daddy to the hospital to pick up the first new baby. I begged and begged until he snapped, "Okay boy, get in the car." It could have been my pleas or the relentless December rain that wore him down. It didn't matter; without grabbing a coat, I ran out and jumped in the back seat of the old humpback Chevy before he changed his mind. The wipers flopped hard across the windshield as water drained from my wet body causing the musty smell of straw to rise from the faded yellow weaved seat cushion. Goose pimples popped on my arms when Daddy switched on the fan of the old heater that hung beneath the dashboard. He focused on steering the car through the wet dark streets as I tried to imagine what my little sister would look like.

There hadn't been a baby in our house for as long as I could remember. When we parked in the lot behind the hospital, I started to jump out but daddy explained that children my age were not allowed. I waited in the car with the motor running to keep me warm. I was as excited about seeing Mama as I was the new baby. She had been away for months. Her pregnancy was spent at Pilgrim State Hospital but the baby was born at Queens General.

Unable to keep still, I bounced up and down on the seat and refereed streams of raindrops that raced to the bottom of the car window. Then, suddenly two silhouettes rose in front of me. In a misty gust of wind the front passenger door opened. My heart thumped hard against my bony chest. "Let me see the baby! Let me see the baby!" I hung over the front seat but the baby was covered.

"Sit back, Little Jimmy," Daddy ordered.

"You can see the baby," Mama said and raised the blanket just as headlights swung into the parking lot. In the brightness, I saw two big sparkling eyes.

"She's looking at you," Mama said, sending a warm tingle through my body.

"Sit back!" Daddy commanded more forcefully. I did as I was told. On the ride home the car was quiet, not a word was spoken between my parents. Still, it was one of my best moments with the two of them. My eyes were fixed on the backs of their heads. I snuggled in a cozy blanket of rain with both parents.

When we got home the entire family gathered around to inspect the baby. "Her name is Frances," Mama announced and peeled the blankets back from head to toe. I grinned, *What a pretty little black girl—just pretty, and I saw her first.*

Mama looked so peaceful holding and rocking and singing to Frances. I thought she was home for good. She seemed fine to me but in a few days she handed the baby to Granny and returned to Pilgrim State Hospital. Again, I saw her only on weekends.

A year later, when Granny and Aunt Carrie Mae hunched their backs in worry, I was beside myself with glee. Mama had brought home my baby sister, Ruthie. I liked being big brother to Ruthie and Frances. Instead of getting into trouble, I became Little Jimmy, who helped out with the babies. Granny and Aunt Carrie Mae's concern about Mama's having babies confused me.

"Granny is just guilty because she signed papers to get Mama's head operated on," I told Gloria.

"Don't be angry with Granny!" my sister fumed. Mama never wanted to marry Daddy and she didn't want any of us."

I thought my older sister's opinions were twisted and deep down I didn't really care what she said. I knew Mama loved me and I was excited about my little sisters.

The fact is neither Gloria nor I really knew fact from fiction. My family history had gotten buried under layers of silence and half-truths. My aunt and grandmother were trying to protect us children from the harsh realities of life, but they were doing more harm than good.

Finally, I exploded at poor Aunt Bertha, Daddy's sister who had come from Florida to live with us around the time of Mama's operation. Day after day, Aunt Bertha charged through the house cursing and slamming doors. With less understanding of her problem than of Mama's condition, and unable to bear the agony any longer, I screamed at the top of my lungs, "Is everybody in this house crazy?" Granny and Aunt Carrie Mae looked at me as if I had lost my mind, but it was Aunt Bertha who had gone to pieces. She was soon admitted to the same hospital as Mama.

We weren't all crazy, but we were all angry: Granny with the doctors and Daddy, Gloria with Mama, and me with Daddy and Granny though I shouldn't have been. They couldn't pronounce the "lobotomy" word they tried to say, and I doubt that my father or grandmother understood the operation described on the paper they signed. Later, all they could say was Aunt Bertha "died from experiments at that hospital."

I didn't understand it at the time but Granny and Daddy were from a generation of poor, uneducated farm hands in a time when doctors were gods who were never questioned. How could they have known that Mama and Aunt Bertha would suffer more from the cure than from their original illnesses? So, papers were dutifully signed that caused Mama, Aunt Bertha and our entire family to become victims of the lumbering mental hospital bureaucracy of the 1950s.

Granny seemed to age every time she talked about Mama, but with the strength that God gives, she took courage whenever her daughter was home. On those weekends, she fed us first, and then spoon-fed Mama special dishes she had prepared. Before sitting down, she gathered all of the children in the kitchen and threatened to beat us with her heavy strap if we interrupted the feeding. We nodded obediently but once I saw the food, all understanding vanished. "I want some of what Mama is eating," I griped. Shielded from Mama's view, Granny opened her purse enough for me to see the belt curled up like a snake ready to strike. I backed away.

Despite my grandmother's brave efforts, things fell apart. Mama was getting better, but Granny was worn down by eight wild children chasing about the house tearing up everything. Added pressure from Mr. Casey, the landlord, did not help. Because he was never without a complaint, I thought he was a mean old White man. It didn't occur to me that he might have had just grievances. After all, we were destroying his property.

My cousins, teenage uncles, siblings and I pulled all sorts of pranks. One Sunday we drilled holes in the floor and dropped firecrackers into Granny's apartment to frighten away the greedy church women who were gobbling up all the coconut pie and apple jelly cake. Big Jimmy knocked the shower door off its hinges and stampeded naked up the stairs along with the church women. The place did not catch fire but burn spots dotted the walls.

As if a mob of destructive children was not bad enough, Granny butchered chickens in the basement. First time I saw her at the bottom of the steps with a live bird from the 111th Street poultry market, wings batted violently against the air, feathers flew and the loud squawks of terror paralyzed me. In one movement Granny's hand slipped upward, tightened its grip and twirled that chicken round and round until, "snap," with a swift jerk of her wrist, the neck broke. With her free hand, she grabbed the butcher knife and chopped off the head. When that headless chicken hit the floor chasing around the room, splashing blood everywhere, I got the heck out of that basement. Not only was I filled with a new fear of Granny's prowess, the moment was also ripe with learning. Afterwards, whenever she threatened, "If you lie to me, I'll wring your neck," I thought about that chicken and told her more truth than she ever wanted to know. She started bragging: "One thing about Little Jimmy, he will tell you the truth."

Granny was a clean woman. After she killed a chicken, she scrubbed everything down. Not a bloodstain, not a feather was left in the place but the friction between Mr. Casey and her increased. He accused her of "running a slaughterhouse" and she said he had "no common sense." Killing chickens just before cooking them was a rural custom practiced for hundreds of years. She couldn't imagine eating store-bought chickens that had been "dead and laying 'round for days." A falling out with the landlord was inevitable.

When Mr. Casey evicted the Toomers, the Blakes fell through the cracks while everybody else landed on their feet. Uncle Jacob moved into the second floor apartment of the house where Aunt Carrie Mae and Uncle Esau rented. Granny found a tiny apartment for herself and her sons, Big Jimmy and Izelle, on 32nd Avenue at 107th Street—just shouting distance from her other children. Within a week the Toomers had settled into their new homes and Granny had taken on a part time job to cover increased expenses. She joined the nightshift assembly line packing tomatoes and other goods at the food company alongside Aunt Carrie Mae and Aunt Reather.

Without a doubt, life got tougher for the Toomers, but we Blakes crashed through the thin net that held the rest of the family together. I blamed Mr. Casey for snitching on us to the authorities. I was unaware that social workers had been visiting our house since Mama's hospitalization, and they made the decision to separate Gloria, Joseph, Carol and I from our family and friends. We were carted off to the Hebrew Children's Home.

Part Two:

Voices in the dark

Flying without wings, my two sisters, brother and I were released into the world. I had heard old people say that family gives children roots to make them strong and wings to fly. Ripped from our home and dropped off at a strange place, the four of us were angry with our mother's family for not keeping us with them.

"Blood is thicker than water!" Gloria ranted. "'You have to sacrifice for your family!' That's what Granny said. Remember? When I was thirteen and wanted to be out with my friends, I got a good beating and she was yelling, 'Family take care of one another!' Well, Granny lied, didn't she? Why the family not taking care of us if blood so thick? Why? Huh? Why they let them bring us to this—this home? This ain't no home?"

.Gloria wasn't the only one who believed everything Granny said. I was ten and didn't know what to think, so I nodded, "*Yeah*" or shook my head, "*I don't know*" to her rapid-fire questions. Carol, a skinny tomboyish eight-year-old, imitated my gestures. Joseph, eleven and sullen, studied her quietly and by nightfall he walked. I started out behind him but he stopped me. The next morning the staff van brought him back and fueled Gloria's fury for another day. "See Granny didn't keep him," she assigned blame. When Joseph left the second night, I did not try to follow because Gloria convinced me that the Toomers would send him back by morning. Sure enough, the van carrying him rolled in before noon. Joseph ran away so often during our first week at The Hebrew Children's Home that I thought he had a ride, but he walked from

Monroe Avenue in the Bronx, across the Triborough Bridge into Queens and along Astoria Boulevard back to Corona.

Gloria wanted to walk too, but stayed to look out for Carol who felt safe with her big sister around. If another child jumped one of us the fight was on! One thing we had learned from the Toomers was how to defend ourselves. Under Gloria's protection, Carol spent hours playing on the little sliding board that she never left unless Bailey entered the yard. For some odd reason the sight of his thick lips and shaven head, a style worn by many boys in those days, sent her racing to Gloria, pointing and crying: "Bald head! Bald head!" Otherwise, Carol was happy with her big sister nearby.

In sharp contrast to my younger sister's experience, my world had crumbled. I wanted to be back on 108th Street 'kicking the can' with friends. Besides, as the new kid in the children's home, I was constantly tested. Eventually, the pranks got out of hand.

One counselor, Mr. Brooks, tried to teach us art. We learned boredom. Sitting on the fire escape leading down to the playground, we watched him paint landscapes when all we wanted to do was play. Whenever he walked away for a minute, our fidgety energy turned to horsing around. During a moment of mischief, one of the kids put his paintbrushes behind me without my knowledge. When Mr. Brooks returned, he went berserk, cursing wildly, charging from step to step, looking behind each child until he reached the top row, ordered me to stand and found his precious brushes. Without warning, he yanked my feet from under me and dragged me down the stairs with my head bouncing against the metal steps and left me bleeding on the cement yard. In my semi-conscious state, I heard Gloria crying and cursing to high heaven.

When Joseph found out what had happened, he wanted to jump Mr. Brooks but I persuaded him to wait for Daddy. In the meantime, I threatened that counselor, "My father gon' kick your butt."

Daddy's boxing activities took on a legendary quality. I bragged to the other children, "Yep! He fought Joe Louis and he gon' kick that counselor's butt. Un-huh, he threw a man over a tree! You watch; see what happens."

When Daddy stepped into the building, neck bulging and muscles rippling under his shirt, a chorus of "Ooooo!" rose from the children crowded around the stairway. They gawked wide-eyed at the boxer's back as he swept across the tiny lobby into the director's office. I huddled with them—our eyes fixed on the closed door. Before long, a crack appeared and Daddy wedged it wider as he backed from the room nodding and bowing. He gently pulled the door shut, turned and walked toward me grinning like a mouse, "Little Jimmy, you listen to these people; they trying to help you."

What happened to the butt-kicking? That counselor almost killed me! My body went rigid with anger. Gloria had put on a better show than Daddy. At least, she cursed Mr. Brooks out. *Weak!* I seethed. Without a word, I broke from the crowd and climbed the stairs to the dormitory. I was depending on Daddy but he was not dependable.

"He's a punk!" I complained to Joseph.

My brother gave a half-smile, "Man, let that go; Daddy ain't no punk. Them people told him you was clowning around and fell. They say you making all this fuss 'cause you want to go home. They lied to Daddy." I knew Joseph was telling the truth. He was never quick to speak but when he weighed in, he was frank, sometimes brutal in his honesty. The talk with him redirected my fury away from my father toward the culprits: the staff.

How could they help us with our problems when they covered up the truth about my injury? At ten, I didn't have the words to describe an unjust system; so, I fumed: "It's unfair!" "I hate you!."

Deep inside me, in a place that I could not touch at that moment, I had learned my first lesson about institutional brutality. Mr. Brooks had done more than crack my head; he had sowed seeds of justice in a place in my heart that Granny had prepared. She had taught me to play fair, to treat people fair, and when that failed, to fight fair.

The physical abuse I suffered from that counselor wasn't fair, so Gloria roamed around like a mother tiger ready to attack. Eventually, her threats about killing Mr. Brooks, Joseph's constant running away, and my persuading Daddy of what had really happened made him get us out of that 'home.'

Daddy piled us into his old Chevy and headed to Corona. I thought we were going to 108th Street but he drove to 97th and made a left turn off Northern Blvd toward 32nd Avenue. "Look at that haunted house! See! See!" I laughed as we zoomed by a rickety two-story unpainted shell of a building. Straining my neck toward the rear window, I lost sight of the house just as Daddy jammed the brakes and shifted into reverse. "This is it," he pointed, and a collective groan of disbelief rumbled through the car.

It was the worst looking house I had ever seen. Faded whitewash, rotten siding and old rags stuffed in broken windowpanes looked out of place among the neatly kept homes on the block. Gutters hung from the roof; the front door swung lopsided from its hinges; and, jagged holes scarred the front facing where bricks and hunks of concrete had fallen to the ground. The only solid part of the house was the concrete stoop.

"This place should be condemned," Gloria bellowed. Daddy ignored her and ushered us up to the second floor apartment. The sagging stairway groaned under our weight like the lid opening on Dracula's coffin. Huge flakes of paint covered the floor and, except for an old oil-burning stove near the side window, only two raggedy sofa chairs slumped in the living room. Each of the two bedrooms contained a full size bed with a lumpy mattress, but there were no heaters to warm the space.

The worst room of all was the kitchen. Thousands of roaches scurried about uninterrupted by our presence. The oven door was propped up with a stick and only one of the top burners of the stove worked. The smell of mold seeped from the rusty icebox and a foul odor drifted into the kitchen through the missing door of the bathroom. For use to flush the toilet, a large white bucket of water sat beneath the kitchen table.

Gloria was right. The place was a dump but my father acted all excited, like it was a brand new house. After a while he left with a promise to return with food. I am not clear where he lived but it definitely was not with us. Granny's sister-in-law, our great Auntie Carry, had been appointed by the court as "the adult of record" to supervise us. Though she was probably fifty-five or sixty like Granny, we called her the spooky ninety-year-old that lived on the first floor. It never entered our minds that she was supposed to be in charge of us.

The social services agency had failed miserably to do its job. The caseworker who approved our release from the Hebrew Children's Home either did not care enough to inspect the place before certifying it fit for children or saw the conditions but looked the other way. So, we lived in squalor, above a distant aunt who was too feeble to care for herself let alone us.

"Suffer the little children to come unto me..." was Aunt Reather's favorite quote from scripture, when she tried to convince me to go to church. Well, we were suffering. I wondered where God was.

Gloria tried to make the best of our situation. At thirteen, she was sort of head of the household. She prepared our meals in a filthy ritual that began with her chasing one of us out of the bathroom. "Don't smell up this place while I'm cooking," she would yell. Even without the stench that crept into the kitchen, eating was anything but inviting. Ignoring the daily call of "Waaatermelllons, fresh vegetabllles," from the horse-drawn wagon that rolled through the block, Gloria heard, "Tomatoooes! Get your ripe tomatoes!" She fed us a variation of tomato dishes day in and day out. It was tomatoes and green peppers over rice for dinner; and, for breakfast, tomatoes and green peppers over grits or, sometimes, bacon simmered in stewed tomatoes. I hated the food almost as much as I hated the house. I was happy when Carol set the place on fire.

The day had started with Gloria scolding our younger sister for breaking some random rule. You can imagine the fairness of punishment meted out from one sibling to another. Everybody was outside shooting fireworks on the fourth of July in celebration of Daddy's birthday instead of the nation's independence. Carol, who knew better than to cross Gloria, was inside. Determined not to miss out on the fun, she created her own fireworks by stretching a Brillo pad to the length of her hand, lighting it, then spinning round and round to make sparks. Up went the kitchen curtains in flames. Carol yelled, "Fire!" Gloria sprang into action. You would have thought she was saving a mansion. She raced upstairs, grabbed the bucket of water from the kitchen floor and doused the blaze.

Ahhhh, shoot! She ought to let it burn. Thoughts of Carol and Auntie Carry's safety didn't enter my mind. I wanted out of that wretched house but Gloria's heroics produced bittersweet results: no one was hurt but we were doomed to a godless year on 97th Street. We had no adult supervision, but Gloria—with Joseph's help—restricted Carol's and my activities to our block.

The October stickball games on the corner from our house were the bright spots in my life. Bands of teenagers gathered every day in "The Valley" where the sloping hills from 96th and 98th Streets converged at the intersection of 97th and 32nd Avenue. Tall, good looking, athletic guys played fierce stickball in The Valley. Cookie was the fastest runner. Duke, Chino, Count, Torch and Lucky were sluggers on the teams before they formed gangs and added the handle, "Big," in front of their names. I was tagged "Kool-Aid." Whenever the fellows took a breather from fielding balls that were sometimes hit four blocks away, they bought a refreshing drink from my stand.

Joseph never went to The Valley; he headed in the opposite direction to Northern Boulevard. He had celebrated his twelfth birthday that past June and was hanging out with a rough bunch of fellows known for crimped down velour hats, bee-bop walking, jive talking, wine drinking, basement parties, and gang banging.

I was proud of my brother. Whenever I ventured onto the main drag, "That's Joe's little brother," trailed me from scattered huddles of cats who robbed, beat and intimidated anyone who crossed their paths. The free pass I got from them made me respect Joseph. I wanted

43

to be like him, but the minute he saw me, he sent me straight home.

Toward the end of October, I turned eleven just as interest in The Valley shifted from stickball to gangs. The cops had started coming through disbanding the dozens of young men gathered for clean healthy fun. Before long, everybody drifted to Northern Boulevard. Boosted by my birthday, I too was ready for the big time with the big boys on the big street that lost its first name and simply became The Boulevard.

There was excitement to be had on The Boulevard. The aroma of hot fish and chips swirled in the cold crisp air. Pretty girls sauntered back and forth eyeing young jitterbugs. Music blasted from storefronts; guys harmonized on street corners; and, though they were from another era, Flash and Dash put on the best shows. Dressed in loud turquoise and purple Zoot suits with gold chains spilling out of their pockets down to their knees, the aging brothers sang jazz tunes and scatted "beeee-bop-dee-bop." Their pointed-toe shoes struck the pavement like lighting as they tap-danced in the middle of the street.

Against a backdrop of lively entertainment, everybody was profiling. "The walk" marked the stride of young "Turks." The dip in every step, the defiance in the slow drag of the right arm said, "I'll kill you if you mess with me." The walk communicated fearlessness. Anybody who failed to fall in step invited a challenge. Walk the walk and back it up with action was the winning combination for individuals and gangs. Groups of dudes floated down the sidewalk dipping to the same rhythm, swaying as one body and giving off one message: we tough enough.

Reputations were gained and lost on The Boulevard and I wanted to be ring-side for sudden fights between legends like Big Lucky, Big Count, Lucius, Big Torch, The Duke, my uncle—Big Jimmy Toomer—and the fearsome Huey Long who had a plate in his head. I wished my brother would stop chasing me home before the rumbles got underway. *Joseph wants all the fun for himself,* I sulked. Without the faintest understanding that he was trying to look out for me, I vowed to get even.

My chance came one day when Auntie Carry summoned me, "Boy, take this hatchet and go chop some wood. I'm gittin' cold." She was confused and probably thought she was in the backwoods of South Carolina. Her husband, Bemon Williams, had died the previous winter and their son Bemon, Jr. was away in the army. I felt sorry for Auntie Carry because she no longer had men in the house to fetch her wood. So, I took the hatchet, headed to the basement, and chopped away at the walls. Where else was I going to find firewood in New York City?

I hacked half way down the first board before the gun fell from its hiding place. It hit the floor with a thud— not the sound of plastic. It was hard cold steel in my hands. My heart thumped. Quickly, I hid it behind another board and raced upstairs to share my find with Joseph. "Come down stairs I want to show you something," I pulled at his blanket. "Get away," he growled, not wanting the cold to crawl beneath the covers with him. I whispered, "Joe, there's a gun in the basement." He bolted out of the bed and down the stairs with me on his heels. "Man, where my gun?" he whirled around when he did not find it in its usual spot. I was dumbstruck. He yanked me by my neck until I got the gun and gave it to him.

"And don't you say nothing to nobody," he tightened his grip.

"Ain't gon' say nothin'," I gasped so that he would let me loose.

After getting my wind back, I finished chopping wood for Auntie Carry, hauled an arm full up to the first floor and built a roaring fire. Because the house was full of holes, the wind froze everything in its path and caused Auntie Carry to all but hug her stove. She was the only person I had ever seen smoke a pipe and chew tobacco at the same time. Her rocker was pulled right up to the mouth of the stove and at regular intervals she lurched forward, took her pipe from her mouth and squirted a brown arrow of tobacco juice through the open door causing the flame to sizzle and hiss. I stayed and watched her for the longest. All the while, I relished the fact that I had a secret to hold over Joseph.

The next time I went to The Boulevard and my brother chased me home, I told Daddy about the gun. He made Joseph get it, and with Auntie Carry's hatchet, he chopped it to smithereens. I got revenge but Joseph's fury ran deep. As soon as Daddy left, he cursed me out, called me a snitch—the absolute worse label in Corona—then stopped speaking to me for weeks. I idolized my brother; being frozen out of his world was torture.

The dispute between Joseph and me smoldered but the clashes between him and Gloria were downright ugly. One Saturday afternoon they squared off cursing, punching, kicking, biting, clawing and rolling on the floor knocking over the little bit of furniture in the living room. It was better than any fight on The Boulevard. I squealed with glee.

Daddy's footsteps went unnoticed until his face, frozen with murderous intent, popped up the stairwell. He reached across the room, snatched Joseph off the floor and held him suspended in the air. Trembling like every fiber of his being had been summoned to keep him from hitting my brother, tears streamed down Daddy's face. "I'm sick of you kids!" he groaned and flung Joseph

46

against the wall. "Don't you say a word!" his thick finger pointed at Gloria. The command was unnecessary; nobody made a sound, not even me, though I was smiling inside. Now, that was the dad I had wanted to see at the Hebrew Children's Home! He turned Gloria and Joseph into scared rabbits and they got busy at the order, "Clean this place up, right now! Next time, I'll beat the hell out of you."

Without Mama or Granny and with quick spot-checks from Daddy, who dropped off food, I was lonely and dejected. However, my spirit warmed with the weather in the spring of 1954 when a Cuban girl stole my young heart.

Margie lived in a huge brick house across the street from Junior High School 127 where I was a seventh grader. Except for a Hawaiian girl and a dark skinned boy who spoke Spanish, only Blacks and Italians were in my class. But Margie stood out. Her olive complexion, straight black hair, and dark eyes excited me. Dressed like some little rich kid, she was clean and fresh and, though I was dirty and tattered, she always greeted me warmly and never made me feel different. Once, she even let me kiss her in the schoolyard and I liked it in spite of her braces.

Margie was a friendly but assertive girl who decided one day to walk me home. "No, you don't have to," I protested. I didn't want her to know how poor I was.

"But, I'm going to," she stated flat out.

Unable to put her off, I let her walk me to the house next door, with its white shingle siding, blue shutters and yard full of bright yellow daffodils. "Well, here we are." I knew Mrs. Jeeters was at work so I stepped inside the gate and lingered in the warmth of puppy love until, "Little Jimmy! Get up here!" thundered across the softness of the afternoon. I cringed at the sight of a wild and bushy-headed Gloria leaning out of an upstairs window that barely held her weight. "You better get off that gate and get up here right now!" Not stated but unmistakable in her tone was, *Or, I'll come down and get you!*

In utter confusion, Margie looked up, then down at the garbage that covered our front yard. "I'll see you later," I mumbled, put my head down and, mad enough to fight, I shuffled into our crumbling house. Margie walked back toward East Elmhurst.

Humiliation pricked a strange memory. In the middle of my shame popped a scene from my third-grade classroom. A substitute teacher stood singing, "You wear a tulip a sweet and yellow tulip and I wear a red, red rose." The substitute was the only Black or male teacher I had had but he offered me nothing but a song. Four years later his lyric rattled the hurtful truth: in my seventh-grade class, I was a bloody, thorny rose among satin yellow tulips.

Embarrassed by my plight, I began to avoid Margie. I spent the rest of my days in Junior High School 127, lonely, hungry and all-but–naked. I indicted my family, my teachers and God for valuing me less than other children. I did not know the word, "poverty" but I understood, "want." I wanted what other children had: clothes, food, and a family that cared for me. I drew inward to the solid ache that had been soothed by Margie's friendship. The day she walked away, her kindness went with her. My interest in school died.

"Touch her, go ahead," my cousin, Wilber, pushed me forward.

"Oh!" I jumped back. "She's cold and... hard." Adults sat somber at the wake but we noisily bumped into chairs as we raced out of Armwood Funeral Home onto The Boulevard.

Auntie Carry had been in the hospital for weeks but I did not miss her until her son, Bemon, came home from the army for the funeral. He looked strong and healthy like one of the soldiers in the war movies at The Dumps. After the burial he stayed in the downstairs apartment for a few days. His presence fed my hunger for a father in the house. He thanked me for helping his mother while he was away and bragged about almost everything I did. I beamed at the compliments but my happiness was fleeting. "The Korean War," he said, and returned to fight in a distant land I had never heard of, for reasons I did not know.

After Bemon left, somehow a social worker discovered there was no adult in the house. To my knowledge, no one from the Department of Welfare had ever visited or noted the unsanitary conditions of our apartment. However, the absence of an adult in the home got the attention of the authorities. The court ordered Daddy to get someone to supervise us and to find a new place immediately.

The Toomers were busy taking care of their own children as well as my baby sisters, Ruthie and Frances. Without a family member in Corona to lean on, my father searched for a relative from his side of the family to come up from Florida. Meanwhile we said goodbye and good riddance to 97th Street. Daddy moved us to a single family house on 107th Street where we had the full run of the place. The fact that we had more space didn't matter to me. I was happy to be near my old buddies on 108th Street.

On 107th Street we lived next door to Pops. Like a glad uncle, he fed my sisters and me without making us feel like charity cases. Most times he sent food over, but also he called us next door for dinner. Though the two houses were the same size, with the same layout, his was everything that ours was not. It was neat, clean, pretty, and filled with the inviting aroma of roasting chicken and baking bread. The place sparkled with glossy photos and mirrors, shiny wallpaper in the bathroom, hard ceramic tile floors in the kitchen and an upright piano surrounded by hi-fi equipment in the living room. The music corner drew my sisters and me to it like magnets. Though I never touched anything, Gloria played the piano while Miss Robinson, a maid around Mama's age, complained about fingerprints. Despite her reprimands, I enjoyed the relaxed orderliness of Pops' home as I gobbled down delicious meals at the kitchen table.

Other times, Carol and I lounged at the bedroom window overlooking our neighbor's backyard. We first soaked up the festivities next door on a breezy summer night in 1954. With elbows on the windowsill, we peered around the yellow and white umbrella table that sat on a small patch of grassy lawn. Along the back fence a six-foot table was loaded with sliced turkey, ham, and dishes that were unfamiliar and uninteresting to me. My eyes feasted on the chocolate layer, fluffy coconut, and buttery marble pound cakes that rested on the smaller table off to the side. Near the kitchen door, a bass fiddler, and two men with brassy horns created sounds I had heard drifting from bars and lounges on The Boulevard. What fun to be serenaded by a live trio!

Bobbing our heads to the music, Carol and I watched men in dark suits and ties tap their feet and slap one another on the backs. Heavy strings of pearls tumbled down the front of midnight lace and satin dresses. Diamonds glittered on the necks of women who threw their heads back in laughter. I had just seen the movie, *Stormy Weather*, at The Dumps and could have sworn that one of the ladies was Lena Horne. For hours we gawked at the fancy people, snapped our fingers to the rhythms, and waited eagerly for cold cuts and sweet cakes that would be ours at the end of the evening.

A parade of friends streamed through Pops' house. No doubt, many of them were celebrities but I never felt like I was in the way. Sometimes the visitors headed up the block to the Silver Rail Bar, a Corona juke joint with a bunch of country people crowded inside. I trailed behind them to the corner of 108th Street and Northern where I met up with my friends, Henry and Billy. We gazed through the window of the Silver Rail and watched the old-timers party.

Pops was cool. He paid Gloria to walk his two Belgian Shepherds and gave me quarters to wash his car. One day I carried a watermelon into the kitchen for him and dropped it on the floor. Miss Robinson scolded me but Pops slipped me a silver dollar. It was heavy in my hand but I had no sense of its value. It could have purchased a three-day supply of food for our house; but, to me, the coin meant a five-cent stamp to write to Mama and an afternoon of fun with my friends.

Squeezing Pops' silver dollar in my fist, I ducked into our ramshackle house and went right upstairs. We hardly used the first floor living room, dining room and kitchen. When night fell or rain drove Gloria, Joseph, Carol and me off the streets, we passed our time in the three bedrooms on the second floor. So, I raced upstairs with my silver dollar, flopped on one of the saggy beds and poured my heart out begging Mama to come home. Though I had stopped praying to her friend, Jesus, her favorite song filled my head as I wrote.

With the letter stuffed deep in my pocket, off I went to 108th Street to show my shiny coin to Billy and Henry. After purchasing a stamp, and buying Royal Crown Colas, potato chips, and sourballs at Mr. Moody's grocery store, enough was left for twelve-cent movie tickets at The Dumps but we sneaked pass Miss Mary, the usher. We devoured our snacks during the five cartoons, then happily settled into double features starring Randolph Scott as a gun-blazing cowboy. At the end of the movies, my buddies and I strutted down The Boulevard like the 'badest' dudes in the West. It was all thanks to Pops.

Unlike other people on our block, Pops traveled for weeks at a time, but his wife—Aunt Lucille to us—would continue to prepare dinner and send it over to our house. The fresh meats and vegetables were a welcome relief from Gloria's tomato dishes. Aunt Lucille was a sweet lady and like her husband, she gave us spending change.

When Pops returned home, he'd pick up his horn and blow sizzling tunes that floated next door and burned away the cold empty spaces of my heart. His music lulled me to sleep many nights but his compassion had the deepest impact. He lovingly drew me into his world. The glimpse of another way of life stirred a desire to reach for something better. Without my knowing it, Pops' kindness planted in my soul charity for others.

At eleven, I did not know that my neighbor was Louis Armstrong. I thought he was a regular cat like the rest of the men on the block. Society people lived in big houses in East Elmhurst, wore white handkerchiefs hanging out of their lapel pockets, doused themselves in loud smelling cologne and came into the garage to order Daddy around. Pops' car was big and shiny like the uppity people; but, like the working folks of Corona, he washed it on the street in front of his house. Except for the parties in his backyard, Pops seemed no better off than our other neighbors. Because he did not brag or put on airs, I did not peg him as a society fellow.

Not only was I unaware that Pops was The Louis Armstrong, I knew little else about what was happening in the wider world. Without a newspaper, a radio or the thought of a television in our house, I had no sense of news except the gossip that passed between my friends and me. I was ignorant of the United States Supreme Court's landmark *Brown v. Board of Education* decision that was about to alter the lives of millions of children. In 1954, America was on the edge of explosive change. The very next year Rosa Parks would refuse to give up her seat on a Montgomery, Alabama bus and set off a historic civil rights movement. At the same time, dramatic shifts were about to take place in my personal life, but I was clueless.

The joy of living on 107th Street plunged with the temperature when the electricity, gas and running water were cut off in early October. Without a working stove, Gloria, Joseph, Carol and I ate cold cans of Spaghetti-Os and stale Finocchio bread that Daddy dropped off once a week. Nights, we slept in the cold, and during the day we scattered in search of warmth and food. Early mornings, Gloria took Carol with her to babysit Ruthie and Frances at Granny's place. Joseph headed to goodness-knows-where. Nobody kept track of his movements. I waited around for the parents to go to work before hanging out at a friend's house on 108th Street. While alone, my thoughts always turned to Mama. I wondered why she didn't answer any of my letters. Sorrowful thoughts of her made me more eager to spend time in the warm home of my friends.

At night, I sometimes escaped the cold with one of my cousins, Elijah or Wilbur. Aunt Carrie Mae loved to cook and feed anyone who knocked on her door. She was really happy whenever I showed up. She would pull me into her tiny apartment, feed me and then get out clean sheets while I fidgeted. I wanted to tell her that Elijah's cot was too small but I was afraid of hurting her feelings. Unable to say that I preferred spending the night across the hall in Wilbur's roomy double bed, I came up with a scheme.

I had noticed how Aunt Reather's eyes twinkled at the mention of Jesus' name. Taking advantage of her love of Christ, I followed her down to First Baptist Church located back then on the corner of 103rd Street and 37th Avenue. Everyone was dressed in Sunday best. The men wore dark suits. The women were clad in deep purple, navy and maroon crepe dresses and had feathered felt hats perched on their heads—except for the five elderly women in the front row who were dressed in white and had tiny lace scarves pinned in their hair. Wilbur, neatly dressed in a pressed shirt and tie, sat on one side of his mother and I sat on the other side, my skinny frame swallowed in one of his oversized shirts.

I imitated everything Aunt Reather did. When the Spirit touched her, he touched me. When she jerked, I jerked. My "Jesus, Jesus" echoed her "Jesus, Jesus."

"Oh look at that little boy praising the Lord," one of the church mothers exclaimed. When an usher rushed over to fan me, I bucked like a wild horse. At dismissal, the sisters lined up to encourage my aunt, "You got to bring him back next week; get him baptized." Aunt Reather nodded her pleasure, then took me home, fed me all the food I could eat, and before Aunt Carrie Mae could make her move, I was on my way to Wilbur's room for a comfortable night's sleep.

My hopes were high the Sunday I walked down the church aisle with my chest poked out in my little white baptismal gown. *I'ma be eatin' good for a long time,* I thought but it was not to be. The moment I set foot in the pulpit, things looked suspicious. The deacons scrambled around rolling back the rug where Reverend Gardener's red velvet chair had been. Then, one by one they lifted boards from the floor until I was standing at the edge of a pool. *Who hid this pool under the pastor's chair?* I wanted to ask, but a brother quickly led me down the steps into water up to my neck. Panic gripped me the way it did when Granny used to dunk my head in the bathtub to wash my hair. I struggled to free myself, but the brother had a firm grip on my arm.

In one movement, Reverend Gardner grabbed me, gave a quick push on my forehead "In the name of the Father, the Son, and..." down I went thrashing and swallowing big gulps of water. I came up coughing and cursing. "Get this little boy out of here," the reverend ordered. He was annoyed and I was furious. Water dripped from my body and profanity spewed from my mouth as Aunt Reather rushed up the center aisle to meet me: "Little Jimmy the Lord don't want you to act like this. You clean now." I pulled away from her and headed straight for the door convinced that she was hanging out with a bunch of child-killers. I never went back to church and I stopped scheming for a warm night's sleep in Wilbur's bed.

For most children, baptism is the beginning of a conscious Christian walk. It was the end for me. When I told Gloria about my terrifying episode at church, she reminded me that I had once attended Sunday school and Wednesday Bible study. I knew nothing about the classes she described but I did remember that women dressed in white uniforms used to come every week to our block on

108th Street, pile us into a black car and take us to Ebenezer Baptist Church in Flushing. In my mind, those trips had been outings for cookies and punch in the church basement. I didn't understand or care about saving my soul. I needed the Jesus who fed the hungry.

I was mad at Aunt Reather and her church for scaring me half to death. Though I didn't have the words to express it at the time, the baptism experience planted in me a distrust of religion that grew over the years. I began to see church people as Sunday-go-meeting phonies because they didn't live the life they talked about. The event also drove a deeper wedge between my relatives and me. For fear of seeing Aunt Reather, I stopped visiting Aunt Carrie Mae too.

For a long time, hunger was the winner. I lowered my expectations, braced my body against the winds and spent many sleepless nights wandering the streets of Corona fighting stomach cramps.

Thank God for Mr. Askew. One day, hungry enough to die, I entered his little store on the corner of 104th Street and 32nd Avenue. "Can I have some food?" I asked.

"You didn't eat today, Little Blake?" I shook my head and he called to his wife, "Make him a bologna sandwich and give him a grape soda." That was the first of many days I entered his store. He always handed me food with the same instruction: "Tell your father I want to see him."

Mr. Askew fed me so often and treated me so nice that he felt like an uncle, but he was compassionate to anyone in need. Like Mr. Moody, he let people sign for their food and pay when they could. It was a small wonder that either storekeeper stayed in business. In my case, payment was nonexistent. I saw Daddy so infrequently that I never remembered to tell him that I was eating at Mr. Askew's store.

Our wide-eyed cousin from the South walked into the chaos of our lives a full four months after the court ordered Daddy to find an adult to supervise us. Fifteen-year-old Gloria was trying to look after us when Betty was put in charge. At eighteen, she was legally an adult and considered old enough to raise a family. Uncle Mike, my father's brother, thought he was making the right move by sending his daughter from Jacksonville, Florida to look after us, but he and our cousin were naive about big city life.

We ran circles around Betty. At night, Gloria sneaked her boyfriend, Frenchie, in and out of the house and, before long, Betty took up with an Italian named Romeo. Free to do as I pleased, I rode the subway all day. Trying to copy my behavior, Carol decided to become a fifth-grade dropout, but the morning she hid in the attic to keep from going to school Granny appeared at the bottom of the stairs. "You can come down or I can come get you," she shouted up to my sister. A tearful Carol crawled out of hiding and off to school wondering, like me, who had called Granny.

There were no antics from thirteen-year-old Joseph. With no deception, he had stopped going to school altogether. He stayed in bed as long as he wanted and got up to hang out with his friends when he felt like it. So-called responsible adults—our father, relatives, neighbors, social workers and school officials—let him live a lie. They pretended that he was old enough at age thirteen to take care of himself.

Joseph's freedom intoxicated me and I decided to grab a few liberties. I was not as bold as my brother though. Every day, I dressed and headed in the direction of Junior High School 16, but stopped short of arrival and hopped a Manhattan bound #7 train at Roosevelt Avenue.

"I'ma have to whip you, Little Jimmy," Betty declared when she discovered I wasn't going to school.

"Whip me?"

"Yes." She came toward me with the wooden ruler from Carol's book satchel. I was baffled. I had been whipped with a belt, a switch, an ironing cord—but never a ruler.

"Hold out your hand," she said. Defiantly my hand jutted toward her. Counting aloud, "One, two, three, four...," Betty smacked twenty stinging licks on my upturned palm. As the count mounted, my hand reddened, and then throbbed, but I did not flinch.

"Are you finished?" I grimaced when she stopped hitting me. Exasperated by my response, she flung the ruler across the room.

"Good, 'cause I'm outta here," I slammed the door on a sobbing, defeated Betty.

After "the whipping," I came and went without question and I didn't return to school. Matter of fact, I was shooting hooky the morning a truant officer stopped me. I would've been rocking my way to Times Square on the #7 train if it hadn't been for autumn leaves sailing to the ground like snowflakes and reminding me of Mama. Her birthday, October sixteenth, was approaching. Though I had not gotten a single answer to my many letters, I went back inside and wrote one more time begging her to come home. With one of Pops' quarters in my pocket, I was off to Mr. Moody's to buy a stamp when the truant officer from Junior High School 16 asked my name and age. "James Blake. I'm eleven," I answered without giving it a thought.

The next day Daddy and I were standing before a judge in Queens Family Court. He asked, "Mr. Blake, are you aware your son has been absent from school ninety consecutive days?" Not knowing what else to do and

58

wanting to appear cooperative, Daddy nodded; and I copied him.

"These absences are in direct violation of New York State child protection laws."

Again, we nodded.

"Ninety consecutive absences is delinquent behavior..." The rest of what he said was gibberish; I was busy trying to figure out what "consecutive" meant.

When the judge finally ended his lecture, Daddy and I lumbered in silence toward the Jamaica Avenue Bus Terminal. After a long while, I asked, "What does consecutive mean?"

Daddy looked at me and shook his head, "I don't know, son, but it sho' must be bad."

Like most poor people we had no lawyer to help us understand the proceedings; so, neither my father nor I were any better informed after the court appearance.

I returned to my old habits, except I started checking on Carol. She was often home alone and had started complaining about "the man with the flashlight." At first I thought she had been tricked by dancing shadows that bounced off the flickering candles we had spread around to light the second floor. Then, on his way to the bathroom one night, Joseph bumped into an old White man and tried to take his head off. It was the landlord who had been living in the basement since we moved into the house four months earlier. Who knew how many times he had crept up the stairs or what no-good deeds were on his mind? Though his return was unlikely after his encounter with Joseph, I hated to take chances with Carol's safety. So, I checked on her every couple of hours.

The heist failed as soon as it got started. Fear swelled in Billy's face when the owner asked to see what was bulging beneath his coat. Unlike Mr. Moody, the Italian storekeeper had difficulty keeping us in line because he did not know our parents. In an effort to make my friend obey, he grabbed him by the elbow. Candy spilled everywhere. Tony and I bolted for the door. Around the corner and across 108th Street we raced with Billy bringing up the rear. We dashed to our old unfinished construction-site play area and scrambled underground into the tunnel we had dug. The storekeeper was dumbfounded when he rounded the corner seconds later and we had vanished.

Without a thought of being buried alive by loose dirt in our makeshift clubhouse, we happily counted the loot from our robbery. Some of the big items on the list—potato chips and Hostess Twinkies—were missing, but we had enough Mary Janes, Tootsie Rolls, Red Hots and Sour Balls for the twelfth birthday party my buddies had planned for me.

After lying low for an hour, I started home with a promise to be back at six o'clock. The swollen jaw on the right side of my face had closed my right eye and pushed my lips apart just enough for the October cold to jab at my aching tooth, but I felt like the luckiest guy in the world. My buddies had risked getting into serious trouble so that I could have a happy birthday. Thoughts of them—my true family—filled me with warmth as I bounced down 107th Street to check on Carol.

A short stocky White woman stood in front of my house. I thought maybe she was going to see Pops. He was the only one on the block who had White visitors.

"Is your name James Blake?"

Oh no, I fretted inwardly. I thought she had found out about the robbery. I'd have to bluff my way.

"Who wants to know?" I asked in a rude tone.

"I'm Miss VanIyke. Is your father home?"

"None of your business!" In an attempt to scare her off, I also told her where she could go.

Totally unimpressed by my tough talk, she calmly informed me, "I'll be back," got into her car and drove away.

Inside, Carol ran up to me, happy she was no longer alone. I opened a can of franks and beans, and let her have the last of the Italian bread in a grand gesture to soften her to the idea of my leaving for the party.

"No, Jimmy, I'm going with you," she cried.

"You can't go. Carol." How could I make her understand? The time Billy brought his sister to our clubhouse, we felt under her dress. I did not want that to happen to my sister. Before I could figure things out, a fierce knocking shook the front door.

"Stay in the corner," I whispered, snatched a kitchen knife off the table, and was ready to pounce when I heard, "I know you're in there!"

"Oh, relax. It's that VanIyke woman," I told Carol as I yelled curses through the closed door. When the banging persisted, I flung the door open to really get her straight but there she stood with two burly cops. They escorted Carol and me out of the house and into the back of Miss VanIyke's station wagon. For a split second, panic-driven thoughts rushed through my mind: *It's not fair. I'm the one who robbed the store. Why punish Carol for my crime?* Then, I comforted myself: *There's no one to check on her while I'm in jail. Maybe it's good they're bringing her too.*

We pulled off from the house and headed to round up my friends, so I thought; but, the car swung east on Northern Boulevard, beyond 108th Street and away from Corona. We stopped half an hour later in front of the

Jamaica courthouse on Union Hall Street where Daddy and I had been a week earlier. Thinking that I would be tried in night court, I mounted a defense in my head: *I won't say a word. If they torture me, I'm not saying anything. I'm not giving my boys up.* I was oblivious to the real danger engulfing me.

Miss VanIyke ushered Carol and me into the building and onto a wooden bench outside of the courtroom where we waited half terrified. Around eight o'clock that evening my father arrived. We stood before a judge who grilled Daddy about the lack of supervision in the household, about my physical condition (pointing to my swollen jaw) and again about my absence from school. Daddy pleaded for time to bring an older family member up from Florida. The judge gave him two weeks to get a mature person to look after us. In the meantime, he sent us to the Queens Children's Shelter, housed in the red brick building next door to the courthouse.

Helpless in the face of raw anger, Daddy's eyes watered.

"I want to go home!" Carol shrieked.

"I'll get you in two weeks," he promised.

The more he weakened the louder she screamed, "I don't want to stay here! You take me home!"

"You're going to like it here. There are lots of little girls your age to play with," the woman behind the reception desk at the Queens Children's Shelter tried to calm my sister, but Carol was way past encouraging words.

Finally, an elderly bald man in a three-piece suit approached us. I later learned he was Mr. Henry, the social worker. "Little girl, if you don't stop that fuss, I am going next door and ask the judge to send you to a reform school for misbehaved children," he threatened.

"Leave my sister alone! You ain't sending her nowhere!" I had been watching quietly but jumped in with a streak of cursing the likes of which he had probably never heard.

What a commotion: my cursing, Carol's screaming, and Mr. Henry's threats. Kids poked their heads into the reception area. Excited whispers drifted to my ear: "The new boy is tall." "You think he can fight?" Carol paid no attention to them; she was relentless in her demand to go home.

Mr. Henry broke the stalemate. "Mr. Blake you're going to have to leave," he instructed.

My father lurched toward the door with Carol hanging around his waist. "Don't leave me! Don't leave me here!" she squalled. Daddy was about to break into tears. A wave of terror ripped through my chest. Once, when he was upset with my mother, I had seen him sob uncontrollably with his big fists pounding the wall. It was a sight I never wanted to see again. I gently pulled Carol's arms loose from Daddy and he stumbled into the night.

"Don't worry. I'll take care of you," I told my sister. She quieted down until two counselors arrived to take us to separate dormitories. Then, the yelling started again. "I want to stay with my brother," she locked onto my arm.

"Girl, stop your foolishness!" ordered Mr. Henry. I wanted to kill him. He showed no feeling for Carol's pain.

I was hurting too, but fear for my sister overshadowed my feelings. "Listen, Carol, listen! I'm gon' see you first thing in the morning and I'm gon' take care of you while we're here. It's only two weeks, okay?"

"Okay." She went reluctantly to her dormitory.

As I was led across the tiny entrance hall, I gave Mr. Henry the finger before climbing a flight of stairs and entering a massive dull green rectangle, called The Boys' Dormitory. Straight ahead three gigantic windows stretched upward toward a cracked ceiling. Twenty beds were lined in two columns of ten. They were dressed in dingy gray and, I would soon discover, itchy wool blankets. Beside each bed was a cubbyhole nightstand for personal items. Directed to the only empty bed on the right wall, I sat down and jumped right back up when the bedsprings gave a rusty squeak.

Most of the children were asleep but a few had waited for me. "New Boy, Alfredo gon' kick your butt," whispered the boy to my left as he pulled the covers over his head. *Who is Alfredo? What...* "Lights out!" barked the counselor who had brought me upstairs. The room plunged into darkness.

I lay awake, angry. *Why they jail me without a trial? I didn't do nothing bad enough to take me from my family... did I? Yeah, I stole the candy for my birthday party but the judge didn't say nothing 'bout me stealing. Why they take me from my family?* "MAMA!" "Oh! Oh! Oh!" "Maaama! " "Uhhhhhh!" Cries of anguish yanked me into the cold reality of my surroundings.

Grinding teeth, squeaking bed springs and mournful whimpers played a sad symphony. Children rocked back and forth trying to soothe the ache of being ripped from their families. I forgot my own plight and, though no one had taught me to pray, I pleaded, "God, please help these poor children." The louder they cried, the more I prayed. With tears streaming down the side of my face, I begged God to remove their pain.

It was my twelfth birthday but I felt old by the time I collapsed into sleep and tossed in a dream where...

My real Father stands over me. I can't see His face but His robe is purple velvet with gold braided trim. His voice soothes like the warmth after drinking a steaming cup of hot chocolate. "Everything is going to be alright," He says. "I brought you here to rescue the children from pain." He closes his gigantic hand around mine; I feel His strength. He leads me to a mountaintop; the sharp rocks cut the soles of my feet. "Speak!" He orders. As far as my eyes can see, a multitude of children stretch downward to the horizon. They scratch and claw like Dodo birds unable to lift themselves in flight. "I'm here," I tell them. "With God's help, I'm going to lead you out of your suffering." Silence falls on the mountainside; then, thunderous applause... jolted me awake.

Peace blanketed the room. My Powerful Father was present and I no longer feared the strange new place where fate had dropped me. That night God lit in my heart a burning desire to help children. I was barely twelve but I began to realize that the less I thought about myself and the more I focused on the needs of others, the happier I would be. Barely discernible in a bed of raw emotions, God-of-love seeds that had been planted on 108th Street by Mr. Moore began to sprout. I drifted into a peaceful slumber.

Next morning, the dream was still fresh but Carol was uppermost in my mind. I even forgot about my toothache. I guess my jaw was still swollen but I did not notice and nobody else seemed to either. Matter of fact I do not recall ever being sent to the dentist. My strongest recollection is the early morning smell of alcohol on the breath of a man who said he was my counselor as he handed me a faded shirt and a baggy pair of jeans. I fastened the oversized clean but frayed clothes with a belt that wrapped twice around my waist, then I headed for the door in search of Carol.

"Hold up, New Boy," the counselor stopped me. "We go to breakfast as a group. Line up with the others in the hallway." I did not know it at the time but it was the first in a series of steps to control my every move. My instinct said resist but I got in line like I was told.

When my group finally marched into the eerie quiet of the school style cafeteria, my neck stretched to catch sight of Carol. She was seated at a table in the back of the room with a group of other ten-year-old girls. Still visibly upset, she gave a slight wave when I shouted her name.

"Okay, since you just arrived last night, you can speak to her quickly but come right back," the counselor consented. "After breakfast, you'll get a chance to talk to her in the yard." I dashed to my sister's table.

"Carol, remember this is only for two weeks, two weeks! You remember that." Her eyes were swollen from crying. She nodded. "I'll see you outside right after breakfast." I rushed back to my seat.

"No talking!" the counselor ordered but it did not stop the boys at my table from pounding their fists in their hands and cutting their eyes towards me. "Alfredo," one of them murmured. I wondered which one of them was Alfredo.

We ate in silence and once in the yard, I met Alfredo. He was a muscular boy, twice my size with scars that crisscrossed his face like lines on a road map. He was itching for a fight. Every time our eyes met he clenched his fists and jeered, "I'm going to get you, New Boy." I was scared.

The kids spent the rest of the day speculating about whether or not I could whip Alfredo. Once I saw how big he was, I really didn't want to fight. I tried to wriggle out of it but as the day wore on it was clear I would be put to the test. It was tradition: a showdown with the new kid determined if the reigning tough guy would retain his power. I had never been a bully and didn't want power over the group; I was only going to be there for two weeks.

Leery about the impending brawl, I jumped when Walter, the only boy brave enough to talk to me, came up behind me at the fence. "New Boy," he said, "Alfredo is going to attack you at nine o'clock when the lights go out tonight. That's when the counselor leaves the floor. He punches real hard. He get you down, he won't stop hittin' you."

Walter was no push over. I had been in enough street scrapes to tell he had skills, but I could also tell by the way he talked that Alfredo whipped him when he was the new boy. I needed a plan.

Nine o'clock drew near. A lump of fear lodged in my throat but I swaggered to my bed pretending to be a tough guy. The lump was dissolving to trembling when Daddy's voice rang in my head: *Calm down boy! Never let anybody know you afraid.* The shaking stopped. *Fake out your opponent; make him unsure.* I bobbed my head up and down, *Yes, Daddy.*

I watched the clock near the exit sign in the hallway. At exactly eight fifty-five, while the counselor was still there to protect me, I executed my plan. With the speed of a tiger and screaming like a wild hyena, I leaped across two beds and landed on top of Alfredo with a solid punch to his face... *another to the top of his head,* Daddy instructed. *Now, end-knuckle punches to the bony parts of the jaw! To the bones in the shoulders! Look him in the eye; let him know you fearless! Let him know you determined!* Alfredo's eyes glared back with naked fear and I would have ended it had it not been for Daddy's sharp rebuke: *A wounded animal is dangerous! Go for the kill!* "I'm gon' kill you." I screamed over and over as I straddled Alfredo pounding away.

"Pleeease! Please, New Boy," he begged. I tasted blood and wanted more.

"My name's not New Boy; it's Spade!" I hurled the first tough guy tag that came to mind.

"Please, Spade." With that pitiful whimper Alfredo's year-long reign ended. When the counselor finally pulled me off him, I was the new "king" of the Shelter.

That night when the lights went out, gleeful laughter replaced the moans and groans of the previous evening. The dormitory room was charged with excited whispering. "Man, did you see that!" "Pow! Alfredo went down!" "Spade, that's your name, right?" "Spade creamed him." The guys heaped praise on me and I openly egged them on though inwardly I thanked God for getting me through that scary fight. Except for Alfredo, who had retreated beneath his blanket, my dorm mates bantered back and forth until a deep, quiet sleep covered the room.

At breakfast, I got the first glimpse at how dramatically things had changed. In the space of twenty-four hours I had gone from Little Jimmy to New Boy to Spade. The boys respected Spade. They introduced themselves with broad smiles and offered me the milk from their trays. I acknowledged their smiles with a nod but refused the milk. Again, my focus was on Carol. I asked the boy next to me if the girls would jump my sister. "Nobody gon' touch your sister; you the toughest guy in here," he proclaimed. At that moment, I understood my power and, though I did not want to be the top dog, I was ready to fight every new boy that entered the shelter if it meant protecting my sister.

I wanted to do something about my dream of relieving the children's pain. Deciding that my authority would be used for good, I outlined some rules. Armed with The Golden Rule—"Do unto others as you would have them do unto you"—and the sincerity of a twelve-year-old with street smarts, I wielded my own brand of justice.

On the third night after lights out, I laid down Rule Number One: "No chump in here better not jump nobody smaller or weaker than him or you gon' answer to me."

"Okay Spade," resounded through the dormitory. It was my very first act as a community leader. After a week, with several successful fights under my belt, the new rule was firmly established and I went back to counting the days until Daddy would arrive to take Carol and me home.

"Get your things and meet me on the stairs," I told Carol on the Saturday Daddy was to pick us up. Happy that we would not have to stay in the shelter one more day, we sat patiently on the lobby steps with our little bundles resting at our feet.

After a while Mr. Henry happened by, "What y'all doing there?"

"My father is picking us up today," I answered.

"What?" His bottom lip quivered, "Nobody's coming for you. Git your little behinds upstairs!"

I could see Carol was about to let loose. "Don't worry. Go back to your room. I'll call Daddy," I reassured her.

"You're not calling anyone!" Mr. Henry scolded.

"Don't pay him any attention, Carol. Go back to your room."

After all the bragging about going home, I crept back to my room in shame. The boys looked surprised but no one dared approach me.

When I asked for permission to call Daddy, Mr. Jackson quickly informed me that I was not allowed to use the phone. It infuriated me. He was the same counselor who stayed out of trouble with the director by coming to me to get the boys to make their beds.

"Rip the covers off," I ordered. Blankets and pillows flew in the air. Within seconds the dormitory was a mess. Mr. Jackson countered my order with threats of restrictions for everyone. Nobody moved.

"I want to see you in the hall, Blake," he commanded. I strolled out of the room. Once in the hallway, he changed his tone: "Okay, you can use the phone but don't let the others know."

"Clean it up," I signaled when I reentered the room. All I wanted was to use the phone but I discovered that my power extended to the counselors.

I called Granny and she had Daddy call me back. "You got it all wrong. It's next Saturday. I'll be there next Saturday," he promised.

A week later he arrived full of excuses. "Ain't got nobody from Florida yet; so, it'll be two more weeks."

I was already at the stairs when a bloodcurdling "Noooooo..." spun me around just in time to see Carol fly into my father's chest. With clench fists she pounded and screamed, "No! No! No!"

"Let's go Carol! Come on!" Though I was weak in the knees, I managed to pull her off him.

"I hate you! I hate you!" she screamed at Daddy's back as he retreated. The encounter must have taken its emotional toll on my father because he never visited us again.

Three weeks into our stay in the Shelter, Carol and I were on our own. Any security would have to come from me. I exacted some privileges too. I was aware that messy rooms always got the counselors in trouble with the director. Faced with the possibility of getting fired, they bargained. In exchange for making their jobs easier, I was allowed to stay up late and go to the corner store for candy. If I deemed another child's punishment to be unfair, I overturned the restriction. Most of all, I made things easier for my sister. I showered her with treats and got Mr. Jackson to arrange extra privileges from her counselor. When a counselor refused to go along with my demands, beds were left unmade and garbage cans were knocked over.

Mr. Jackson adopted a new hip attitude toward me. With a dip in his walk, he extended his hand, "Hey man, give me some skin. Get that room in order, you know."

"Yeah, just have my pass ready," I reminded him.

"You straight, man. Cool."

Everybody was happy: Mr. Jackson, the director and me with my privileges. This early ability to manipulate the shelter's structure helped me understand power relationships in institutions. Everybody has a boss and

71

pleasing the boss leads to money or privileges or both.   At the shelter the counselors pleased the director, the director answered to the administrator, the administrator appeased the Board and the Board catered to the funding agencies for which we children were placed on display.   In this way, three weeks drifted into six.   With Christmas fast approaching, I began to settle down because I had learned to work the system.

Eight to ten civic organizations and churches in Queens donated Christmas presents to the shelter children.   To work picking up gifts meant a chance to see the packages while they were still prettily wrapped and an opportunity to get out of the shelter for the day.   All the boys wanted the job but only three of us were chosen.

We climbed on the back of an open-bed truck and made our rounds to Lions Clubs, Shriners and Veterans of Foreign Wars.   I liked the VFW post on Merrick Boulevard in Jamaica because it was Black.   Matter of fact, it was the only Black organization on our entire route.

At some stops, it took two adults working for thirty minutes alongside us three kids to load the many gifts.   I was amazed by the number of presents we had collected by the end of the day.   The outpouring of compassion from people who wanted to help caused feelings of appreciation to surge in my chest, but gratitude never took hold. When we carted the gifts to the shelter attic, there were already piles and piles of neatly wrapped boxes tagged "girl-8," "boy-10," "girl-6."

"Who are all those presents for?" I asked, Mr. Roy, the driver.

"Oh," he sneered sarcastically, "they been up here for years. This is where the staff Christmas shops for free."

Once we finished unloading the new gifts, I went straight to Miss Corbett, the head administrator. "There are presents in the attic. Why don't we get them?" I demanded to know.

"You want something, go get it, Jimmy" she snapped without looking up from the papers she was studying.

I returned to the attic to find the staff hovering over the fresh heap of gifts like seagulls at a garbage dump. Giving the most liberal interpretation to Miss Corbett's response, I ignored the staff, and tore into boxes marked, "boy-12." When I could no longer find gifts appropriate for my age, out of curiosity, I ripped open other presents. There were lots of White dolls, basketballs, footballs, sleighs and other toys to make a child's eyes light up. After an hour's rampage, I left the attic with three heavy flannel shirts, a baseball and catcher's mitt, a train set and a cowboy gun and holster that I had wanted since the time Joseph got a cowboy outfit for his birthday.

"Ooooo! Where did you get that?" the other children crowded around when I entered the dormitory.

"Back off!" I barked.

"Why you get that and we can't get something?"

"I got it 'cause Miss Corbett said so. Now, get lost."

They crept back to their bunks too afraid to challenge me. I spent the rest of the evening playing with my new toys but the best gifts were the colorful plaid shirts. The warm browns and bright reds sparkled next to the dull institutional clothes we were forced to wear.

After my shopping spree in the attic, I decided never again to sing for gifts like we had done in the cafeteria for Halloween and Thanksgiving. I hated the sight of the women who rushed around the room before our performance chirping with red, red lips, "How cute." "How precious."

I longed for an on-going relationship with a caring adult. Even back in the 1950s Big Brother and Boys Clubs of America were well established organizations that offered the kind of one-on-one attention that I yearned. However, I never had a mentoring experience with either group, nor did I get to know the good hearts of the charitable ladies who came to the shelter. I jerked back when they leaned down to smile and pat me on the head. Confusion crossed their brows but, by maintaining a posture of rigid anger, I managed to escape what I considered their pawing. They moved on to a more complacent child.

The dreaded Christmas party was fast approaching. Once in the cafeteria, there would be no getting out of the caroling. The inevitable line-up before a sea of strange faces would end with us chiming "Joy to the World" when we felt anything but joy. I already had my presents. I vowed to stay in the dorm the day of the party.

Christmas 1954 was the saddest ever. I missed my family. If I could not be with Mama and Daddy or Gloria and Joseph, then I wanted to be left alone to think about them and that is exactly what I was doing when Mr. Jackson started rooting everyone out of the dormitory. The other children protested but, eventually, they left whining and complaining about going to "that stupid old party." I flatly refused to budge. After a while Mr. Jackson gave up. Alone at last, I pulled the blanket over my head and imagined myself at Aunt Carrie Mae's holiday table covered with meats, vegetables and her delicious macaroni and cheese. Just when I was about to *run outside and ride Wilbur's shiny new bike*, the cover was lifted from my head.

"What you doing little boy? Don't you want to go to the party?" A blond, who looked to be in her twenties, peered down at me.

"Leave me 'lone." I snatched the edge of my blanket from her hand.

"Don't be like that; why you so mad?"

"Don't ask me why I'm mad. You got a damn home to go to and I don't."

She sat down on the bed and started rubbing up and down my leg; tears glistened in her blue eyes. *What's this?* I wondered. Next thing I knew she was under the covers with her hands in my pants. When it was over, she stood up, smoothed her silky hair, and walked out of the room without a word. I lay on my bed staring at peeling paint on the ceiling and feeling nothing in particular.

Richard, a White guy a couple of years older than I, was the first to come back from the party. He got all excited when I told him what had happened. "How was she?" he wanted to know.

"What you mean?" He had to do a lot of explaining because I was unfamiliar with any of the terms he used.

Up to that point, my exposure to the opposite sex had been indirect. Early on, I would sit in the car and between sips of gin my father would groan, "Ummm-umph!" whenever a female passed. First time I noticed this reaction to women, *what's wrong with him?* I puzzled but never questioned. So, the extent of my education about women was, "She's a tiger," or "Look at her, Little Jimmy; she's a fox."

By the time I was eleven I had seen Daddy kissing women at the garage. Whenever I entered he would wink. On several occasions, he sent me to fetch his favorite girl: "Jimmy, Jimmy, do me a favor; take this ten-dollar bill and tell Barbara to meet me at the garage." Barbara would tuck the money in her bra and follow me. Daddy would give me a quarter to buy treats.

Watching my father made what happens between men and women seem the most natural behavior in the world, but men with men was a whole different thing. Corona had one openly homosexual guy and everybody teased him because he switched like a girl and wore his hair in frilly curls. "Howie, Howie. Howie, the Cowie!" Or, for no reason, jeers "Sissy!" "Faggot!" "Queer!" followed him down the street. Though I never knew Howie to harm anyone, my friends and I made a solemn oath *to take the head off a faggot that tried any stuff with us.* This attitude went with me to the shelter and fight off male counselors, I did.

When I first arrived, one counselor used to sit on the shower floor, call the boys in and lather their private parts. "Don't soap me! I'll soap myself!" I knocked his hands away.

"Aw, don't be so difficult," he pouted. "It's easy. The others like it."

With images of Howie in my head and Daddy's voice ordering, *"Little Jimmy, don't let no faggot touch you,"* I assumed an unmistakable fight posture. That counselor never bothered me again and, once I gained a measure of power over counselors as the reigning new boy, he left the boys in my dormitory alone too.

At age twelve, I thought I was a tough guy, but I was defenseless. Instead of stereotyping predators, I wished Daddy or somebody had told me more about women. Without knowledge of the opposite sex, a person innocent in appearance abused me. Of course Daddy had no idea of the dangers of the shelter, and I was unsuspecting when it came to would-be good Samaritans who take advantage of kids in institutions. Contrary to today's openness, in 1954, there was no media blitz encouraging children to "tell an adult you trust if someone touches you." Even if I had possessed such awareness, there were no adults I trusted. Without an outlet to express my confusion, the Christmas molestation was just another experience that did not quite measure up to the pain of losing my mother.

Failing to make sense of what had just happened to me, I nonchalantly returned to my presents from the attic. In the distance I heard young voices ringing out "Silent night, holy night. All is calm; all is bright/round yon' virgin, mother and child."

Several grades were lumped together. At best, we received two hours of instruction a day in the shelter school. Different groups—girls, boys, preteens and adolescents—rotated in and out of a single classroom.

"You're smart," said my teacher, Mr. Dan. "Talk to Miss Corbett. You don't belong in my class. You should be in a program where you can be challenged."

I would turn fourteen that fall and was old enough to attend high school. However, the idea of being on grade level was not uppermost in my mind; I simply wanted to walk to school like a regular kid.

I had developed a closeness that made it easy for me to approach Miss Corbett about my schooling. "Mr. Dan said I am wasting my time in his class; so, I want to go to public school," I told her.

"No Jimmy, you can't go out to school. We have never done that before," she grinned like I couldn't be serious. Her off-hand reply annoyed me. As far as I was concerned, the request was the same as asking to go to the corner store, which she had never refused. When I pressed the point, Miss. Corbett explained that attending a public school would be a "serious departure from shelter regulations." I did not understand: so, I persisted. Days passed before it sank in that my request had been denied.

I lost interest in everything. I stopped going to Mr. Dan's class despite Mr. Henry's threats of taking me to family court. Invitations to Miss Corbett's house for the weekend were declined. Cooperation with the counselors ceased and the dormitories grew filthy as fights erupted around me. In short, I released control over the other children and the placed became a zoo.

Finally, in mid-September, Miss Corbett agreed to let me attend Jamaica High School. Mr. Henry was furious. "Don't reward him for his rebellion," he argued. "You need to drag that hard-headed hoodlum into court and send him to reformatory school."

Despite the anger of the head social worker, Miss Corbett stuck to her guns. Later, Mr. Jackson pulled me to the side and informed me, "She forced Mr. Henry to file the court petition for you to attend public high school." I was the first child from the shelter granted such a privilege. Beyond the personal benefits, my protest paved the way for other children to attend public school.

Miss Corbett's decision also altered my life in another significant way: it closed a reformatory school door that had been swinging wide open to receive me.

Cowards! They made me break the news to Carol. "Why can't I go?" she asked. Her wide-eyed fear almost choked me.

"They don't accept girls," I half whispered.

"Then, why are they taking you if they don't accept girls."

"I don't know, Carol."

"I don't want to stay here, Jimmy. If I got to be in some stupid old place, I want to be with you. Why they got to separate us?"

It felt like a big hoax. My pleas to stay at the shelter or at least to keep Carol and me together had fallen on deaf ears. Miss Corbett hadn't explained why my sister and I were being separated. She had rambled on about how the new place was the best for me: I would have a room with one roommate; I would be allowed to leave the facility to attend a public high school.

None of it made sense. I had already started the fall term at Jamaica High School, had won my first battles with the want-to-be tough kids and I liked it there. Miss. Corbett had not convinced me that I would be better off at another school but most of all she had failed to explain why Woodycrest, a home with other eleven-year-old girls, was not accepting my sister.

On the day I left, just as I was walking out, Carol, who had been hiding, jumped out from nowhere screaming, "Jimmy don't go! Don't leave me!" It took three people to hold her back. She thought a big enough

fuss would force the staff to let her come with me.   I
wanted to calm her but there was no time. Right outside
the door sat the car with a female passenger in the front
seat and an impatient driver revving the motor. I was on
the verge of crying, but did not want to make it worse for
my sister. I charged out of the building and into the car.
The driver sped off.   Shrieks of "Jimmeeeeeee..." trailed
behind me. My heart shook like a rattling boiler about to
explode.

I was half way to the Bronx before a clear thought
formed. *Why?* I kept asking myself as the station wagon
zoomed across the Triborough Bridge. I wondered what
would happen to Carol without my protection and what
this Woodycrest place would be like.   I was trying to
steady myself when a wiggle against my rib cage startled
me: "Frances! Ruthie!" Lost in pain, I had not noticed my
baby sisters on the back seat of the station wagon.
During my two-year stay at the Queen's Children's
Shelter, I had seen them on infrequent weekend visits to
Corona. After months of separation, Frances had crawled
over, without warning, and snuggled up against me. *How
cruel!* Some unfeeling social worker had stuck her and
Ruthie in the car.

"What they doing here?" I asked the driver.

"We dropping them off at a foster home.   Don't
worry; I'm taking you to Woodycrest first."

"Oh, they going to be in the Bronx too?"

"I can't tell you where they going. Speak to your
social worker." He was stern, like he had been through
the routine many times. *Cowards!* All the adult
responsibility had been shoved into my lap: I had to tell
Carol I was leaving, then brace for a second separation.

Ruthie and Frances were bright-eyed, playful three-
and four-year-olds—pretty little girls too young to know
what was happening. I thumb-wrestled and sang "John-

Jacob-Jinglehiemmer-Smith" songs with them until we stopped in front of Woodycrest. Of course they clung to me when I started out of the car. Promises of visits and candy did not calm them. They cried. I cried.

Leaving the female passenger in the front seat and without attempts to comfort me or my baby sisters, the driver got out of the car and escorted me up the stone steps to the massive building that sat at the top of Woodycrest Avenue like a haunted castle from a Dracula movie. Carved above the heavy wooden doors were the words, "American Female Guardian Society's Home for the Friendless."

Though everybody referred to the orphanage as Woodycrest after its street location, its official name was rooted in the 1830s when the American Female Guardian Society was founded to aid destitute women and children. It was a time when most Blacks in New York were slaves and would not have been considered for the services of the new organization. In 1849 the Society merged with the Home for Friendless Children and other charitable organizations. In the early 1900s, the institution moved from Manhattan to the building at 936 Woodycrest Avenue in the Bronx. By 1956, children from various ethnic and racial backgrounds were admitted and there I stood reading the inscription, "...Home for the Friendless." The name fitted my emotional state. I felt like I did not have a friend in the world. I couldn't even summon Mama's song, "What a friend we have in Jesus," to comfort me.

To make sure that I was handed over to the proper authorities, the driver of the station wagon entered the building with me. The expansive lobby dwarfed us. A crystal chandelier sparkled fifteen feet above the gray marble floor. It reminded me of magazine pictures I had seen of the White House. Like walking in an echo chamber, the clop-clop of our footsteps chased us across the lobby to a woman who stood smiling at me from the bottom of a wide winding stairway. "Helloooo, James Blake," leaped from her lips and circled the room in a vibrating echo. No place—Children's Center (where I stayed for a week before going to the Hebrew Children's Home), the Hebrew Children's Home itself, nor the Queen's Children's Shelter—was comparable to Woodycrest in size and grandeur and no place felt as cold. Not a single child was visible. I was small and alone.

The unnamed woman took me to an office on the second floor where Mrs. Ferguson introduced herself as my social worker.

"How are you?" she fired the totally ridiculous question.

How do you think I am? I raged inwardly. The last fragments of family had just been ripped from me and blown to God-knows-where.

Week one, I learned the downsides of living in a large institution where hundreds of people from different backgrounds were thrown together. To insure order, the place was run military style and "Move with the group" was the number one rule. I hated it.

Week two brought an unfamiliar challenge of group living. I scratched and swatted, then switched on the bedside lamp. Tiny bugs crawled all over my body. Some scurried when the light hit them but others dug in, biting the mess out of me.

"Bugs! I got bugs on me!" I ran screaming to my counselor, Mr. Craft.

"Oh my God! You've got lice! Come! Come! Come!" He took me to the nurse, who poured a cold lotion over my body, shaved my hair and isolated me from the other boys. Never had I seen anything like it in Corona or the shelter. It was my first lesson on health and hygiene in group living. I was subject to catch anything— unexplained rashes, viruses and a slew of colds. When one person was infected everybody was unsafe. So, I was quarantined and the medical staff prodded, poked and jabbed me with needles for the good of us all.

Week three, I moved to Roberts Hall, named (as were all the dormitories) for a family or organization that had given big money to Woodycrest. Because my group ranged from age fourteen to eighteen, we were privileged to live in a separate building from the younger boys. We slept two to a room, had our own gymnasium and pool, and attended school off the premises. To keep me from falling behind in my high school studies, I was transferred from the eleven-to-thirteen year old Gould-Tuthill boys to Roberts Hall a couple of weeks before my fourteenth birthday. To mark the milestone, counselors allowed an initiation in the locker room area of the pool where other new guys and I were herded like cattle through pitched darkness and beaten.

The Gould-Tuthill boys had filled me with scary initiation tales of kids bumping into things, fainting and getting hurt during the hazing. They warned that I would have to be brave if I didn't want to be teased or taunted or labeled a crybaby. Determined to avoid such a fate, I went through the line with my fists clenched. Voices rang out in the dark: "Let's see what this kid is made of." "Is he going to be a crybaby?" "Come on you little bastard, let's see what you made of."

"If you touch me, I'ma kill you!" I shouted.

"Oh. We got a tough one." "Tough one," echoed around the locker room. A hand pushed me to the floor and I came up swinging, but it was a lost cause. Their eyes had adjusted to the dark and they dodged my blows. In contrast, I had just left the bright lights of the first floor and, virtually blind, I punched the wall.

My right hand swelled along with my resentment against the Roberts Hall boys and the counselors, supposedly responsible individuals who watched a rowdy group of teens inflict violence on their defenseless victims. Fights on the block in Corona and "new boy" scuffles in the shelter were fair one-on-one encounters, but the cowardly mob in Roberts Hall had hidden in the dark and ganged up on me. A wall rose between them and me. The hazing marked the beginning of my days as the institution's rebellious bad boy. I distanced myself from the other boys and decided to ignore Woodycrest rules.

Coach Ramseur was the first to feel my wrath. He had observed me on the court weaving, jumping and making baskets when I was a Gould-Tuthill boy. "Blake, we gon' get you a uniform," he declared.

"I ain't playing." I was defiant.

"Yeah, you good; you gon' play for Woodycrest."

"No. I'm not gonna do it."

"What's wrong with you, Blake?" My stubborn refusal baffled him. However, because I was really good at basketball, he wouldn't give up. He attempted to wear me down by making me attend practice every day. At first, I detested the idle time on the bench but after a while I got joy out of watching Zachariah, a little short Greek guy, drift down court, spin three times and go airborne in a jump-shot. What he lacked in height, he made up for with agility and speed. Then, there was the real star, Charlie, who skillfully bobbed around four guys to make a lay-up. My spirit quickened at the glory moments of those great players and then slumped again.

I plodded through Woodycrest in passive isolation until the day Alfred swirled around on the dinner line and punched me in my chest with all the force he could muster.

"What the hell you do that for?" I yelled.

"Who do you think you are?" he mumbled.

The fight was on! We had tumbled onto the floor before the staff separated us and restricted us to our rooms. An empty stomach that night and the threat of no breakfast simmered us down. By the middle of the next day Alfred and I were laughing and talking. His anger had nothing to do with me. He had returned from his weekend visit home knotted in pain. The only way he knew to release the anguish was to punch somebody.

The tussle with Alfred taught me to be on guard. Because I was surrounded by all kinds of personalities, I never knew when someone would explode and hurt me. Family brawls back in Corona were terrible, but it was downright brutal when thirty or forty strangers with different backgrounds and different problems lived in close quarters. We went for blood. In such an environment, my easy gait and relaxed way of moving in the world got displaced.

Alfred's punch also caused my focus to shift. Like in the shelter, my own suffering began to take a back seat to the pain of those around me. Most of the children, even the older boys of Roberts Hall were intimidated by a kind of staff manipulation where some guys were favored and others were rejected. This was especially cruel for children who were completely cut off from family and relatives. They were the hungriest for acceptance and the most vulnerable to exploitation because Woodycrest was their only family. This need for acceptance bred an atmosphere of competition and submission that made guys, in an attempt to avoid the cruel sting of isolation, pretend to like people that they despised. The environment was the perfect incubator for the staunch rivalry that developed between Charlie and me.

Charlie was a scholar-athlete decades before the current widespread emphasis on this dual achievement. Defying the stereotype of the dumb Black athlete, he excelled in his studies and dominated in sports. He was the quarterback for the Woodycrest football team. When he walked onto the field we swelled with pride. As the lead man for the basketball team, not only did he get the ball from the opponents, he weaved past slashing arms and around sweaty bodies to make spectacular plays that brought us yelling to our feet. In softball games, he played short stop and nothing got past him—line drives, ground balls, nothing; and homeruns were guaranteed when he stepped up to the plate. He was good enough to play in an exhibition game at Yankee Stadium with youth from all over the city.

Charlie had such athletic ability. Even in water sports, he was the king. During the winter, he swam like a fish in the Roberts Hall pool. In summer camp canoe races, he stood tall rowing side to side with steady strokes while the rest of us bobbled up and down and sometimes fell overboard. He ruled the waterfront and his prowess landed him the title Waterfront Director.

You name it—archery, ping-pong, horseshoes; Charlie was good at it. Most of all he was fast with his hands. Even with my skills as a fighter, I could not whip him. Except for Richard, who was older and a boxer, nobody could beat him.

Charlie was the man! He was fifteen and good looking. His muscular body swaggered and his light complexion glowed in an era when "yellow was mellow." Girls were crazy about him. He had everything the fellows admired and Woodycrest held him up as the perfect model of conduct. The role must have made Charlie uncomfortable but I never considered how he felt. All I knew was, if he liked you, you were in; if he didn't, you were ostracized.

Having just arrived from an institution where I had been the kingpin, I cared less whether Charlie liked me or not. In my mind the important question was whether I liked him which I did not and I let everybody know it. My attitude left Woodycrest without leverage over me. When asked, "Why can't you be like Charlie," I retorted "'Cause I'm me."

Even though I was not one of the top fighters, the other guys respected me for my fearlessness. I said things to counselors and administrators that they wanted but were afraid to say: "Get the hell out of my face." "Ain't cleaning that damn room." "I'm sick of this schedule." "Why we always got to line up?" "This food stinks." "I can't stand this place." "I'm restricted, so what?" "Oh, I'm not going home for the weekend? Well, you know what you can do with that." I even knocked away the hand of the director's wife when she tried to straighten my tie. I told her, "You ain't my mama; I got a mama!" when she asked me to call her Mommy. I became the voice of the other children's misery. There was no question that Charlie could whip me physically. He was a bodybuilder and I was the skinniest guy in the place but I seized the moral high ground. The competition was on for the leadership of the group.

I had no favors for the fellows, but I encouraged them to stand up to the staff: "Don't call that woman, 'Mommy.'" "Don't let them push you around." "Why they restricting you? That's not right. He hit you first, didn't he? Go back and tell 'em it's not fair." Though they never followed through, the guys were comforted by my expressions of outrage about presumed mistreatment. I became the voice of justice.

My desire for justice was sincere, but really I resented Charlie because he posed a threat to my gang-banging ways. The more I watched him moving with ease through Woodycrest's maze of regulations, the more I rebelled against rules set in place to reshape me. I had no idea of good or bad limits; any control over my behavior was viewed as an attempt to rob me of my identity. The truth was, I could have learned from the discipline Charlie displayed but I was too angry to see it.

Angry or not, I was forced to bond with the group of guys in Robert Halls that attended Taft High School. Herman, Curtis, Tommy, Charlie, Zachariah, Alfred, Carlos and I walked in a drove down Woodycrest Avenue, alongside Macombs Dam Park and past Yankee Stadium to the 161st Street – River Avenue subway station of the D line. At seven-thirty in the morning the train was full of pretty girls from Walton, a predominantly Black all-girls high school. They chewed gum, giggled and sometimes winked. I winked right back. When one of them whispered, "Oh, he's cute," I flashed a broad smile, held her gaze and gave a second wink.

When another asked, "Who's he?"

I leaned in closer, "I'm Jimmy Blake, baby. What's your name?"

Five minutes later, we scrambled off the train at the 170th Street station. In the half-block walk to the school, our excitement turned to dread. A crowd of White students hung out in front of Taft. Guys with Elvis hairdos and leather jackets smoked cigarettes along the sidewalk and grooved on the steps with girls who wore poodle skirts and pulled their hair into silky ponytails.

With the approach of our racially mixed group, the atmosphere changed.

"Here come them niggers." "Monkeys!" they jeered.

"Yeah, call us 'niggers' but you better not put your hands on us," we shot back. With fury we entered the building and scattered to different classrooms. The only Black in my class, I adopted a defensive attitude toward classmates who seized every opportunity to remind me of my race.

Charlie was the Woodycrest guy who got along with the student body at Taft. His athletic and academic abilities served him well. Students swooned over him; he walked their walk and talked their talk. Charlie breezed through the school day while the rest of us counted the minutes to dismissal. I was unaware of it at the time but Charlie was the first Black child to be admitted to Woodycrest. He had taken the lumps and bruises of racism as a very young boy and by high school had learned to navigate a predominantly White terrain.

For the rest of us Woodycrest boys, the week crawled to our only enjoyment at the Friday after-school sock-hop in the gymnasium. Even though Tommy Sands and Elvis Presley records played instead of Little Anthony and the Imperials, we risked being jumped by the Fordham Baldies gang for the chance to dance with the hand full of Black girls who attended Taft. Without fail the dance party started with girls lined on one side of the gym and boys holding up the wall across the floor. Because I was a good dancer and kind of cocky, I was the first to cross the divide, grab a girl and pull her to the center of the floor. The party got swinging. That's the wonderful thing about music—any music—it breaks down barriers. Though we never danced together, Black and White students dropped their guards and had fun for an hour. Never mind the Baldies, I rocked to Elvis.

Every week my Woodycrest brothers and I took a big risk staying at those sock-hops. The Fordham Road section of the Bronx was ruled by the Baldies. I had heard that it was a gang that wore jackets with the image of a hanging Black kid plastered across the back. Small bands of them rode the trains with razor blades between their fingers and randomly slashed anybody with dark skin. Other times, a huge swarm attacked small numbers of students as they left Taft. Rumors circulated among students: "The Fordham Baldies are coming today."

It wasn't just a Black thing. The Taft student body was mostly Jewish but they too were jumpy about the Baldies and other gangs that were cropping up. Newspapers sensationalized notorious incidents of gang violence. Influenced by those articles, the Woodycrest staff instructed Roberts Hall boys to come straight back to the dormitory after dismissal from school. Though we were nervous, our closest encounter with the Baldies was indirect. The gang scarred the face of a Black student, who was usually on the D-train when we boarded it for school. His misfortune forged a tight bond among the Roberts Hall boys. We watched one another's backs and I developed a small circle of close friends at Woodycrest, despite my resistance to all things institutional.

Worried about my sisters, I told my social worker, "Mrs. Ferguson, if you don't let me see my sisters, I'll walk away from this place." My one-month probationary period as a new boy at Woodycrest had ended. I was eligible for weekend passes home and would have more opportunities to run away but I was more concerned about finding my baby sisters. Mrs. Ferguson surprised me. Hoping to reduce my chances of running away, she responded to my threat, "Can you take two buses, if I write down the directions?"

"You bet I can!" I left that office pumped with excitement.

The very next Saturday I got off the bus in a crowded section of the Bronx. The exact location of Ruthie and Frances' foster home has faded but the muffled sounds behind the closed door of the house are etched in my memory. The place must have been packed with people. I knocked and explained who I was. Minutes later a hand pushed my sisters through a slightly cracked door and onto the porch. Then, a set of eyes peeked at the window while we visited. That was our routine every other week for a year.

Not once did I enter that house and I never got a look at the woman that I assumed was the foster mother to my sisters. On warm and cold days Ruthie, Frances and I spent short visits perched on the stoop under the watchful but hidden gaze of the mysterious woman. She made me feel like an outcast who could not be trusted with my sisters, but I pressed past my annoyance and played little games with them. They loved guessing which of my fists held the Tootsie Roll or Mary Jane that brought squeals of delight. After precisely an hour, the door cracked and a detached voice bellowed, "Time's up."

I had heard Granny and Aunt Carrie Mae talk about people who took in foster children for the money. Ruthie and Frances' foster mother was so peculiar that I concluded she was definitely in it for the money. I wondered why the government didn't give that money to Aunt Carrie Mae. She had taken care of my younger sisters from birth and had grieved their loss when they were taken from her. "They been with me for a long, long time and I hate to give them up, but, I ain't got nobody to help me," she had cried. "I have to go to work and pay the rent. I have to look after Elizabeth and Elijah too. I can't help any of them if I'm outdoors. I have to go to work," she repeated over and over as she resigned herself to letting her nieces go. Instead of assisting Aunt Carrie Mae in her efforts, the child welfare people took Ruthie and Frances from a loving family member and placed them in the hands of a stranger—a seemingly coldhearted stranger at that.

There were days my imagination ran wild. I envisioned all sorts of horrors inflicted on my sisters in their foster home. At the tender ages of three and four, they were unable to tell me about their living conditions or the treatment they were receiving. On my visits, they conveyed only two emotions: happiness when I arrived and sadness when I left.

Nowadays, when asked about the Bronx home, Frances can't remember the names of the foster parents or how many other children were in the house or the room where she slept or the food that she ate. "All I can remember is being lost," she says. "I was lost and no one knew where to find me. I wanted Mommy and Daddy to find me—especially when I saw other children with their parents."

In a year's time, Francis and Ruthie were abruptly removed from the Bronx home. The day I discovered they were gone, I fumed all the way back to Woodycrest. When I stormed into Mrs. Ferguson's office, she told me that my sisters were with "a wonderful family in Wyandanch, Long Island." I had never heard of the place. Even if I had known how to travel to their new home, I had no money. So, I swallowed the pain of loss and endured the separation in silence.

During one of my early weekend visits to Corona, I discovered that Carol had refused to eat or participate in any activities after I left the shelter. She went three days without food, forcing Miss Corbett to call Granny who read her the riot act before promising to bring her home on weekends.

It seemed like it would have been easier for Granny to let Carol live with her than to shuttle back and forth between Corona and downtown Jamaica. Nevertheless, she repeatedly pulled her three-hundred-pound, sixty-year-old body on and off the eight buses that the two roundtrips with transfers required. Every weekend she rose early on Saturdays to pick Carol up and took her back to the shelter late Sunday afternoons.

Something was up. On the return trips to the shelter, Carol never failed to cry and beg to live with Granny. Though no reason was ever stated, fear of eviction or the loss of a government check or one of a thousand secrets must have prevented my grandmother from taking my sister into her home. So, she stubbornly maintained the grueling weekend schedule.

Eventually, Granny's persistence yielded results. With me gone, the trips home made weekdays at the Shelter bearable for Carol. Oh, she still hated the place but, to protect her weekend privileges, she stopped giving the staff grief.

The new calmer routine went on for a year before change pushed in again without warning. Miss Corbett called Carol to her office and announced, "We got a place for you." Loud and persistent, but empty protests, followed. Within days my sister was in the back seat of the same gray station wagon that had transported me to Woodycrest.

"They didn't even bother to give me a suitcase," Carol complained. "Just stuffed my things into a pillow case and shoved me into the car with a stone-faced driver who took me to the end of the earth without a single word." She was headed to Hillcrest, a home for girls in Bedford Hills, New York. The grounds at Hillcrest were beautiful but the place reminded my sister of a prison. "Removed from society out in the middle of nowhere," she grumbled. To her twelve-year-old way of thinking, meanness made the shelter send her too far away to visit her family.

At Hillcrest, Carol released her rage on anyone. She also reverted to her old tactics of not eating and refusing to participate in activities. This promptly earned a trip to Mrs. Earp, a skinny little social worker in her forties.

"You have to participate; it's not healthy," Mrs. Earp stated in a stern tone.

Sobbing uncontrollably, Carol screamed, "It's not healthy for you to keep me from my family!" Then, she lunged over the desk and began choking the social worker.

The loud commotion brought a rush of staff to pull her off that poor woman.

Instead of labeling the attack an assault and threatening Carol with reformatory school, like Mr. Henry certainly would have done, Mrs. Earp turned mayhem into mishap. She must have read in the records that Granny could put an end to my sister's tirades. Calmly, she dialed and handed the phone to Carol.

"You put your hands on anyone else, I'll come up there and ring your neck. Now, you eat your food and listen to those people." Of course, it was too far away for Granny to visit but the threat worked. With a "Yes, Granny," my sister settled down.

Resigned to her fate, Carol began to participate in activities. On the track team she ran the hundred-yard dash and received countless ribbons and trophies. She even joined the drama club and landed the role of Pitti-Sing, one of the maidens in Gilbert and Sullivan's opera, *The Mikado*. Mayor Wagner came to see the performance on opening night, but Carol didn't meet him because she had promised too often to tell the world about the horrors of Hillcrest if she ever got the chance. The staff carefully steered her away from the mayor though Daddy met him while she was backstage.

When she peeked from behind the curtains, Carol was shocked and very pleased to see Daddy sitting among the other parents. Because the children were in costumes and make-up, it was impossible to identify them during the performance. Afterwards, when she ran over to him, he did not recognize her behind the slanted eyes painted on her face. Once he realized it was her, with a big smile, he bragged to everyone, "This my daughter; she can act."

On the surface Carol adjusted to institutional life, but anger smoldered underneath and she continued to give Daddy a fit. Her letters to him read: "All y'all people ain't no good. I hate you all. Don't even bother to come see me. Don't write me either."

Daddy cried to me on one of my weekend visits home from Woodycrest: "Go see your sister, Little Jimmy. She ain't doing too well." Though my situation was just as bad as hers, on my next weekend pass, I visited Carol because I knew what she was going through. I showed up trying to be a fourteen-year-old Daddy to my twelve-year-old sister.

"What's wrong with you?   Why you keep writing them letters?" I asked.

"Nobody won't visit me."

"I'm here. What's the matter with you? We got to do this. It'll get better."

"I hate this place. It's a prison. I want to go home, Jimmy."

I softened my tone, "Oh, it's not so bad; look how beautiful it is up here. Come on. Show me around." She was reluctant at first but fell into a perky tour guide role as she pointed out the track where she won her ribbons.

As we strolled, Mama's melodic voice gently rebounded across the neatly clipped grounds and over the rolling hills of time: *You'll take the high road and / I'll take the low road...*/ *Me and Little Jimmy/ will meet again / on the bonnie, bonnie banks / of Loch Lomond.*   Carol chattered away and I wondered if our family would ever gather on the "bonnie, bonnie banks." It sounded like such a peaceful place.

By the end of our visit, Carol had settled down but it didn't stop her from handing me a list of demands for Daddy: 1. You better come see me. 2. Bring me a portable radio. 3. I need money.

Except for the time my father saw her in *The Mikado*, he never visited but he sent the radio on my next visit. She put it on the shelf over her bed and dared anyone to touch it. Nobody stole the radio or anything else from her because no one wanted to deal with the aftermath of screaming, yelling and crying.

On another of my visits to Hillcrest, Daddy sent money. He had only four dollars and I had already pleaded for money. The fair thing would have been to give two dollars to each of us but he replied, "No, Little Jimmy, I got to give it all to Carol; she'll be upset. You understand, don't you?"

"Okay, Daddy." I agreed, not because I understood but because I did not want a tearful scene from her or him. Dutifully, I gave Carol all four dollars.

Today, Carol teases me about my visits to Hillcrest: "You thought you were somebody, stepping up there in a three-quarter length top coat with your stingy brim hat crimped over one eye. You looked good though." Indeed, I did. I took great pains in dressing because I knew I was going to a place where there was nothing but girls.

On weekend trips home from Woodycrest, I usually stayed with Gloria. I looked to her to fill the void my mother had left. She had defended me when I was a little boy on the block, at school and in the Hebrew Children's Home. I had always counted on her to be there when I needed her and, in 1956, she was still shouldering the responsibility that Black families expect of the oldest child. I remembered when she got the shellacking of her life back on 108th Street. She had been hanging out with her friends when she was supposed to be watching us. Granny stripped her naked and whipped her. With every lash Granny yelled, "Take responsibility!" My sister might as well have been told, *"Be a mother! Be a mother!"*

Finally, Gloria was a hardworking, scheming teen mom. After Carol and I were removed from Corona by Miss VanIyke, street-life caught up with Joseph and he was sent to Warwick State Training School for Boys in Orangeburg, New York. Gloria and Betty both came up pregnant but had remained for several months in the frigidly cold house on 107th Street. Following the birth of her son, Richard, Betty moved out, leaving Gloria alone. Struggling to live up to the sister-mama role, she had continued to go daily to Aunt Carrie Mae's to baby-sit Ruthie and Frances who were both toddlers. Her struggle to survive independent of my father and our relatives began with the delivery of her son, Eddie.

When I first laid eyes on Eddie, he was a fragile infant lying in the dresser drawer my sister had converted into a bassinet. Back then I was still in the shelter and Gloria and her baby were living in a little apartment on the corner of Northern Boulevard and 97th Street. I asked her how she managed to find her own place, "Whoosh," she answered, "It gives me a splitting headache to think about it." I changed the subject.

We talked instead about happier times on 107th Street. Gloria reminisced about horseback riding. She showed me the beautiful leather riding boots Pops and Aunt Lucille had given her. She laughed at the falls, bumps and bruises she suffered learning to ride. Footprints of our childhood lingered in those memories of 107th Street.

During weekend visits from Woodycrest, Gloria and Eddie were always a few steps ahead of homelessness. One night she slept on the streets but unable to bear having her son out-of-doors, she knocked on Dorothy La Lande's door and her friend took Eddie, thinking that she was simply babysitting for the evening. Next morning, as if nothing was wrong, Gloria returned to pick him up with gratitude, easy laughter, and merry conversation. By nightfall she had somehow secured shelter.

Eddie was the firstborn of a new generation in our family. Hopes of our future rested in him. In the three years since his birth, my nephew had already taken on his mother's unshakable spirit. He was a child stripped of material goods but, like Gloria, he shared what little he had. "Uncle Jimmy, you want some eggs," he would offer. After making a big fuss over him, I would decline. He barely had enough for himself, but that was Eddie—free-hearted, the little man around the house trying to protect and cheer his mother. With awkward humor, he tumbled into screwball somersaults trying to make her laugh whenever she looked sad.

Gloria moved so often that I had to hunt for her whenever I came home. When I found her, no matter how tight the furnished room or how cramped the tiny apartment, I had a place to sleep. I was unfazed by my seventeen-year-old sister's nightmarish fight for survival. I was even unaware that she was trying to mother me. I did realize, though, that she wanted the best for me and that she shared my dream of reuniting our family. She talked about starting her own business, becoming a beautician or a nurse and getting a huge house where all her sisters and brothers would live. It was a fantasy. I was only fourteen but I could see that caring for Eddie took all the energy she could muster. There was no need for her to worry about my future. I was satisfied with the haven she provided whenever I showed up at her door. She was my lifeline to Corona.

T he crisp fresh part of the day rolled across Lake Cohasset in swirls of sunlight but the beauty of the scene was marred by a tide of dread that swelled inside of me. Woodycrest had packed up its whole operation and moved out of the city to Harriman State Park for the summer.

As I stood shivering beside the totem pole in front of the camp mess hall, my mind drifted back to the previous summer when the shelter had sent me to The Fresh Air Fund's Camp Trailblazers. On that first trip to upstate New York I was angry because I was forced to leave the city. However, the minute I stepped off the bus I noticed a skinny kid, tall like a basketball player, with a velour hat cocked to the side the way we wore them in Corona when we wanted to show we were tough gang members. My attraction to him was instant. I rushed over, "Hey. What's happening man?"

"Nothin' happ'nin'." His surly response meant some well-meaning adult had snatched him off the streets and sent him to the boondocks.

"You Chaplain?"

"Yeeeah, what's it to you?" His voice shifted to a hip tone.

"I'm Chaplain too."

"Yeah?" he perked up. "Man, where you from?"

"Corona."

"Coroman?" He messed it up. "Where's that?" he asked and I explained.

He was two years older than I was but our gang connection made us fast friends. This rough dude from the Brevoort Projects in Bedford Stuyvesant, Brooklyn told mesmerizing stories of bat brigades and stomping attacks that took me back to Corona. I responded with accounts of life at the shelter. Touched by the sorrow of my separation from family, he promised that his mother would take me in and his gang would look after me if I ever decided to run away. He even invited me to bring my boys from Corona to Brooklyn without fear of being jumped. I had never had anyone express such forthright compassion for me.

My newfound friend and I dubbed Camp Trailblazers "Camp Corny" and refused to participate in any activities. *Let them sing their songs and roast their marshmallows; we have one another,* was our attitude. As we bonded, the tough guy dropped his guard and underneath the hardened veneer, behind the front, was a gentle spirit. He reminded me of my brother, Joseph: he did not smile often but when he did it was beautiful the way his eyes danced and his whole face lit up.

When we parted this guy that I had known for only two weeks showed me a picture of his sister—a really pretty girl—and said he would introduce me to her when I visited him in Brooklyn. Deep down I knew I would not see him again but I promised to definitely look him up. I pledged never to forget him and I haven't, but for the life of me, I can't remember his name.

A year later, there I was back upstate. Standing on the cliff of Camp Woodycrest overlooking the lake, I braced for an entire summer with no visible ally. Camp Trailblazers had pulled children from all over the city and provided opportunities to meet new people, but Camp Woodycrest was a closed circle. My heart longed for a new sidekick but there was no way to duplicate the friendship I had developed the previous summer. I was stuck with a bunch of guys I already knew, who had no fascinating stories of street life to help me escape the drudgery of my second "Camp Corny."

Wound up like an old-fashion clock, I ticked off my disapproval of Camp Woodycrest. First of all the staff changed our group names. They tagged Roberts Hall, the Boone Boys, and branded the Gould-Tuthill preteens, The Apaches. How corny could they get? Whether it was basketball, boating or swimming, I ridiculed those who got involved in activities under the banners of lame group labels. "Why you acting like you White? You Black," I mocked guys lounging on the diving board tanning when their natural hues ranged from deep bronze to blueberry black.

To emphasize my disgust, I looked for every opportunity to oppose camp rules. By then, I had accepted my bad boy label and anybody in trouble was a comrade of mine. Chuck, one of the Apaches, was constantly in a jam because his mouth was always running. On display as an example to other campers who might become disruptive, time after time he sat in front of the dining hall on the massive rock that jutted out of the earth.

"What's going on man?" I would inquire.

"I'm on the rock again. I can't go swimming, can't go boating, can't do anything."

"Don't worry about it. Here take this paint can; hit this beat: 'Boom-pop-pop, boom-boom!'" I demonstrated.

Over the course of the summer, Chuck got really interested in the drum and time on the rock became pleasurable. I got satisfaction from helping him sidestep penalties for petty infractions and, though it may be the farthest thing from the truth, my ego tells me that I had a small hand in Chuck's later success as a member of the Last Poets—a renowned group of rhyming, rapping, drumming bards of the 1970s.

My sole mission was to irritate the counselors and staff—that is, until the second week of camp when the Boone Boys began weekly hiking ventures. Roughly twenty-five rowdy teenagers trekked downward from Camp Woodycrest. The tightness of my body loosened the minute I set foot on the vertical path. Being naturally agile, I had a talent for the charge down the mountain. Others tripped and tumbled, but with the wind on my face, I leaped from rock to rock without losing my balance. As we sped ahead, our counselors quickly fell behind. Their shouts drifted on the wind, "When you get down to the lake, wait up!"

The most daring quest on our spiraling descent was the black snakes curled beneath sunny rocks that dotted the mountainside. We moved a rock; a snake ran out; that snake was dead. Armed with sticks, we pounded its head, and then paraded it around on the end of the longest branch we could find.

We were young and totally ignorant of the critical roles that snakes play in the environment. We didn't know that they controlled the population of insects, rats and other pests that bred along the lake's edge and crept into our barracks to make our lives miserable at night. Our counselors were also unaware of the important link of snakes between lower and higher orders of the food chain. With nobody to enlighten us about these and other creatures encountered in nature, an opportunity for a great open-air education was squandered.

Nature has a way of striking back; the snakes got their revenge. Snakebites were common on our excursions. Thank God, we carried an emergency kit with a sharp knife and a suction cup. When a kid suffered a bite, the counselor sliced a tiny X over the two holes where the fangs pierced the skin, suctioned the venom out and bandaged up the leg. One of the counselors took the injured hiker back to camp for the nurse to take a look while the group kept to the trail.

The snakebites never made us cautious. On every hiking adventure there was the invariable snake hunt. If we cornered an adult eight-foot long Black Rat Snake, we told tall tales for the rest of the week. "You see the way Blake grabbed that snake?" "That snake was hissssing!" "I saved your life, Blake." "No, you didn't. I was careful. I knew exactly what I was doing. That snake had'a bit me, I'da grabbed him around the neck and squeezed." "Yeah-yeah, right!" With the briefest exchanges, the squabbles ended. The big bragging sessions were saved for nights around the campfire. We also tired quickly of our prize conquest, slung the snake carcass into the bushes and moved on.

Once the trail curved into the woods, golden flecks of sun flickered through the lush canopy of treetops. Steadily, we made our way along the dark shady path. When we came upon a clearing or a roadside, the blinding light startled us. "Ooooh, it's bright out here!" "Boy, must be noon!" "Is it time for lunch?" Usually, it was not time to break and eat. We crossed the road and reentered the dark coolness of the woods. Away from the grime and humidity of the city, I felt refreshed and energized. The songs of robins, the buzz of bees and the piney smell of cedar caused my lungs to explode, "Yewww! Yew! Yew!" My ears cocked for the returning echo.

Hiking possibilities were endless. Though we were in our teens, Cowboys and Indians was the war game of choice in the summer of 1957. Half of us ripped off our shirts and smeared our chests and faces with mud, let out battle cries and attacked the cowboys who barricaded themselves behind dried brush piled against groves of young trees. Occasionally, we stumbled upon a raccoon or a possum. Sometimes a deer leaped across the trail and we became hunters in hot pursuit. Of course, we did an immediate about-face if we got close to a deer. Anything that moved in the woods was a target. We inspected insects, chased squirrels, stirred beehives to shouts of "run, run, runnnn!" With no nearby lake to plunge into, most of us outran those bees.

One kid got popped by a bee and in a matter of seconds his lip blew up like a balloon. It was the most bizarre sight, his bottom lip hanging down almost to his chest. The counselors hovered around him administering some mysterious on-the-spot treatment. To me he was just another casualty taken back to camp as our expedition advanced.

Frequently, we came upon cave-shelters—tin sheds along the Appalachian Trail where campers and hikers stopped to rest, eat and sleep. We poked around looking for treasures of flash lights and hunting knives but found discarded frankfurter wrappings, empty cereal boxes and crumpled cigarette packs. Failing to unearth any real bounty, we turned our attention to the pipe of running water that was a main fixture at each shelter. We splashed our faces, filled our canteens, got off the main path with its guide markers and moved deeper into the woods.

In uncharted territory heavy with mounds of dry leaves, we imagined ourselves explorers trampling through dense forest where human feet had never trod. One afternoon, we veered off the trail, through the underbrush and into a yard where a bearded man in overalls stood holding a shotgun. We took off running. "He's gonna shoot! He's one of them woodsmen," we screamed. Actually, the man had not threatened us. We had simply heard too many campfire tales about woodsmen who shoot people for trespassing. Before long, we settled down and happily made our way back to the marked trail. Our adventures of fear and hope continued deep in the woods.

By the time we started the climb back up the hill to Woodycrest, the sun was setting over the lake and the Jokosee kids had gathered on the campground next to ours. They gawked like we were a bunch of animals crawling up out of a cave. They acted like we had no right to be in the area. Under the snooty gaze of upper middle class exclusively White campers, our racially mixed group initially mumbled resentment. After a while we conjured up a more creative response:

> One, two three, four, five, six, seven
> All from Woodycrest go to heaven.
> When we get there we will yell
> Jokosee! Jokosee! Go to
> Hey there. Hi there.
> Baby in the high chair.
> Who put 'em up there?
> Ma? Pa? Shish-Cum-Bah!
> Woodycrest! Woodycrest!
> Rah. Rah. Rah

Once armed with the chant, even when we were dog tired from a day of hiking, we squared our shoulders and marched by Camp Jokosee like a drill sergeant was breathing down our necks. It was our way of saying: *we're just as good as you.*

I found peace in the woods. Thoughts of separation from my family, fights against authority, the pain and complaints of my fellow Boone's Boys were wiped away. I released tangled emotions in outbursts of positive energy. Those summers in the woods were the cave-shelters of my adolescence. Praises to Woodycrest for sprinkling my youth with serene episodes in the wild.

Lights flashed in my eyes and I froze in the chill of the September night. "Hey! You Joe Blake's son?" the officer asked after looking me up and down. He recognized me because of Daddy's work as an auxiliary policeman.

"Yeah." I kept my cool.

"Where you going, Blake?"

"To my sister's house."

"You better get the hell on home," he ordered not realizing that I was a part of the gang they were hunting.

Jose of Woodside had jumped my uncle, Izelle, because they both loved the same girl. To get even, four hotheads from Corona went with me to Woodside, randomly snatched guys out of stores, off park benches, out of parked cars, did them in and fled on the #7 train.

Adrenaline pumped on one end of the subway car. On the other end, two young cats with BB guns talked in snobbish tones about their homes in St. Albans—the leading upper middle class Black neighborhood of Queens. *Uppity jerks!* We grabbed and busted up their guns, dragged them off the train, onto the platform and down the stairs. At the base of the steps, in a dimly lit area under the elevated tracks at 103rd Street and Roosevelt Avenue, we whipped them until they were wobbly and left them wiping their bloody noses on their coat sleeves.

My crew and I drifted up 103rd Street toward Northern Boulevard. Like a menacing slow moving storm, we rolled in the middle of the street between rows of parked cars and away from the bunched up storefronts that hid behind heavy wrought iron gates. At the first corner, I pulled away and turned left onto a dark avenue and headed to Gloria's place on 99th Street. That's why I was alone when I froze in the glare of police lights.

"Two kids were dragged off the train and beat up tonight. We rounding up the thugs. You better get your behind off the streets," the cop repeated. Not only did I hurry to Gloria's house, the next day, instead of stretching my visit to the last second, I returned to Woodycrest Sunday morning.

The following weekend I discovered that my boys were in jail and the police were looking for a tall skinny fifteen-year-old named Spade. No one told them that Spade was James Blake. Not one of the guys gave me up. People in Corona had a sacred code: "Don't rat one another out." Even if one of them had broken rank, it was not likely the police could have traced me to Woodycrest. Only Cody, the least likely to squeal, knew that I lived in a children's home. They all knew, however, that I frequently stayed at my sisters' house but the cops had not questioned her.

Saturday, Joseph also spent the night at Gloria's place. It was the first time we slept in the same bed since 107th Street. Lying in the dark, I asked him, "What happens when you get arrested."

"Man, they beat you." His voice was barely audible, like he was far away. "They ask you questions then hit you before you can answer because they not interested in answers; they just wanta beat you. They call you all kind of names and hit you in the chest, stomach or on the arms, but not in the face where it'll show."

"How many of them, just one?"

"No. Two or three hold you down while one punches you over and over."

"Did you get beat?"

"Yeah."

"Why? What did you do?"

"Nothing. They didn't like me looking at them; they wanted me to keep my eyes on the floor but I never took my eyes off them; so, they beat me in shifts."

"Then, why didn't you stop looking at them?"

"Because I wanted to know what was coming my way; I didn't want any surprises. I saw them sucker punch some of the guys."

The image of three burly policemen beating my brother made my stomach boil. They had beat Joseph and they weren't even trying to get information from him.

Horrifying thoughts of what was happening to my friends raced through my head. Withholding my name from the cops made them heroes in my book. I was too young to understand it at the time but their protecting me saved my life as surely as going to jail destroyed theirs.

Today I'm much older and wiser but I'm still haunted by images of my brother and friends brutalized inside jail cells. I cringe whenever I see twelve and fourteen-year-old children in handcuffs, or a young brother stopped and frisked for no reason of his own. It's also disturbing to watch the trend toward criminalizing the mistakes of school children. Correcting errors is essential to the learning process. Yet, in the names of law and order school buildings are policed and mistakes are stomped out at young and tender ages. In doing so, we send children to an emotional and mental death row.

Of course I didn't think this way as a teenager. Back then, happy that I had escaped arrest, I concocted a plan to stay free. I refused to make my bed, cursed at everybody and did whatever I could to start trouble at Woodycrest. "Ain't no janitor and I ain't mopping no floor," I bristled at Mr. Green.

Clueless that he was playing into my hand, "You not going home 'til you do it," he guaranteed me.

In order to get a weekend pass my chores had to be finished no later than one o'clock on Saturday. I let the hour slide by and, predictably, Mr. Green suspended my pass and eliminated my need to explain why I did not want to go home.

Relieved as I was to hide out at Woodycrest for the weekend, I hated being restricted to Roberts Hall. While the other children swam in the indoor pool, played basketball in the gym, then bundled up and went to the movies, I was stuck in my room, except for mealtime and one hour a day of television in the Social Room.

The deafening quiet of the building got to me. Right at the end of my confinement, I scurried to the corner Jewish deli and spent fifty cents Daddy had given me on the best liverwurst sandwich in New York. To my utter dismay, Mr. Green caught me sneaking back into Roberts Hall and tacked another week onto my punishment.

Mr. Green, our new Roberts Hall counselor, had been one of my counselors at the shelter. He took on the mission of quelling my rebellion at Woodycrest. He proved to be a hard taskmaster when it came to rules and chores but cleverly balanced his strictness with compassion. He was aware of my interest in the piano because Gloria had banged on the old upright in our house back on 108th Street. He also knew that I had watched with envy when she picked up a few notes from Louis Armstrong. He used this knowledge of my fascination with the piano to reach me.

A talented, versatile musician—drummer, pianist, singer—Mr. Green hummed Broadway tunes but never made it to the Great White Way. Because theatrical opportunities were virtually closed to Blacks in the fifties, he worked in small clubs around the city. At Woodycrest, convinced that music could harness my energy, I became his creative project. At the height of my anger over the extended restriction, Mr. Green pulled me into the Social Room. "Sit down," he ordered and then he played *Misty*. Immediately, I was soothed. The piano reminded me of home and the lyrics to the song, *"I'm as helpless as a kitten up a tree; / never knowing my right foot from my left..."* described my predicament.

For the rest of my restriction, I entered the Social Room eager to see Mr. Green at the piano. When I caught up with him, he surprised me. "Try it," he pushed me toward the piano stool.

"No," I pulled back.

"But you have beautiful hands, long fingers made for the piano." I was a kid who had received few compliments. Those simple words made me want to play. During my second week on punishment, I spent almost all of my time at the piano, but poor coordination hampered my progress. Just when I was ready to give up, Mr. Green gently pressed, "Keep trying; you can do it."

After my restriction ended, I continued to rise before six in the morning to practice. With Mr. Green teaching me a note at a time, I learned to play *Misty*. Next, he taught me to play *Summertime*, another superb song choice: "Oh, Your Daddy's rich and your Mamma's good lookin'/ So hush little baby / Don't cry." The mournful tune captured my deepest yearnings. Daily, I practiced at the piano. Oh, I still squabbled with Mr. Green over chores but time at the piano was timeout from rebelling.

When I returned to Corona and my boys were still in jail, I decided to sip scotch with Gloria and her friends. For as long as I could remember I had had little tastes of alcohol from my father and other men in a macho mood: "Here little Jimmy, try some of this; it'll put hair on your chest." The firewater burnt a trail all the way to my stomach but, glad to be treated like a man, I accepted the nips. By the time I was fifteen, drinking came easy.

To celebrate my homecoming, an Italian girl that everybody called White Betty dropped off a bottle of J&B Scotch at Gloria's apartment. She lived in Corona Heights, the neighborhood just south of ours. She had befriended a few Corona girls when they were classmates at Junior High School Sixteen and had taken to hanging out in front of Wheat's Candy Store on The Boulevard. She had money and in a poor neighborhood money attracts lots of friends. Gloria and I cultivated her.

Like everyone else, White Betty assumed I had been away in reformatory school and, because it eliminated the hassle of explaining my situation, I was happy to let the lie stand. When she heard I was home, she made a beeline to Corona, dropped off the bottle of scotch and kept moving.

Joseph arrived as I headed to the store for bread and bologna to make sandwiches to go with the drinks. "Man, don't touch my J&B," I said. No answer. I repeated myself. He nodded. When I got back, he was drinking my liquor. With a smirk on his face, he let the challenge fly: "I touched it! So what you gon' do?" I was furious but knew my brother would get the best of me in a fight. To retaliate, I gulped the whole bottle of scotch down without giving him another drop. Last thing I remembered was his sarcastic smile.

Gloria rushed me unconscious to Flushing Hospital where they pumped my stomach. Without today's computerized networks and notification requirements designed to protect children, Woodycrest was in the dark about the emergency room visit. Also, with no one to teach me about the devastating effects of alcohol, I drew my own lessons from the ordeal. I became a "smart" drinker: hard liquor for social occasions and beer— which

I considered non-alcoholic—for mealtimes, snacks and watching television.

The weekend following my drunken episode, I couldn't find Gloria when I arrived home, but there was no reason to panic. Searching for family members was common. Threats from the landlord over back rent had probably sent Gloria packing. My hunt for her started with Aunt Carrie Mae and Granny who had no information on her whereabouts. Next, I headed to The Boulevard and inquired about my brother, Joseph, and was pointed to 32nd Avenue and 103rd Street. I was shocked when a strange woman answered the door and shouted over her shoulder, "Joe, your son's here."

"Hey, come on in Little Jimmy," Daddy smiled as if I routinely entered the other side of his world. By the time I flopped on the couch, the nameless woman had beckoned him to the bedroom.

"He ain't got no place else to stay, damn it! He got to stay here," I overheard my father say. He was right. I had nooo-where to go, so I bedded down on the sofa.

My presence caused Daddy and his woman to bicker into the night. Listening to him argue passionately for me to stay in a house where he obviously had little authority, made me keenly aware of his suffering. Mournful pleas for peace shed a whole new light on his womanizing. My father and most of his contemporaries talked big about "a man's nature," but that night I saw the downside of chasing women. The humiliating argument between him and his woman flooded my heart with compassion for Daddy. I was in for a long evening.

The Friday night of squabbling droned on while a pretty little girl kept peeking around the corner of the living room wall until I fell asleep. Next morning, encouraged by the sight of the five-year-old happily talking to me, Daddy sheepishly confessed, "That's your sister,

Susan." The revelation stunned me but motivated him to share longer held secrets.   Giving me no chance to respond, he named two other of his children by another woman.   Pearl and David were neighborhood friends my age. I had almost dated Pearl back when I was in the shelter. Thank God I hadn't come home enough to pursue the crush.

By the time I left in search of Gloria, puzzling questions had been answered regarding where my father lived and why he was unreliable.   Three families were more than he could juggle and his problems were compounded in an era when men took a passive role in childrearing. Contrary to today's terrific Mister Moms, the day-to-day details of raising children were left exclusively to wives, aunts, grandmothers and older sisters.   In my father's case, the southern women in his family had tended to the offspring and he expected the same from my mother's family.   Perhaps his greatest failing was his inability to recognize that city living had strained the Toomer women to the breaking point and that the primary responsibility for raising us had fallen to him.

Our neglect was inevitable.   Without a cultural reference point or an example of how to handle his circumstances, Daddy made erratic attempts to care for his children. I have no doubt, however, that he loved us. I must also give him credit for being a constant presence in my life.   Sometimes, he surprised me by coming through when I really needed him like the night I slept on his woman's couch.

Finally, a light switched on in my head. I had to face the unavoidable fact that my family had disintegrated.   In 1958, months went by without my staying in one place.   I bounced from Aunt Carrie Mae to Aunt Reather to Gloria and, infrequently, to my father's place. Once I stayed with Joseph, who lived in the basement beneath the first floor apartment of a woman ten years his senior with four young sons. By his eighteenth birthday, my brother had moved in with Mattie Mae and I saw less and less of him. I was left without any consistency in family relationships.

Weekend visits to Corona became a matter of finding someone at home. Too often, my Fridays and Saturdays were spent wandering the streets homeless. Woodycrest turned out to be the dominant influence in my life despite my resistance to being defined by the institution. Along with family, other critical aspects of my life—friends, food, music—were replaced with a host of institutional rules and shift-workers who tended to my biological needs like I was a widget on an assembly line.

Woodycrest prided itself on being a compassionate organization and a few staff members like our activities director, Lula King, did express genuine love for children. She listened to our problems and tapped our talents in variety shows, dance recitals and plays. In her summer 1958 production of *Show Boat*, I belted out, "There is nothing like a dame..."

"Jimmy Blake, you can be on Broadway," she proclaimed and, though I knew I could not sing a lick, her praise pumped me with pride. In my heart I was Miss King's favorite but actually she was skillful at making all us children feel good about ourselves. In craftily designed creative activities, she helped us release some of our bottled up emotions. Unfortunately, Lula King worked only during the camp season. The rest of the year I was left to administrators, social workers and counselors who mostly ignored the rage I felt over being snatched out of my community.

Nobody understood how removal from the bad elements of my environment simultaneously severed the cultural richness of family and community. Jive talk—*It's your world squirrel*— ripped through my mind dragging behind it memories of hand jive—*Hand bone, hand bone where you been / down the road and back again...* I could feel rhythmic hands beating against thighs and chests conjuring up sounds and movements of stomp, tap and African step dances. Nothing in the institution came close to replacing the loss of these experiences and no one addressed the emotional turmoil left in the empty spaces.

Conversations with social workers were methodical and sterile in nature. Their main concern was about adjustment—or in my case, maladjustment—to institutional life. The other children and I were in Woodycrest because of major disruptions in our families, but the staff did not build on that common bond; and, though I was close with some of the kids, we never ever discussed among ourselves what brought us to Woodycrest. Unlike the shelter where children cried out in the night, a suffocating silence blanketed Roberts Hall. There was nobody to talk to and no relief from the pain. My many fights against institutional rules and regulations were attempts to break through the wall of silence. I wanted communication. Instead, I was punished as counselors rendered their favorite verdict: "You're restricted."

"So what? I'm already 'restricted' by being in this place!" I'd fire back and find myself doing time in my room. While the other children went out for the day, I wrestled with the hard reality of isolation. Why couldn't the staff soar above petty policies and grab hold of the spirit of what was happening with me? It had been two years and Woodycrest remained an uncomfortable fit. The place made me doubt myself. At sixteen, I felt strange, different, odd.

When on restriction, I'd search my mind for some memory to make me feel less peculiar. During one long solitary punishment, I thought back to my baptism and how Aunt Reather's church had been alive compared to the dry vesper services at Woodycrest where the director's wife, bounced around cooing, "Straighten your tie for Mommy, dear." I wanted to shout: *Somebody please make her shut up! Doesn't she know we miss our mothers?* Just as dreadful were the mournful tunes pumped from the pipe organ and the slow dragging songs that bore no relation to my condition.

No doubt religion had its answers, but deep pools of suspicion had formed in my soul. I wanted a religion that spoke to my life. So, I lay in bed during those painful restrictions trying to jar loose meaningful memories of trips to Ebenezer Baptist Church that Gloria had mentioned back when I was younger. It was a futile effort. I couldn't get beyond the image of me munching cookies in the basement. No choirs singing, Sunday school classes, or memorized Bible verses, materialized. I needed something real, but I was left with the limited knowledge of church principles and images of rituals assembled from the make believe world of movies at The Dumps. What I wanted was a set of rules to justify my rebellion against an unjust system that controlled the lives of the neediest children.

Yes, I was a troublemaker and I was punished for it. I didn't know that Mama's friend, Jesus, was a troublemaker who transformed the world with love. At sixteen, I felt that love had no place in fights against hypocrisy and injustice. Without an understanding that justice could be realized with compassion and forgiveness, my fights were without mercy. The lack of balance in my actions led to criticism by the staff and many of my peers.

Woodycrest stifled rather than developed my spirit. None of the scriptures read at worship services emphasized the value of standing up for what's right; nor were we presented with examples of righteous men who went against the grain of their times in efforts to ease human suffering. My values were shaped almost exclusively by the harshness of my experience and that was not enough to sustain me. My self-esteem took a big hit.

Oooo... What kind of twisted social worker am I getting now?

"You uh ugly little bastard," is how he started.

I wanted to punch him in the mouth.

"I'm Tilley," he introduced himself.

I sat sizing him up. His cologne was loud and for such an immaculate, manicured man, his manner was shocking, or, it would have been if anything could have shocked me. The other workers clearly emphasized their adult status: it was Mr. Merrill, Mr. Enderly, Mr. Green, and my previous social worker was Mrs. Gardner, but this cat was just, "Tilley." I decided not to waste my time playing whatever little game he had in mind; I got right to the point. "Well, Till-lee," I said sarcastically, "Mr. Enderly took away my weekend pass and I want it back."

"You mean that pervert, Enderly, did that?" he raised an eyebrow and added a curse to emphasize his outrage.

"Yeah, he did that." I threw in my own choice words.

"I tell you, I can't stand him."

"Me either." I slipped into an agreeable disposition. Never had I heard anyone, especially a social worker, express my sentiments toward the administration in such blunt terms.

We tossed obscenities at various members of the staff until he shifted my attention, "And that 'Uncle Tom' Charlie, I can't stand him either." Tilley must have been studying me because he knew exactly what buttons to push.   When I think back on it, Charlie was no more Uncle Tom than today's Black children who are labeled "White" or "nerds" by their peers whenever they follow the rules or apply themselves academically. Tilley knew that Charlie was smart but he also knew how to bait me. I responded with a barrage of vulgarities directed at Charlie.

It was liberating to share my raw feelings with an official at Woodycrest. After I had vented every pet peeve I could dredge up, Tilley secured my pass. *This cat's okay.* When I left his office I felt like I had been kicking it with one of the boys on the block.

The first several sessions with my new social worker were filled with grievances about people who annoyed me and about the unending restrictions Woodycrest imposed. It was summer before we got to the heart of what was bothering me.

Like most breakthroughs mine emerged in a haphazard fashion. I was up in camp and Tilley was back at the Woodycrest offices in the Bronx because social workers, maintenance people and clerical staff stayed in the city to prepare for the school year. While off in the woods, I sprouted a big Afro, a full ten years before the style was fashionable. Insisting I had to get a haircut, Mr. Enderly drove me down the mountain from Camp Woodycrest into Monroe, New York, a little rural town steeped in dairy farming and mining history. The moment we jumped out of the car and made our approach, the barber rushed to the door and flipped the "OPEN" sign to "CLOSED."   Mr. Enderly turned red but he did not try to stand up for me. By the end of the fifteen-minute ride back up the mountain, I was at the boiling point. I could not wait to call Tilley.

"These people don't respect us; they think we are monkeys and they won't cut my hair," I screamed into the receiver.

"Give Enderly the phone," he ordered. Angry curses rattled loud enough for me to hear. When Enderly passed the phone back to me, Tilley went on venting, "There're no Blacks in that town and Enderly knows how those people are. Besides, they don't even know how to cut our hair. Don't worry about it, Blake; I'll make damn sure you get out of there for a haircut."

He sent a station wagon up from the Bronx to bring me back to the city. The minute I stepped into his office, he came around his desk, "I got a barber for you. Come on, I'm taking you to 145th Street." We hopped a subway to Harlem. It was the first time Tilley and I had been together outside of Woodycrest and something about the change of setting freed both of us.

"Why you so angry?" he asked once we got settled on the train.

"You'd be angry too if someone ripped your family apart?"

"Nobody ripped your family apart! It just fell; it fell apart."

"What do you mean it fell apart?"

"That's what happened; it fell apart. Your mother is sick; she can't take care of your little Black behind. Your father is running around with other women and he can't find anyone to take care of you. That's why your little butt is here. You ain't got nobody to blame."

"What the hell you talking about?" For the second time, I wanted to punch Tilley. Nobody had ever described my family situation in such vivid details.

"Look, you were running in the damn streets. I got everything in the records: you never went to school; you were hanging with gangs; you were getting in trouble. Your little behind would be in Warwick if you had stayed in that environment. You had no food in your house; the place was full of roaches and rats and you had no lights!

It's all in the damn records.   You were out of school
NINETY consecutive days!"

"Well, they didn't have to take me from my family."

"No! They had to take you. They had to take you
from the neighborhood because you had no family."

"Well, I want my family and I'm going to get them
back."

"How?"

"I'm going to get out of Woodycrest, get me a job,
save my money, find me an apartment and bring my
family back together! That's how! I'm going to do it as
soon as I get out of this place."

"Well then, you're going to need an education."

"I'm going to school."

"Yeah, but you're not doing anything in school."

"Yes I am."

"No, you're not. You're barely passing, and you're
smart. You'll never be able to help your family if you
continue doing whatever you want whenever you want. If
you want to help your family, you got to change your
ways."

"What you talking about?"

"You got to stop fighting with these people at
Woodycrest because ten years from now they won't mean
a thing to you. So, you need to stop fighting them. These
cats are about to send you to Warwick!"

"I got a lot of friends at Warwick. That's where they
want to send me, I'll go to Warwick!"

"Yeah, but them friends in Warwick ain't going
nowhere. It's a training school. They watch you twenty-
four-hours a day. You think Woodycrest is a jail; they
don't even let you out of that place. You can't do a thing
up there in the sticks; ain't nothing up there but trees."

Whooaa! Visions flashed in my head of a year-
round camp with guards instead of counselors.

The D train rocked toward 145th Street and I drifted back in time: *Daddy washes cars; Mama sings in the kitchen; friends play on the block.* Abruptly warm memories dissolved into dread: *Ruthie and Frances' bodies press against mine; we shiver on the porch of their first foster home.* Then, *Carol yells, "I can't take it anymore; somebody got to get me out of here, Jimmy."* Recollections swirled into aching and I broke the silence.

"Okay, what do you think I can do to bring my family back together?" I asked.

"Well," answered Tilley, "first thing, whenever you get angry, come see me. Then, we'll take it from there."

Despite the sting, Tilley delivered the swift kick in the pants I needed. He helped me to adopt a can-do attitude. For the rest of the summer, I participated in camp activities and amazed everyone by earning the most improved camper trophy for 1959. A surge of pride came with the accomplishment and it was all because my social worker spoke my language. He understood the power of patience and openness in addressing problems. The two of us became partners working to repair the damage caused by separation from my family. We set a plan that included my doing my very best in the academic program at Taft High School and keeping a cool head at Woodycrest. The cloud of rage that blinded me began to lift.

In the fall of 1959, in addition to a better attitude about my own personal development, I began to understand how I could make a dent in the suffering of others.

Apparently my wall of resistance had begun to show cracks. Otherwise, I would have batted away the comment from Mr. Harris, counselor for the seven to ten-

year-old Colgate boys. "Little Blake, you can fight with
your hands but you don't know how to fight with your
mind," he referred to my dwindling, yet explosive
rebellious acts against Woodycrest. Mr. Harris suspected
I was ripe for the kill. He invited me to his room; said he
wanted to show me something. I agreed, but was
suspicious because abuse of kids by counselors was
rampant.

By the time of Mr. Harris' invitation, I had
discovered the reason my sister Carol had not been placed
at Woodycrest with me. The admission of girls was being
phased out because of an alarming rate of pregnancies.
The scandal was characterized by an unspoken truth.
Everyone knew that mixing between girls and boys was
limited to Friday socials where we gathered for cookies,
punch and dancing under the watchful eye of counselors
before they hustled us back to our separate dormitories.
So, I concluded that it had to be members of the staff who
were getting young girls pregnant. In fact, I had witnessed
a female counselor having sex with one of the Roberts Hall
boys. I wasn't the only one to reason that the girls must
have also been molested, but no one uttered a word.

There was also homosexual abuse. Gould-Tuthill
boys, who respected me because I stood up for them,
confided in me about their experiences with male staff. I
did not betray their trust, but unable to speak out about
the abuses, I blasted the institution about other issues.
Actually, much of my rebellion at Woodycrest stemmed
from the hypocrisy that cloaked its dirty little secrets.

The names of four homosexual men surfaced during
my confidential conversations with the younger boys, but I
had never heard anything negative about Mr. Harris. He
smiled infrequently, never joked, and never hung around
Woodycrest after he finished work. His group, the Colgate
boys, was always clean and orderly and they respected

him. Still, I was not taking a chance of going to his room by myself. I invited Tommy and Curtis, "Come with me. Mr. Harris wants to show me something and if this guy breaks bad, I'ma need some back up." Like me, Tommy and Curtis were considered oddballs and staff members usually did not mess with them. Unlike me they were muscular. The three of us could easily handle anything that went down.

"Shhhh! Come in." It was after bedtime when Mr. Harris ushered us quietly into his quarters. A pale light cut across the dark room. I could not figure if he had put the flashlight on for effect or to keep from waking up the younger kids. Whatever the case, the mood was intriguing—like peering into a forbidden realm.

With flashlight in hand, Mr. Harris pulled out a magazine. The light fell on the cover. *Buy Black* commanded the bold letters stenciled across the top. In the center of the page stood a stately African warrior, spear in one hand and a massive shield in the other. The caption beneath him proclaimed, "Shaka, the Zulu King."

"Do you know that this king ruled over thousands of African warriors? They beat back the British in South Africa." Harris flipped the page and the light rolled slowly over another picture. "This is Timbuktu. It's an ancient city with massive libraries. This is the home of our forefathers. They built these temples and schools. They were the founders of mathematics, and this guy here crossed mountain ranges with elephants and fought the Romans." The spotlight dropped on a sketch with "Hannibal" typed below it.

"Whaaat?" We were beside ourselves with excitement: "Look at this!" We were close to finishing high school but never had we seen or heard anything like what Harris was showing us. Our only images of Africa and its people were taken from Tarzan movies.

Back in my room later that night, images of Harris' warriors caused me to think about the heroes in my life. They were people who knew how to fight with their hands, handle a razor and hold their liquor. Torch, Count, Chino, Cody and Tombstone were in my valiant group, but the champion of them all was Lou Benson, a boxer ten years my senior. Lou was fierce but protective of young upstarts on The Boulevard and we respected him. I crossed him only once.

Always the rebel, when Sam Switzer had approached me about club dues, I was foolish enough to listen. "Yo, Spade, about the money: Lou got the dues," was his opener. "He's not giving it up, man."

"Why don't you ask him for it?"

"Man, you know Lou. I don't want him to explode."

"Yeah, but it's our money."

"But, it's Lou man," Sam cautioned.

"Well, I'll ask him."

"You crazy, Spade."

"But, we have a right to know what's happening with our money." Full of fool's courage, I went looking for Lou with Sam tailing me. The minute I saw him I blustered, "Hey Lou, about the money, man: the club wants to know what you doing with the dues?"

"Don't worry about it. I got it," he said in a low, steady voice.

Increasing my belligerence, I persisted "You got it, but we want it!"

With a long stare and a sharper tone, he said "Spade, I told you I got it."

"Yeah, but we want it!"

Lou started blinking fast, fast—the sure sign that he had reached his threshold and somebody was about to get tagged. *Awww, man!* The image of him knocking a cat's teeth out flashed in my mind. I backed up real slow, like inching away from a growling pit bull.

"Spade man, let's go!" Sam Switzer's voice snapped me into overdrive. We made a hasty retreat along with the crowd that had gathered. Nobody wanted to be within arm's reach when the fury erupted.

I had not gotten hurt that day because Lou really loved me and because he was a principled person. He only fought when pushed; stood up for the weak, and most of all, tried to re-direct the energy of a group of rowdy youngsters who were out to establish supremacy on the streets. He had recruited several of us from gangs, and was attempting to build a positive social club that would serve as an alternative to violence. By the time Mr. Harris approached me, the money I had been demanding from Lou was already being used for parties and athletic activities for the club.

Lou was my Charlie; he was the reason Woodycrest could not hold out a model for me to imitate. I had my group and it had a leader. Elroy was the only cat at Woodycrest to bridge the gap between my two worlds. I had taken him to Corona and introduced him to my boys. He got a taste of my gang activity at a social in the Baptist church basement the night ten guys from Astoria invaded our turf. One of them tried to talk to Tombstone's girl. We rumbled while Elroy stood on a chair shouting over and over, "They killing them all." Actually, nobody was seriously hurt; it was just another old fashion fisticuff.

Elroy would have really been upset had he been present the night Daddy-O died. The Syndicate (all the gangs of Flushing, Corona and Corona Heights) locked down the community. Hundreds of people were on the streets but nobody moved in or out of Corona. The Dukes, one of the White gangs, halted all trains on Roosevelt Avenue. It was not racial; it was territorial. Someone had come in from Manhattan and stabbed one of our own and everybody united. Despite the unity, Daddy-O's killer was not caught. His death had a profound impact on turf wars. It marked the time when gangs in Corona began to arm themselves with knives and guns.

Though there were no weapons the night Elroy ranted about killings, the skirmish had been too wild for the chaperones to restore order. The police were called and everybody scattered. I grabbed Elroy and sprinted to the subway. In witnessing this and other scrapes, he was the one Woodycrest brother who came close to understanding my allegiance to guys left in the neighborhood.

Tilley was right. I didn't have a traditional family but he was wrong when he narrowly labeled my Corona buddies "gangsters." They were family in the sense that we wore the same name, ate together, laughed and cried together, and we maintained a united front against the world. When members of my "family" banded together, we survived. When we separated, we got picked off one by one.

Ironically, the night I left Mr. Harris' room, I lay in bed trying to wrap myself in the unity of a group that had already vanished. My boys protected one another on the streets but had no protection against the system. They were upstate in detention centers like Warwick and Otisville. The "family" I knew best had collapsed but I still fantasized that Torch and Cody, who knew that I was in Woodycrest, would spring me—their war counselor, the most popular guy in the group. I was ignorant of the cold reality that they were spending longer and longer stints in juvenile facilities and would soon graduate to adult prisons. Unaware of this trend, I remained steadfast in my refusal to integrate into other groups—that is, until my senior year of high school when Mr. Harris started talking to me.

Mr. Harris stretched my definition of hero to include men who fought with their minds. By pointing out the rich heritage of Black people, he awakened in me a desire to belong to a community other than Corona. His description of the African Nationalist Pioneer Movement roused my interest, but what really grabbed my adolescent mind was a picture he showed me of Black men in uniforms. They were serious men who stood for the liberation and advancement of my people. It was a new way of thinking. Up to that time, I had never viewed warriors in terms of race; Black gangs, White gangs were pretty much the same. The thought of Blacks as an oppressed race of people in America was completely alien to me. "A race of people, who needs to be lifted from their status," Mr. Harris told Tommy, Curtis, and me. Even so, I related to the men in the picture as gang members in uniforms.

"Look, would you like to come down to meet our leader?" Mr. Harris asked in one of our many conversations.

"Oh yeah!" I leaped at the chance. In my mind, I was going to meet his war counselor, the leader of his gang. He had already schooled us about Carlos Cook, the successor to Marcus Garvey, whom he described as a fierce leader of tens of thousands of Black people. He had even showed us pictures of throngs of people parading behind Garvey seated in a 1920s style convertible, in military garb with ropes and tassels hanging from his shoulder and a feathery plume rising from his hat.

Mr. Harris had told us about Garvey's creation of the Black Star Line that was to transport Blacks back to Africa. The heir to this great work was Carlos Cook, who held meetings at the now defunct Central Ballroom Annex on the corner of 125th and Fifth Avenue in Harlem. If Tommy, Curtis, and I wanted to attend, Mr. Harris would take us to the meetings but only if we promised not to tell the other kids. That made the idea even more appealing. No longer would the three of us be a mere clique in Roberts Hall. Our group was being elevated to a secret society with a secret meeting place with uniformed Black men. Of course we would keep quiet.

Once or twice a month we traveled to African Nationalist Pioneer Movement meetings in Harlem and listened to talks about "the motherland." We were told "Black is beautiful" long before it became a slogan of the sixties and seventies. On Garvey Day we marched down 125th Street with hundreds of men and women and sold *Buy Black* magazines along the parade route. When we returned to Woodycrest, we walked pass Mr. Harris in the cafeteria and exchanged knowing smiles and winks. However, we never said a word that might get him into trouble and, more importantly, we guarded the precious secret of our new society.

Before long Tommy and Curtis were huddling in my room listening to the beat of bongo drums that I had brought from Corona where Afro-Cuban music was the rage. Dizzy Gillespie, who lived in our community, was a pioneer in fusing jazz and Afro-Cuban rhythms. In the late fifties, he held the same sway over old and young in Corona that he had held over the rest of New York since the mid nineteen forties.

In 1959, I was seventeen and too young for admission to the Palladium. I learned my Latin moves from Lou, Big Torch and Carter. They danced at the ballroom on Sunday nights, returned to the neighborhood and eventually displaced street corner quartets on Northern Boulevard with demonstrations of the Mambo, Meringue and Cha-Cha. Carter, the smoothest of them all, could have been considered disabled. He had a wide angular face on a head that was too big for shoulders that were too high. Extremely pigeon-toed, his knees knocked when he walked but Sundays he cut the steps that won dance contests at the Palladium. In his Saturday afternoon warm-ups, Carter released subtle hypnotic moves to every throb of the jukebox outside of Wheat's Candy Store. Young cats imitated him: three steps up, right foot behind left calf, down, back, one, to, three, left heel up, spin; we learned the "Carter Step."

While most Black communities were rocking to Rhythm and Blues, Corona was swaying to the Afro-Cuban beat. The neighborhood was a blend of African American, West Indian and Cuban cultures that made no distinctions among the groups. All the teens crowded into the basement of Corona Congregational Church and danced to Machito's hit record, "Babarabatiri." We couldn't Mambo at the Palladuim but Joseph and I were mesmerized by the passion of the drums. A man at the church taught him to play the congas and the bongos, and he in turn taught me. As an expression of African pride instilled by Mr. Harris, I brought the drums to Woodycrest and beat them at every opportunity.

With newfound self-esteem, I ceased being openly rebellious and became quiet, even cooperative. A more reflective style of dialogue replaced vulgar street talk as I quoted with an air of wisdom what I had heard in African Nationalist meetings.

Mr. Green scolded, "You'll mop that floor until I am satisfied."

Without raising my voice, I replied, "You will never be satisfied because you are part of a system that wants to keep Black people down."

He looked at me like I had lost my mind. "Where did you get that mumbo-jumbo?" he asked.

"Mumbo-jumbo to you because you don't understand who you are," I said and walked away. Previously, I would have cursed him out.

From the very beginning, the beat of the drum irritated Mr. Robertson, the Director of Woodycrest. He could no longer contain his annoyance once Tommy, Curtis and I started talking to the other children about Africa. We quizzed: "Do you know about Shaka? Do you know about the talking drums? Do you know about the great African kings and queens?"

We provoked the director to speak out in the cafeteria: "Yeah that Jimmy Blake, Curtis and Tommy are up there in that room beating them drums. They talk African jungle bunny stuff. Don't y'all listen to that stuff! Stay away from them jungle bunnies."

I did not recognize his statement as blatantly racist because, at the time, his was the commonly held view of anything African. I saw his reaction as just another attempt to punish me by isolating me from the other children. However, instead of withholding a weekend pass or restricting me to my room, he belittled the richness of my culture. His words did not have the desired effect though. Matter of fact, the outburst gave me satisfaction. Once I realized that it infuriated the administration, my quest to learn more about my history was added to the arsenal I used against them.

After Mr. Robertson's comment, some of the guys in Roberts Hall started calling us "jungle bunnies" and mocking our drumming. My behavior did not alter one bit and I didn't stop trying to teach my peers about their heritage. A more serious response to the director's remarks came from counselors' who increasingly portrayed Tommy, Curtis and me as troubled youngsters with severe social problems when, actually, our behavior had shown marked improvement. When I told Tilley about their depiction of us, he laughed and said, "Don't worry about idle talk from counselors."

Without mentioning Mr. Harris, I went on to describe to Tilley the positive views I was forming about Black people. He lent a sensitive ear because of his experience growing up in Durham, North Carolina where racially segregated Black scholars, financiers and lawyers thrived. He himself was the graduate of a Black college and was pleased to see that my hunger for African history was beginning to filter into my schoolwork.

Tilley and Harris were the first individuals in the child welfare system to build a one-on-one relationship with me. They helped me see my hidden abilities and potential. In his own way, each man made me realize that time is the most precious investment in children. Yes, money is necessary but nothing restores broken lives like the knowledge that you are worthy of someone's attention. Interactions with Tilley and Harris made me aware of having something of value inside of myself.

"Yes, you can! If Charlie can get a scholarship, so can you."

"I'm not going to college," I answered. "I'ma get my family back together. Besides, Charlie is eighteen and still living here at Woodycrest. Man, the dream is to be free: no more rules, no more regulations, no more Woodycrest. When I turn eighteen I'm getting out of here as fast as possible. I can't understand why Charlie doesn't want to be free too."

Tilley shook his head in frustration, "You know how much they give him? Five hundred dollars plus a thousand for his summer camp work. You can get the same thing if you go to college."

Fifteen hundred dollars was a lot of money. It was nearly enough to buy a brand new Volkswagen. *Maybe I should tell him I'm going to college, take the money and split*, I thought but said nothing.

"Well, at least get the application to NYU. That's where Charlie is going," Tilley gave a little extra jab.

After a long pause I agreed to fill out an application although I had no concept of college. To me, additional schooling of any kind meant an extension of my dreadful Taft High School experience. Even worse, school would lengthen my stay at Woodycrest and that I could not tolerate.

My hand was on the doorknob when Tilley added, "They didn't want to give you a scholarship but I fought hard for you. Just because you not Charlie doesn't mean you shouldn't go to college." He ignited the flame of the old rivalry and I was boiling by the time I closed the door behind me.

In June 1960, I graduated high school with a general diploma because I failed the New York State Regents Examination in History. My preparation had focused on English, Math and Science because I thought my in-depth study of African empires would be enough for the History exam. Naturally, the emphasis was too narrow. It omitted huge segments of American and World History which, if studied, could have landed me an academic diploma as well as provided a perspective that would have deepened my understanding of my own history.

Overwhelmed by my dilemma, I headed to Tilley's office. "I'm not going to get an academic diploma unless I go to summer school," I grumbled.

"No! We're not going to say a thing about this," Tilley declared. "I fought these bastards too hard. They agreed to give you a scholarship. They don't need to know." He went forward with plans for me to attend college and I headed upstate to Camp Woodycrest for the summer.

I was assigned to my old group, the Boone Boys, but this time as their counselor. Taking charge of guys who were my friends was more than a challenge; they tested me at every turn. Finally, in desperation, I took them on a twenty-mile march. Like a platoon of foot soldiers, they stepped in mud, climbed rocks and wiped sweat from the backs of their necks. When they slouched to the point of dropping, I straightened up the line and counted in cadence, "...your left, your left, left, right, left!" The moment I brought them back to the camp barracks, they fell onto their bunks panting while I pranced around in a false display of energy. Even though the hike wore me out, I came back the new boss of the Boone Boys.

Without the worry of controlling my group, I relaxed with my roommate and co-counselor of the Boone Boys, Mr. Archer. A stern little disciplinarian from Trinidad, he was in his mid-thirties and didn't need to struggle for authority. His evenings were spent listening to jazz tapes. Matter of fact, the previous summer when I was still a Boone Boy and he was my counselor, he had introduced me to the music of jazz greats: Charlie Parker, John Coltrane and Miles Davis. As a treat for earning the "most improved camper" trophy, he had taken me to Sterling Forest Gardens to hear The Modern Jazz Quartet with Strings.

It had been a magical evening. Rich people in formal attire assembled in the woods at sunset. With long stem wineglasses in their hands, they strolled among brilliant flowers. The humming of brass horns summoned everyone under a huge tent where the quartet kicked off its performance, "If I were a bell..." and sent my heart tingling. What impressed me most though was the all-

White audience and string orchestra that focused on four Black men: Milt Jackson, John Lewis, Percy Heath and Connie Kay. It was the most wonderful musical experience of my life.

A year later, the memory of the enchanted evening at Sterling Forest Gardens sent me bouncing to the Blue Room—a jazz spot envied by campers and created by counselors who had strung blue Christmas lights between four trees. As a high school graduate and counselor I was finally welcomed to the club. "Kind of Blue" slipped from Miles' trumpet like satin smoke and drifted to the stars. Deep into the night Mr. Archer, the other counselors and I listened to tracks of Miles Davis, Thelonious Monk, Lester Young, and of course, Louis Armstrong.

Mr. Archer, called The Big Bopper when in the Blue Room, made me want to know more about jazz and more about life in general. I was full of questions about Trinidad and discovered that his information on Black history coincided with much of what I had learned from the African Nationalist Pioneer Movement. However, the scope of his knowledge was much more comprehensive. In addition to music and history, he drew from science, literature, and a variety of perspectives.

On an afternoon when the Blue Room was closed and I had a couple of free hours, I strolled down to the lake to chat with a newcomer to the counseling staff. As a friendly gesture, I went boating with him. He had a book tucked under his arm.

"What's that?" I asked

"My college yearbook."

College? Supposedly, I was on my way to college. I asked to see the book. It blew my mind. Page after page of students and teachers were pictured inside classrooms, libraries, theaters, and gymnasiums. Candid snapshots showed uniformed bands and football teams dashing across an athletic field. Everybody was Black like in the sketches of the ancient African empires Mr. Harris had showed Tommy, Curtis, and me. I thought places like that only existed long ago in faraway lands. It was shocking to see my empire in glossy photographs taken just months earlier.

"Man, this really college?" I asked

"Yes, it's North Carolina College where I graduated."

"This Negro really a professor?" I pointed to a man wearing a white jacket in a chemistry laboratory.

"Yes," he said. "I've never had a White teacher."

"I've never had a Negro teacher," I half-mouthed to myself as I continued to scan the photographs. It hit me hard—seeing so many accomplished Black people.

The next day I phoned Tilley, "I want to go to North Carolina College in Durham."

"My family lives in Durham!" he answered with obvious delight. The wheels of change were rolling.

I could have gone by subway but Bemon drove me to the Port Authority Bus Terminal. He pressed a twenty-dollar bill into my hand. "Buy yourself some food," he said. Back then a twenty was worth more than a hundred of today's dollars but I didn't need the money. My Woodycrest scholarship had taken care of tuition, room and board; and, after buying a few clothes, I had enough cash left from my summer job to buy my bus ticket and for spending money. In addition, Tilley had arranged for The Federation of Protestant Welfare Agencies to deposit five hundred dollars at the college business office for books, school supplies, and incidental expenses during the fall semester. Still, touched by Bemon's compassion, I accepted the twenty. He was the only one in my family who understood the major change occurring in my life. I could have easily taken the subway to the Port Authority Bus Terminal, but Bemon drove me to underscore the important milestone of leaving home.

"Buddy, take care of yourself and watch your back," was his wisdom statement as I scooped from the back seat of the car the tattered brown cardboard suitcase that held barely more than three changes of clothes and a frayed overcoat. Filled with excitement, I was on my way.

The waiting room loudspeaker blared, "Washington, D.C... Richmond, Virginia... Durham, North Carolina..." I was the first to climb on the bus. I took a seat midway on the right side and watched the other passengers push down the aisle. They were mostly Black people weighed down with old suitcases, overstuffed shopping bags, pillows, blankets and children hanging on their elbows. As the bus filled, the aroma of fried chicken and freshly baked cakes mingled in the air. Laughter rang out and friendly singsong chatter rose in a chorus as the handful of men aboard assisted the women in balancing their belongings in the overhead racks.

When the bus pulled out of the terminal, paper bags began to rattle. "Child, pass me some of that potato salad." "I need a cup; you got a cup?" I listened unaware that travel time was mealtime for Blacks who were refused service in most restaurants and cafes across the country. After stuffing themselves, people settled into a restful quiet punctuated by snoring from scattered corners of the bus. I lay my head against the window and tried to imagine what college would be like as we zoomed into the dusk.

I would be eighteen in a month but was leaving New York State for the first time. Friends had pumped me full of stereotypes of southern Blacks: "They talk slow and you gon' come back saying 'yonder.'" "The men walk around in overalls with straws hanging from their mouths." "Why you want to go down there? They a bunch of dumb country boys." Their warnings stirred a streak of defiance: *They not gon' change me; I'm a New Yorker.* I twisted my Applejack cap to the side of my head and closed my eyes.

The whir of bus wheels was broken by quick stops in small towns. Five hours later, the driver announced, "Washington, D.C.; we'll be here for forty-five minutes. If you want to get off and stretch, get something to eat, you have to be back in exactly forty minutes. We're not going to wait for anyone." The thought of getting lost in a strange city kept me glued to my seat while everybody else got off the bus. The driver, a heavy-set friendly White guy, walked back to me.

"You getting off?" he asked.

"No."

"You can get off; get yourself something to eat."

Thinking it would be best to get something in a smaller town along the way, I shook my head.

"Okay, I'm getting off; once I close the door, you have to wait 'til I get back." I nodded. When the door suctioned shut, all the lights went out. I watched people outside milling around in the dark.

In exactly forty minutes, the driver returned. Continuing passengers from New York re-boarded with sodas, cookies and other snacks. They were followed by a new group of riders. A second wave of gaiety and feasting started.

The smell of food gnawed at my stomach and all the stores were closed in the dark little towns where the bus stopped. By the time we pulled into Richmond, Virginia around one-thirty in the morning, I was hungry enough to eat my bus seat.

"Change here for Durham, North Carolina," the driver instructed. "Take all your belongings. Your bus will be here in an hour."

Never mind my stiff body, I grabbed my bag and made a beeline to the brightly-lit café inside the depot. I was the first to place my order:

"A hamburger, French fries and a Coke."

The woman waited on the man behind me.

Whew. I must not be speaking loud enough. "Hey!" I raised my voice to a near shout, "You hear me? I want a hamburger, French fries and a Coke!"

"Tap-tap-tap, Tap-tap-tap," an old Black woman beckoned in my direction but I ignored her; I didn't know anybody in the South. I swung back to the counter ready to do battle, but the annoying pecking on the window intensified. My head twisted toward the woman who gestured violently in my direction.

"Me?" I indicated with a thumb curved toward my chest. She nodded vigorously and I lip-read, *"Yes, you!"*

Impatient to get back to my order, I shuffled over hurriedly and the minute I was close enough to hear, she shouted, "Son, you from the North, ain't you?"

"Yes. I'm from New York."

"I figured so," she continued. "If you want something to eat, you have to go 'round yonder. You have to read the signs," she pointed.

I looked above the waiting room door and read, "White Only."

"Gone 'round yonder; that's where they feed colored."

When I turned away from her, a sea of White faces glared at me. *Oh! This is what I've been hearing.* Never had I experienced such a clear-cut division between Whites and Blacks. At that moment I understood why

Blacks on the bus had so much food. They were bypassing one of the many indignities of travel.

In the back of the terminal I discovered a grimy smoky room with its sign declaring "Colored." Behind a makeshift counter was a Black man with a cigar in his mouth, and a dirty brown (once white) apron hugged his pot belly. He flipped burgers on a greasy stove that looked like it had not been cleaned since I was born. The sight turned my stomach. I forgot about eating, and took a seat in the dingy "Colored" waiting room. I thought hunger was making me queasy but I learned after a while that the colored waiting area and eatery were full of exhaust fumes from the two bus lanes right outside the door.

The bus to Durham arrived not a minute too soon. Again, I headed for a seat half way to the back on the right side, but I was too tired and hungry to notice or care that the seating pattern had changed: Whites in the front, Blacks in the back and me in the middle. I fell asleep.

Next, morning, I peered out the window. A cranberry sun peeked through scraggly pines that lined the rear of an open field where a dewy mist rose from the ground like smoke. For miles, a strange quiet rested on the landscape. Then, "Cocker-doodle-doooo!" a crude imitation rooster's crow shattered the stillness of the morning. "This is yo' boy-eee, country boy. Wake up everybody. Cocker-doodle-doooo!" The driver had switched on the radio. I was accustomed to New York's fast-talking Jock-O. "Hey. Cool. This is Jock-O, playing some hot sounds for you." The cackling of "yo' boy-eee, country boy" caused my heart to sink, *Oh my God, I'm in another country.* I slowly exhaled a deep dread.

My spirit rallied somewhat when I rode into Durham and discovered a lazy little southern city instead of the tobacco fields and barns I had anticipated. Outside the small depot, a man pointed me to the Alston Avenue bus that ran by North Carolina College. When I boarded, the driver beamed, "Good morning," before I handed him my fare. I did not answer. The woman I sat next to sang a cheerful, "How're you this morning?" Ignoring her as well, I grumbled beneath my breath, *Crazy. Speaking to people they don't know? This is certainly going to be different.*

Part Three:

Roller coasters

I **marched** spryly among the pretty women. They sang, "Hiiii," and I pushed out my chest: *I must be hot stuff. All these females speaking to me!*

"Man these women really digging me," I later told my roommate, who was from Creedmoor, North Carolina.

"Why you say that, Blake?"

"They all grinning and cooing, 'hello.' Man, I..."

"Jim... Jimmy, th... that's the way... it is down here," Freddie keeled over with laughter. "Everybody speaks to you. Man, you not up North. We friendly down here."

"Oh," I said, perplexed but not a bit put off. "Well, folksy or not, I like the friendly women and I'm gon' get to know them."

It did not take long for me to develop a reputation as a player. I had a woman in every dormitory. Early evenings, I walked my freshman girl to Annie Day Shepherd Hall in time for her seven o'clock curfew, and then rushed across campus to McClain Hall to pick up a sweet little sophomore. Later, I chatted in the lobby of her dorm with my junior honey who thought I was coming from the James E. Shepherd Memorial Library. At the end of the evening I headed to the library where I knew I would find my senior girl studying hard in preparation for a January graduation. On weekends, when all the campus girlfriends were available and looking for me, I pretended to be studying for exams, but actually, I went partying with the off-campus females. Why did I have so many women? Because I could! The ratio of females to males on campus was five to one.

No, my grades were not up to par. I had been liberated from Woodycrest and had gone buck wild. I desperately needed a road map. Four children's homes had spent a total of six years recording my life in fat files, but not one of them had taught me how to live. I lacked common knowledge about basic necessities. Folk wisdom like "Don't spend all your money in one place" would have served me well because, in a month's time, I had emptied my five hundred-dollar expense account on partying. Someone should have drilled into my head that "Cleanliness is next to godliness" because I did not know how to wash and iron my own clothes. At Woodycrest I had put my dirty clothes outside my door on laundry day to be returned to me fresh and neatly folded. "A stitch in time saves nine," would have been a useful motto too. For, I wore my pants until they turned shiny; then, a tiny rip grew to a gaping hole that I ignored and wrongly assumed that nobody else noticed. Most importantly, long before Tilley pulled my coat, someone should have stressed good study habits.

In short, I arrived at college ill prepared. Routine terms like major, minor, registration, bursar and curriculum were foreign. At the end of my first semester, before I could search for my name among the grades posted on a wall in the basement of the Administration Building, one of my classmate yelled, "Hey Blake you got a lot of Ds. You might as well pack and go home." To spare myself such public embarrassment in subsequent semesters, I muddled through my administrative affairs and studied just enough to avoid academic probation and the loss of my scholarship.

Despite my many shortcomings, I had entered college with one definite advantage: I knew more about people than the average kid. Placement in shelters and children's homes had forced me to learn all sorts of personalities in order to survive. I am sorry to say though, that I wasted my keen people skills on trifling social affairs.

One semester unfolded like another. My sophomore year was a repeat of my freshmen mode of operating; and, on a warm fall Sunday morning, my junior year got underway with a predictable routine. Bopping down from Chidley Hall without breaking a sweat, I floated like a cool breeze on my way to find some girls. When I came around front of the cafeteria, my best friend, Harold Fowler, stood alone in the usually crowded center of the campus.

"Man, where's everybody?"

"I don't know, Jim."

We were puzzling over what had turned the campus into a ghost town when I spotted a classmate headed towards the cafeteria. "Hey man, where's everybody?" I shouted.

"Out on Highway 55; they trying to integrate the Howard Johnson Motel," he yelled and kept moving.

I had heard about sit-ins and demonstrations and about how North Carolina College students had stepped up their involvement in the fall of 1962. However, I was not impacted directly because the protests took place outside the Black community. I hate to admit it now but back in college I felt no need for integration. I had landed in Black heaven. The stately B. N. Duke Auditorium offered movies, plays, and concerts that kept me entertained. The marching band paraded in daily rehearsals and led rousing pep rallies before football games. Our winning basketball team rocked the

McDougall Gymnasium and the weekly dance socials in the recreation rooms of the girls' dormitories culminated in a lavish winter ball. Finally, whenever I tired of cafeteria food and could afford to eat out, the Green Candle and College Inn were right up the street. Life had not been this good back in New York where things were supposedly integrated.

Was I opposed to the Civil Rights Movement? No. It was worse; I was disinterested. Protesting to integrate the Howard Johnson was not on my list of priorities. The hourly-rate Pettigrew Hotel was just fine for my needs. Matter of fact the protests were cramping my style.

"Come on Harold; let's go pull some women from that demonstration," I quipped. We phoned Smooth, our buddy with wheels. In no time, we were rolling down Highway 55 in a carefree mood. In the distance, students milled around the Howard Johnson parking lot and a wall of policemen stretched across the front of the building. As we got nearer, the faint sound of singing grew into a thunderous roar:

> Ain't gon' let nobody
> Turn me 'round,
> Turn me 'round.
>
> Ain't gon' let policemen
> Turn me 'round,
> Turn me 'round.

It was amazing. A police van was loaded with students piled on top of one another like bags of dirty laundry. Beneath the front wheel of the vehicle lay a young man who, when lugged away and pitched into the back of the van, was hurriedly replaced by another student. Like a giant magnet, the scene sucked me in. Glued to the front fender of the vehicle, I watched while the incredible chanting thundered on:

>Ain't gon let policemen
>Turn me...

"Blake! Blake! Stop the wagon! Don't let the truck move! GET! UNDER! THE WHEEL!" Like a flash of lightning, I hit the ground without conscious awareness of my action until "thud, bump-bump-bump," my head bobbled against the pavement as two burly policemen dragged me by the feet, hoisted me up and pitched me into the back of the truck on top of female students. *This is a helluva way to meet girls,* I sighed.

On the harried ride to jail, we managed to untangle and scramble to our feet. Our spirits were high.

>Ain't gon' let no jail
>Turn me 'round,
>Turn me 'round!

The bars to the cell clanged shut. We screamed raw passion:

>Ain't gon' let no jail
>Turn me 'round,
>Turn me 'round!

The cell door opened, closed, opened, closed, opened... Students were pushed in until the rib cage of the guy next to me pressed into mine. A girl let out a shrill "I can't breathe!" Panic scraped my throat dry. A deadly silence settled over us and we dared not look one another in the eyes for fear of the terror we would find.

"They closed all the windows," someone murmured. "Fans off too," whispered a voice from behind me. The temperature must have been a hundred and twenty degrees inside the cell. Some of the female students fainted but there was no room to fall to the floor, no arms free to fan them. The night inched by in tight little seconds. Students fainted, somehow revived themselves, and fainted again. I wondered if any of them were dead.

Around eight the next morning, the cell door opened. "Y'all get on outa here!" a bulldog sheriff drawled. There were no charges, no judge—nothing. They just let us go. We tripped over one another trying to get out of the small confined space. It was not a rush toward the door but an awkward stumbling to free arms and legs caught behind a cellmate's ankle or stuck between the narrow spaces of an iron bar. Outside, red eyes glared against the bright sunlight, stiff bodies stretched and jerked; numbness dissolved into pain. Crooked necks rotated, aching backs arched, and sore arms reached for the sky. My head throbbed with the intensity of a migraine as a tidal wave of relief slammed against my brain. Though there had been nobody to call for help, miraculously, we had survived the night without serious injuries, hospitalizations or deaths.

The people who should have protected us were the enemy. We had no rights. For the first time, I fully understood The Civil Rights Movement. It was about much more than where I ate or slept. It was about human dignity and equal justice under the law. I had stumbled into the Howard Johnson demonstration but left that jail cell a committed civil rights worker.

For a while students stood around in a daze, then slowly we left the downtown area and started back to campus. It was Monday morning and I headed to my first period class. At first I was dejected, but the more I walked the more I swelled with pride. I had done something remarkable. Even though I did not set out to do so, I had stood up for justice. The other students and I had spoken truth to the powerful forces of segregation. I burst into Corporal Jones' class and swaggered to my seat.

"Unh-unh," he cleared his throat, "Mr. Blake, you are late."

"Yes sir," I beamed, "Last night I was in jail all nightlong fighting for freedom." I relished the words rolling off my tongue.

"Do you have your assignment?"

"No sir, like I said I was in jail all night." *Didn't he hear me?*

Professor Jones peered at me over the rim of his wire glasses and studied me until I fidgeted in my seat. "Well, young man," he finally spoke in a deep rich baritone, "you get a zero for the day. The next time you go to jail 'aaall nightlong,' take your books with you." Then, he resumed his lecture on the implications of the emerging African nations for the American Negro.

Of all the teachers at North Carolina College, I respected Corporal Jones the most. He had gone against the grain and established himself as an African history scholar who was sought after to lecture at Black and White colleges. His response puzzled me. At the end of the class period, I stopped at his desk, "Professor Jones, why did you give me a zero when I was fighting for freedom?"

"If freedom comes tomorrow, Mr. Blake, will you be ready?" he turned the question back on me. It took a minute for his point to penetrate. It is good to fight for freedom, he was saying, but it is equally as important to be prepared for freedom when it comes.

That day, Corporal Jones kept his promise. On the first day of class he had warned us, "If you have any excuses, write them down, put them in your back pocket and bring them to me at the end of the semester after the grades have been submitted." His policy amazed me. I had never had a class or any situation that allowed "no excuses." As with my other professors, Corporal Jones demanded excellence. In an environment of high expectations, I discovered that my success or failure depended more on my choices than it did on the behavior of others. Lessons from Corporal Jones were not lost on me but I pushed his gems of wisdom to a quiet corner of my mind and held onto the pride I felt about standing up against racial injustice.

Partying and chasing women remained a big part of my life, but protesting against segregation slowly overshadowed social interests. I got involved with student activities after Professor Norris, an English teacher who thought I had "a flair for writing," suggested that I check out *The Campus Echo*, our student newspaper. Harold Foster, student editor and a truly great writer, was unimpressed with my literary skills and issued a blunt, less flattering assessment. He was clever though. Aware of my popularity, he appointed me circulation manager and put my social skills to work as a volunteer distributor for the publication.

"**M**aclom X on campus? The State is already upset about you students demonstrating. If you bring him to campus, we will not give you the auditorium." The president of the college summoned me to his office late spring 1963 to issue his ruling. He sought a quieter summer term when the majority of students would be back in their hometowns.

Malcolm would be debating Floyd McKissick at the W.D. Hill Center in Durham. I had called New York to ask him to speak to students at North Carolina College while in town and he had agreed. The president's decision was one in a series of frustrating turns of events. First, the city fathers of Durham had canceled the reservation for the debate to take place at the city owned recreational facility because of Malcolm's reputation as a blistering speaker on racial issues. It was also rumored that several Black churches had refused the use of their sanctuaries. Ultimately, the debate took place in an overcrowded hall over a cab stand.

I headed over to Roxboro Street with the bad news about the cancellation of the college event. When I entered the meeting room, the audience of a hundred mostly Black students was seated behind a few professors and students from Duke University. Following the normal arrangement in the segregated South, I was taking a position against the back wall among other students when a group of bald-headed bow-tied Black men walked calmly down the center aisle and firmly beckoned to the Whites who followed their directions. Neither they nor we knew what was happening until seconds later when the brothers directed Black students who were standing as well as those in rear seats into the vacated seats down front. To see the social order turned upside down blew our minds. A rush of pride swept over us. We were privileged with front row seats and Whites sat behind us. It was a first in my North Carolina sojourn. The audience was still reeling when the program got underway.

The topic of debate, the evening of April 18, 1963, was "Which Way for the Civil Rights Movement: Integration or Separation?" Black students had turned out for Floyd McKissick, an activist civil rights attorney, a supporter of the Howard Johnson demonstrations, and a firebrand known for his oratory. He was our hero and leader.

Malcolm was introduced, then Floyd McKissick. Black ministers, a sizeable segment of the audience, cheered, "Amen, Brother Floyd!" "Brother Floyd!" It was obvious they were depending on McKissick, with his reputation as a tough debater, to counter any Muslim theology that might be spread among the people; but they made the mistake of letting Malcolm speak first. Instead of blasting Christianity, he used Biblical examples to score points about the suffering of Black people under a cruel Pharaoh as he likened the Honorable Elijah Muhammad's call for separation to the flight of the Israelites out of Egypt.

Malcolm's speech was riveting, at times spellbinding. He was hard-hitting about the evils of racism and we students could not help turning in our seats to glimpse the reactions of Whites. They sat stiff as boards; rage glowed red on their faces. Our Black professors, even more appalled than the Whites, shifted back and forth in their seats. I believe they would have turned purple if they could have. When Malcolm finished, you could hear a pin drop—then, thunderous applause and hoots from Black students.

It was McKissick's turn at the mike. He walked slowly to the podium and spoke in a deep southern drawl, his speech punctuated by short pants: "I want to tell you... what Malcolm had to say... well, there is... not much for me to add." The ministers were UP-set! We students went wild! When the audience finally quieted, McKissick proceeded in a conversational tone, pointing out disagreements in strategy. The debate turned into a discussion between two men who had obvious respect for one another.

I was not surprised by McKissick's response. I had met him indirectly in 1961. His daughter, Joyce McKissick, was a classmate of mine. All the students knew that her father was a bold leader in the struggle for social and economic advancement for Blacks. That fact coupled with her good looks made her one of the most popular girls on campus.

Back in my sophomore year Joyce had phoned me at Chidley Hall, "Hey Jimmy Blake. What you doing? Want to go to the movies?"

Whaat? Out of all the guys on campus, she had chosen me to take her out. I was on it! "I'll meet you in front of the B. N. Duke Auditorium in ten minutes." My feet could not carry me across campus fast enough. When I came around to the front of the building, Joyce was waiting by the entrance with a big smile.

"Let's go downtown," she sweetly tugged at my arm.

"Okay. Cool." I was happy she wanted to break the routine and make it a special off-campus date. We strolled down Fayetteville Street hand in hand in the middle of a Saturday afternoon. I was scoring big points. Guys drove by, slowed down, "Jimmy Blaaake," they nodded their approval. The ones out walking slapped five in my free hand with a, "Well, alright!"

Once we reached The Carolina, "You buy the tickets." Joyce dropped a dollar bill in my hand and pushed me forward.

"Two tickets to see..."

"We don't sell tickets to Niggers!" the woman grimaced.

Did I hear her right? Happy with my theater on campus, I had never ventured downtown.

"Niggeeer!" she shrieked the second time I attempted to give her the money.

Come on now! I wasn't there for that. I wanted to get my tickets and get on with my date. "Listen, just give me..."

"We want our rights! We want our rights!" I swung around and Joyce was jumping up and down, her arms flaying in the air.

"Joyce, what you doing?"

"We want our rights!"

"Joyce!"

"Niggeeers!" rebounded from the disgruntled White crowd that was gathering.

"We want our rights! We want our rights!"

"Niggeeers!"

"Let's go Joyce!" I grabbed her by the arm.

"We want..."

"Shut up Joyce!" I snatched her to my side and we began to move slowly away from the growing mob of twenty or so. They mumbled, "Niggers." We walked faster. Our pace broke to a trot. They growled at our heels.

"Run, Joyce!" With all the speed in us, we sprinted for the railroad tracks.

Yelling and throwing sticks, rocks and whatever they could get their hands on, the pack gave chase. Then, the most amazing thing happened: a wall loomed ahead of us. Joyce and I were on a collision course. Thirty Black men stood shoulder to shoulder like troopers strung along the tracks. They blocked the entrance to the Black community but just when we were about to crash into them, one man stepped aside to let us pass before closing ranks again. The advancing mob came to a screeching halt. They glared at the men and hissed racial slurs but turned around and headed back downtown.

The Muslim temple was on Pettigrew Street in the slum right across the tracks from the downtown area. Most likely the brothers had heard the ruckus and, believing as they did in defending themselves as well as women and children, they had quickly assembled to protect us. In doing so, more than a confrontation with White segregationists occurred that day. The two dominant civil rights strategies of the sixties—integration and separation—collided when Joyce and I fled behind the protective wall of Muslims, but I had been too terrified to note the significance of the moment.

I cursed Joyce out. "You crazy," I ended my tirade. I had been looking for a date, but again I had stumbled into a struggle. Nowadays, when people praise me regarding my quest for justice, I remind myself that, in the beginning, I was not looking for justice. I was looking for pretty girls. I went back to campus and found myself a real date.

I had forgotten the incident with Joyce until I witnessed her father and Malcolm in the much-heralded 1963 debate. McKissick's daughter was an agitator for justice and perhaps she had shared with her father how the Muslims had saved her that Saturday afternoon back in 1961. In any case, during the debate McKissick and

Malcolm showed an unmistakable appreciation for one another's views. It was a different matter, though, for the Black ministers and professors in the audience; they were livid. Ignoring them, I cheered with the rest of the students as McKissick took his seat.

When we finally settled down, a distinguished looking professor, with a full head of silky red hair and a beard to match, stood to ask the first question. Actually, it was a comment: "Minister Malcolm, I just want to say," he pulled slowly on his beard, "that I was over there in Egypt. I walked through the Djara Cave and I did not feel any of the hostility from the Egyptian Muslims that you are articulating tonight."

"Sir, did you say you walked through the cave?"

"Yes-yes, that's what I said."

"Sir, you can't walk through that cave, you have to get down on your belly and crawl." It was a homerun. We howled.

Of course, both Malcolm and the professor were posturing. They were probably describing what they had read about the famous cave in the western desert of Egypt. Also, both men were correct in their descriptions. In order to enter, the professor would have knelt on the desert floor and scrambled down to the limestone formation. Once inside, he could have walked around. Nevertheless, these facts were unimportant to Black students. We did not care that Malcolm failed to address the meat of the professor's comment. We loved his setting that pompous man straight.

Don't get me wrong. Malcolm was well read and he had his facts together as he demonstrated later in the session, but the psychology of his responses had a greater impact on our young minds than the facts he presented. He and his Muslim brothers were masterful at gaining the psychological edge in a verbal confrontation.

At the end of the evening, students were charged up. There was a buzz around the room about "the expressions on those White people's faces" when we sat in front of them. We had never seen Black men stand up to White people. With all the excitement, I hated to inform Malcolm that the auditorium at the college would not be available.

When I pushed my way through the crowd with the bad news, he chuckled "Well brother, I have never been to North Carolina College. Maybe I will stroll through with my camera and take a few pictures. While there, I will speak to anyone who wants to speak to me."

As I rushed off to prepare for his arrival on campus, I recalled that throngs of students had enjoyed a pleasant spring afternoon on the grassy quad in front of the cafeteria the previous day. With a long extension cord connected to an outlet inside one of the nearby buildings, I could place a microphone in the area. Harold Foster, *The Campus Echo* editor, helped me with the set up.

Contrary to the previous days, a sweltering ninety-five-degree heat scorched the quad the afternoon Malcolm grabbed the microphone and began, "My beautiful brothers and sisters, it is time to wake up. For four hundred years you have been blind, deaf and dumb to self. You don't know your name; you wear the slave master's name. You have lost your language; English is not your language..." A couple of hundred students listened mesmerized.

The sun beat into his face for an hour before I interrupted, "Excuse me Brother Malcolm; we have enough extension cord to take this mike and put it under the tree over there."

He stared at me so hard and so long that I started to squirm. I thought maybe I had caused him to lose his train of thought. Finally he answered: "Brother, thank you for that offer but the Honorable Elijah Muhammad teaches us that a Black man should never stand under a tree in the South." The crowd roared with laughter and he spoke for another half an hour before concluding his talk.

Malcolm's was a strange message for southern students involved in the push for integration, but, for me, he sounded chords of the African Nationalist Pioneer Movement. In any case, it was absolutely astounding for a Black person to stand in the cradle of segregation and speak with frank forcefulness about the evils of racism and the beauty of Blackness. We students were part of an integration movement that espoused loving our enemies and turning the other cheek. Midstream in our quest, Malcolm challenged our thinking: "Integrating with your enemy is like a chicken integrating with a fox. Why would you want to integrate with someone who hates you?" When he left the campus, seeds of dissension had definitely been sowed among students regarding how best to gain justice and equality for Blacks in America.

I spotted Malcolm turning off Astoria Boulevard onto 106th Street. He lived in East Elmhurst six or seven blocks from Gloria's house where I was staying while home from school for the summer. When I waved, he stopped and motioned for me to get in the car.

Immediately, he peppered me with questions: "Any discussion after I left campus? What did students say? Do you think...?"

"Before I answer your questions," I interrupted, "I want to know why you studied me so long when I asked if you wanted to move the microphone under the tree? You made me uncomfortable."

Malcolm doubled over the steering column coughing up belly laughs. Clearing his throat several times, before regaining his composure, "Brother," he looked at me, "it was so hot that day I almost disobeyed my leader and teacher."

As we cruised away from Astoria Boulevard—the great divide between Corona and East Elmhurst—I recalled the first time I had heard Malcolm speak. It was 1957 and I was a fifteen-year-old ditty-bop just arriving home from Woodycrest on a weekend pass. While waiting around Wheat's Candy Store for some of the fellows to show up, Emma, a strikingly beautiful twenty-four-year-old friend of Gloria had come into the store. "You want to go hear this guy, Malcolm, speak over in East Elmhurst this evening?" she asked.

"No, I'll stay here, get some wine and kick it with the fellows," I brushed her off. East Elmhurst was the last place a poor kid like me wanted to be.

"Oh Spade," she used my street name, "You might enjoy it." Again, I declined her invitation.

"Well, if you change your mind, it's at that social club down on Ditmars Boulevard. You know, the one near the tennis courts." I knew the place. It was a little house near the spot of the current LaGuardia Marriott. Back then, the Black elite of East Elmhurst met there with civic organizations and political leaders. To go to the lecture I would have to cross "the border," as we called it. Those "siddity" Blacks had pegged the kids from Northern Boulevard as a bunch of wanna-be gangsters headed nowhere. They didn't want us talking to their daughters or hanging out with their sons and that was fine with me. I had no intention of subjecting myself to their scorn— especially to hear a speech from some Malcolm cat I had never heard of.

I waited but none of my boys showed up at the candy store. Finally, someone told me they had all been arrested for gang activities. To pass the time, I decided to walk on over to Ditmars to check out Emma. Man, she was gorgeous! My adolescent hormones raced at the thought of spending the evening with her.

As I bopped toward the exclusive social club, the modest houses and barren streets of Corona were replaced by stately homes perched along tree-lined Ditmars Boulevard. Only once had I conquered my fear and entered one of those houses. A classmate at Junior High School 127 had invited me to a party at his home. When I arrived he led me into a dimly lit living room, but as I walked I caught glimpses of side rooms that resembled magazine photos. I sank into the plush couch and reached for the tiny white mints in the sculptured bowl that rested on a deeply carved coffee table. I chucked a handful into my mouth and coughed them right back out. "Man, them cigarette butts!" My so-called buddy laughed and teased me for the rest of the evening.

With the earlier humiliation fresh in my mind, I hesitantly entered the meeting hall on Ditmars in 1957. Five neat lines of chairs were carefully spaced on the hardwood floors in a modestly furnished room with a plain mahogany table up front. I sat on the back row and scanned the room. The place smelled of perfume and cologne. Men were clad in suits and ties. Women wore soft flowery dresses. Then there was me—fifteen, unkempt, wild wooly hair, dirty nails, out of place and uncomfortable. Apparently Emma had not attended. The two or three people I recognized, I despised. My father washed their cars and I hated the way he humbled himself to them for a dollar.

The woman sitting next to me shot curious glances my way like, *what are you doing here?*

You're right! What am I doing here? I glared at her. Just as I was about to leave one of the men announced nonchalantly, "Malcolm X is here everybody." People scrambled into their seats making it awkward for me to go.

Malcolm walked briskly to the mike and thundered, "As-Salaam-Alaikum!" I had no clue that it was a greeting of peace, nor did anyone else. In that powerful second, those haughty people were reduced to my level.

Malcolm got right to the point: "I know some of you are scared and want to run out of here. You think your boss will find out you were here and you will lose your fancy houses. But, they are not your homes; everything you own belongs to the White man: your house, your car, your job. You depend on him for everything. That's why you are afraid and ready to run. 'Ooooo, the White man might find out I was in a meeting with Malcolm X,'" he mocked them.

"You are in the hands of a thief and a robber." That struck me. I knew about robbing. "He robbed you of your language, your culture, and your history," Malcolm continued. "You're like the man hit in the head and robbed on the road to Samaria. Everybody is walking by you; nobody wants to help you, but I'm here to tell you that you have a Good Samaritan in the Honorable Elijah Muhammad. He is here to help you, to restore you, to tell you who you are."

When the meeting was over the atmosphere had changed. Boisterous laughter had been replaced with thoughtful murmuring. As others gathered around Malcolm, I left. I was young, but I knew I had just witnessed a legend in action. Before that night, I had known gang legends such as Big Count and Big Lucky who commanded the same reverence and had that same ability as Malcolm to change the temperature in a room

165

merely by entering. *This Malcolm X must be a tough cat,* I pondered on my walk back to Corona.

Back when I was fifteen, Malcolm had placed the untouchable middle class of East Elmhurst within my reach. He disrobed them, left them naked and allowed me to see them for who they were: people like me who didn't have power but were seeking it. They no longer intimidated me. After all, they did not own those big houses or the cars they hired my father to wash. That evening Malcolm erased from my head the dividing line between Corona and East Elmhurst and with it went the fear and resentment I had harbored for middle-class Blacks.

After Malcolm's speech my eyes began to open to good aspects of the East Elmhurst community. I became aware of their strong family ties. They had the kind of family unity I wanted for myself. Also, I took note of their community service projects—some of which reached out to Corona youth. Most of all, I thought a community that embraced this guy, Malcolm, had to be a whole lot better than the men I had seen in my father's garage. At fifteen, I learned not to condemn an entire community for the behavior of a few.

That first encounter with Malcolm back in 1957 had given me a sense of him as teacher. "You can become more than the material objects with which you identify," was his message. However, back then it had been unthinkable that, six years later, I would invite him to my college campus to lecture or that he would give me a lift from East Elmhurst to Corona. Yet, in a remarkable turn of events, in 1963 I was getting out of his car.

Malcolm, who lived in East Elmhurst, was headed to the Muslim restaurant on Northern Boulevard near 105th Street. It was the street corner where I felt the most comfortable in the world. The intersection was the hub of

Black male life in Corona. Before the Muslims took over the property, their restaurant had been Wheat's Candy Store, the place where I had held gang war councils in my teens. Next door was Graham's Barbershop. On the southeast corner was another popular barber, Pete. Directly across the street from Pete's, Big Count—a terror to his enemies and lord to his friends—worked at the auto tire shop.

The vastness of Northern Boulevard and its people still held sway over me. Whenever I came home from college, the first chance I got, I went to The Boulevard to check out the fellows. Though doo-wop groups no longer harmonized on the corners, cool cats in sunglasses with their hats cocked to the side, bopped past. They still had The Walk, and boisterous voices enhanced their war tales as they drifted down The Boulevard. However, my gang hangout, Wheat's Candy Store, had been transformed to the place where Malcolm held court.

He and I entered the Muslim restaurant to sweet aromas of cinnamon and nutmeg from rows of bean pies and carrot cakes on display at the bakery counter to our immediate right. The interior of the place was a tight but cozier spot than when I was fifteen. Next to the pastry display case, men from the neighborhood sat on the three swivel stools at the counter and wolfed down fried fish sandwiches on homemade whole wheat bread. Barely an arm's length across the room, two booths were empty but Malcolm escorted me to the lone one in the back next to a jukebox that played "A White Man's Heaven is a Black Man's Hell" by Louis X (later named Louis Farrakhan).

While bantering about the oppressive heat of North Carolina, Malcolm ordered a bowl of bean soup as we slid into the booth. With customary swift and polite service, a brother in a white shirt and black bow-tie placed the soup in front of me. I bit into the freshly baked whole-wheat roll on the side saucer and Malcolm began again to pump me with questions about his appearances in North Carolina. He wanted to know if students liked his speeches, exactly what they had said and my thoughts about his delivery. I gave him a blow by blow account telling him that the students liked the speeches, but most of them had never heard anyone speak in such bold terms about racism. I was frank in sharing that the majority of students took issue with his calling the White man a "blue-eyed devil." I concluded by telling him that all of them were shaken by his message. "You left the campus in an uproar. They are debating about integration and separation." He listened without defending any of my statements and only interrupted to seek clarification. He was particularly pleased to know that he had raised questions in the minds of students regarding integration.

During our twenty-minute chat, several brothers waited to meet with Malcolm, but he did not rush our conversation. It was my only one-on-one interaction with him and I was amazed at how different he was from the fiery orator who tripped up reporters, challenged "Uncle Tom" leaders, and condemned racism as demonic. But that afternoon with me, he was relaxed and easygoing.

Being with Malcolm was like hanging out with my big brother. I did not feel guarded the way I did with most people though I was not yet aware of our common bond: both of our mothers suffered from mental illness and we both grew up as wards of the state. Even without specific information about his upbringing, I thought, *this is a person who understands pain.* The overlapping facts of our lives would not emerge until I read *The Autobiography of Malcolm X* several years later. Still, while in his presence, some sixth sense alerted me that similar brands of pain ignited both of our passions for justice.

Malcolm and I huddled in the booth. He wore a dazzling smile. The only hint of fire was in the probing eyes that never released their grip on me. The intensity made me hunger for deep wisdom but I dared not break the intimacy of a moment when he was disarmed and simply wanted to know like the rest of us, "How am I doing?" It was my privilege to tell him.

Malcolm profoundly impacted my involvement in the protest movement. He had said to students at North Carolina College, "You let a man take your hat, the next thing he will take is your coat. If somebody hits you and you hit back, they will think twice before they hit you again." I decided no longer to let anyone hit and spit on me. My decision ran contrary to the passive resistance code that required protesters to restrain themselves or leave without making it difficult for others. For a while, I stopped participating in sit-ins and marches.

I stayed home the summer of 1963 and watched the March on Washington on television mostly because I had no money but partly because I thought it was a big push for integration. I did not want to melt into a White world and lose the identity I had struggled so hard to maintain while in children's homes. I wanted to meet Whites on an equal footing—both of us comfortable in our own skins.

After seeing on television that the March on Washington was for jobs and freedom, I realized that Dr. Martin Luther King, Jr. had broadened the focus of the civil rights struggle. Though he had not yet announced his Poor People's Campaign, his attention was shifting to the devastating effects of economic inequities. Their tactics were different, but he and Malcolm had more in common than I had thought. Both leaders had a focus on jobs and so did I.

While in Corona that summer, I took note of cats like Cookie, Sleepy and Cody who had experienced a political awakening at the beginning of the civil rights movement but were unable to find jobs. All too soon, drugs had cooled them out. It was sad to see my buddies—once strong in sports, strong in gangs—now slumped in heroin nods. Inspired by Malcolm's message from the Honorable Elijah Muhammad to "wake up, stop depending on others and do for self," some of them eventually joined the Nation of Islam and got clean. They also got jobs selling Muhammad Speaks for a small profit, as well as working in the Nation's bakeries, restaurants, and schools. I saw how hope in an economic future had transformed their lives. In fact, Cody was such a hard worker in Nation of Islam enterprises that Messenger Muhammad personally named him Elias Muhammad.

Concerned about my many childhood friends who remained slaves to drugs, I asked Elias, "Man, I don't get it; what makes them jab needles in their arms?"

After a long pause he answered, "Think about the best sex you ever had, multiplied a hundred times. That's the way you feel the first time you cop a high. The trouble is you never get back to that level again though you keep reaching for it. That's how you get hooked; trying to relive that first high."

I shuddered. Boy was I glad I had never messed with that stuff. I could see why my buddies were dropping like flies. The roll call of friends lost to drugs included Chino, Big Lucky, Turk, Torch, Duke, Tombstone, Solitaire, and Cookie.

Like most of my remaining buddies, I was also destitute in the summer of 1963. Big Jimmy gave me a job helping out with his landscaping business. Blazing hot hours spent cutting grass, trimming hedges, and sweeping up debris allowed plenty of time to think. Malcolm's words to students, "Life is bigger than your social appetites," kept drifting through my head. For the first time, I wanted to withdraw from the wild social life that had dominated my three years in North Carolina.

At night, thoughts of settling down crept into my sleep: *A girl walks up to me. I see her face, feel her spirit and know her personality. "Jimmy! You need somebody to get you moving. I have a lot for you to do!" She does not speak but the commanding voice engulfs her.* It was a short recurring dream that always lingered after I woke up.

When Harold Fowler came to New York for a visit, I poured out my heart, "Harold, I'm tired of being a player. I'll be a senior this year. I need some stability in my life. I'ma get me a 'main drag.'"

"Yeah. I'ma get me a steady girl too," he agreed.

I swore to start respecting women. My boys and I had become accustomed to the five-to-one female-male ratio at North Carolina College. "Got my quota, brother," we'd bragged to one another. Unwittingly, we had been exploiting the statistic that signaled the hellish condition of Black men who had fallen behind. The image of my wolf pack swaggering across campus looking for prey began to disgust rather than excite me. Partying was not the reason I had gone to college.

Unbelievable! I jumped to my feet. Everything about her—the slender body, soft brown complexion and shoulder length hair flipped up, and framing a serenely beautiful face—everything was identical to the girl I had seen in my dream.

"Here she comes! That's the girl I'm going to marry," I pointed.

"Jim, you don't even know this woman." Harold stood up from the rail near the cafeteria where we had been lounging and checking out the new crop of freshmen girls going in and out of Annie Day Shepherd Hall.

"No, this is the girl I'm going to marry," I said so earnestly that a worry line creased his forehead and his head jerked back in an effort to adjust his loose glasses.

"But Jim, you don't know her," he repeated.

"Yes I do; it's my wife."

"Let me talk to her," Harold offered in an attempt to save me from myself.

"Not this one, she's my wife."

Clarity washed over me but, unable to turn on my usual charm, I stepped awkwardly in front of her and we collided. Confused and discombobulated, she acted like she had run into a tree. "I don't mean to startle you. I just want to say you a FINE looking woman," was my best line at the time. I asked and she told me her name was Lorene Waites; she was from Shreveport, Louisiana; and no she was not a freshman but a graduate student with no number, no address, no way to be reached. Then off she glided into the warmth of the September sun without the faintest clue that she was mine.

"Come on, let's go find some girls," Harold suggested.

"No man, you go ahead; I'm going back to the dorm."

"You sure you don't want to come?"

I shook my head. There was no need to follow him; I had found my *dream*-girl.

Lorene's refusal to tell me where she lived sent me on a hunt: to the cafeteria, to the library, to the female dormitories. I even hung out in front of Anne Day Shepherd hoping to re-enact our meeting, but had no luck. On the fourth day of my search, I went to breakfast and there she was sitting in the private dining room. *What's she doing in there?* Though I knew she was a graduate student, it surprised me to see her seated in an area forbidden to me, an undergraduate.

I waited and caught up with her as she dashed out of the cafeteria. "Hey, remember me? We met the other day?" She gave a blank stare that said she did not remember. It was clearly a brush-off. I fumbled for words; she rushed away. It was a blow, but her public rejection did not make me give up. For days, I wandered the campus in relentless pursuit of Lorene while the whole student body watched and waited for me to come to my senses.

"What's the matter with you? You don't want to party anymore?" asked Joy.

"You haven't called," pouted Wilma, who thought she was my girlfriend.

Every day Harold called and every day I declined his invitations to hang out.

My friend, Smooth, rolled up with a car full of guys, "Hey man, let's go get some women."

I said, "No.

"Oh, you got your sneakers on, huh?" was how he referred to my chasing after Lorene. In disgust he hit the accelerator and burned rubber.

Despite their protests, I knew my boys had mixed feelings. They wanted me to have the "main drag" each of us longed for but they did not want to lose me from the group. They were also annoyed that I had shed my macho-cool-cat image to mercilessly run after a girl. As the highly visible leader of the wolf pack, I had upped the ante and my boys were afraid their women might demand too much attention.

When September turned to October and I was still moping, Harold attempted to snap me out of it. "Come on, Jim, man," he pleaded. "People are saying you lost your mind. They say that girl's got your nose open."

"Yeah, my nose is open. It's so wide open that a drop of water could drown me."

Harold was either touched by the sincere love I expressed or he pitied me. He tried to convince me that Lorene was wrong for me.

"Look man, you don't want to waste your time on her; she's a church girl."

"A church girl?" I had no point of reference for his meaning.

So, he broke it down in simple terms that I could understand: "Man, you ain't gon' score with her."

"Oh, that doesn't matter."

Harold shook his head and, for what he did next, I will always cherish his friendship. He took me by the elbow, "Tell you what, let's go find her."

We covered every inch of the campus before giving up and heading to the Green Candle for the Friday special—a plate of "stew beef" and a garden salad. As we made our way down Fayetteville Street, he spotted "my girl" turning into the College Inn with a friend.

175

Not wanting to appear anxious, I entered the café but waited before I walked up to their booth. "Mind if I join you?" I asked. Immediately the friend moved to the wall to make room for Harold and they fell instantly into light chatter. After an awkward wait, my girl threw herself against the wall like a rag doll, leaving no doubt that she would hate every minute that I sat next to her.

Now and then Harold would cast a what-you-gon'-do-man look at me and I would chuckle. Back and forth we snickered, while Lorene sat, elbows on the table, chin resting in the palms of her hand, scorn on her face. *We must look like two goofy dudes,* I thought. Determined to ride it out, I offered what I considered a courteous gesture.

"Want a beer?"

Confused wrinkles curled her brows.

"A beer?" I repeated.

"A bear?" she echoed.

"A beer. A beer." Exasperated, my hand movement indicated an upturned bottle.

"Bessie, he's saying 'beer,'" her friend, Peaches, translated. It was the first hint that we were from totally different cultures. I had a crisp New York slick way of talking; she the soft drawl of a southern church girl.

"No. No," she waved her hand declining the beer. I ordered a cold one with a bag of potato chips. In an attempt at conversation I asked why Peaches called her Bessie. She explained that her first name was Bessie but she preferred her middle name, Lorene.

"You don't look like a Bessie or a Lorene, you look more like a Donna," I stupidly offered the name of my girlfriend in New York.

Bessie mouthed a dry, "Oh really," before the curtain of silence fell again.

Harold sporadically cleared his throat and adjusted his glasses with a quirky head movement and we continued to exchange nervous chuckles. What a predicament!

"Excuse me!" Without warning, Bessie started pushing her way out of the booth. I jumped up to let her by.

"Mind if I walk with you?" I followed her out of the door.

"The sidewalk is free!" she snapped. I treated the rebuff like an invitation and fell in step beside her.

I can't come my usual way; I have to find something intelligent to talk about, I searched my brain. *A graduate student: she probably likes books.* "Have you read *When the Word Is Given* by Louis E. Lomax?" I asked. Inspired by Malcolm's speech the past spring, I had read Lomax's book about the Muslims.

"No, what is it about?" she asked with mild curiosity. I recounted the 1958 incident where a line of Muslim brothers stood at attention in front of a Harlem precinct seeking medical attention for one of their members who had been beaten by police and then arrested. Behind their ranks an angry crowd was growing ugly and the police captain asked Malcolm to help calm the situation. According to the book, Malcolm astonished the captain; he simply raised his hand and the street cleared instantly.

Bessie thought it was "an interesting story" and said she would read the book. Encouraged by the response, I proceeded to tell her about the Nation of Islam's belief that a territory should be set aside in America for the Black man to build his own government. I rattled on about how Muslims thought the former slaves were wasting time turning the other cheek for integration.

The quick reply, "That's a case of reverse discrimination," signaled debate against a formidable opponent. I usually muscled my way through verbal disagreements with fast talk but Bessie was slow and methodical. "Where is it going to stop if you use the same tactics as they do?" she queried.

"Where is it going to stop indeed?" I shot back. "It's been four hundred years."

"Yes and we don't want another four hundred years of Black domination. If you fight fire with fire you are going to end up with the slaughter of Black people or a roaring inferno where innocent people of both races die."

"Power is never handed over, you have to take it," I stressed.

"There can be peaceful redistribution of power. Gandhi was successful in India with non-violent protests and civil disobedience and that's the model we're following. Besides, the Bible says, we should love everybody," she summed up.

For someone so smart, she's kinda naïve, I thought to myself. I had not consciously considered that the God of justice who came to me in dreams and urged me to help people who were treated unfairly might also be a God of love. The pain I endured from my childhood obscured her image of a God who lovingly administered justice.

Now that I look back on that first conversation with Bessie, I realize we were young, full of ideals and both of us were downright naïve. She had a passion for ideas; I had a passion for justice, and neither of us was impressed with the other's views. She was touched, though, by my interaction with every child we passed along the sidewalk. As we made our way from the College Inn to her house, I patted one boy on the head and said, "Hey little fellow," to another. It was enough to get me a date.

Friday night when Bessie greeted me at the front door of her off-campus apartment, I apologized: "I don't have a car."

"Oh, that's okay. I love to walk."

Well alright, a girl who actually likes to walk! My transportation problem solved, we strolled to the nearby bowling alley and watched other students bowl while I pondered how to spend the two dimes in my pocket to best effect.

"What would you like to do now?" I asked.

"I want some ice cream."

"Ice cream? Did she say ice cream?" I hit the jackpot! Girls I usually hung out with wanted costly cocktails. Why, at two scoops for ten cents, she could have all the ice cream she wanted. *This church girl thing is alright!*

Fayetteville Street was quiet and dark except for an occasional passing car and dimly lit street lamps that glimmered through willow oak branches. I pumped Bessie for information about herself and learned that she was the second oldest of five children; her mother was a nurse; her father lived with the family but she was candid—even blunt—in stating that he was not a provider. She had come to North Carolina to get her Master's degree in American Literature and planned to return home to help her mother. Never had I met such a direct and unpretentious girl.

Instead of simply enjoying the warm fall evening, I probed, "You have a boyfriend?"

"Yes, I'm engaged."

Poor fellow, he just doesn't know, I relished a silent chuckle but said, "How did he let you get away from him?"

"Get away from him? We didn't break up. I'm here for school, nothing else."

"No way would I let you out of my sight; I would've followed you up here."

"I'm not looking for a boyfriend." Her big eyes rolled toward me with irritation.

"Oh, we're here!" Not a minute too soon, we were standing in front of the ice cream shop. I gladly steered her inside.

"Two scoops of Vanilla!" I ordered like I had a roll of dough. Bessie quietly tackled the heaping dish of cream and I rambled on about current events, various books, the plight of the Black man in America—anything to stay away from personal topics. Wanting to stretch my role as the big spender, when she cleaned the dish, "Have another one," I insisted.

"Jimmy," she laughed, "I just ate a pint."

"You sure now? I'll get you some more." I made it clear that I was prepared to take care of business.

"Nooo!" she ended my showboating.

On a pleasant walk back to her place she agreed to a second date. When I left her at her door, I felt rich though I only had a dime in my pocket.

Saturday night the Africans were having parties. In the fall of 1963, North Carolina College had several international students—all Black due to segregation. The foreign students were mainly from Liberia, Ghana, Nigeria, and Kenya and they clustered together according to nationality. The Liberians, Ghanaians and Nigerians had money, while the Kenyans struggled to cover tuition and expenses. John, a tall wispy guy from the Kikuyu tribe, washed dishes in the cafeteria to pay his way. He had the physique of a graceful warrior and a stern demeanor that said he was ready to battle. He thought the other students were laughing at him, and they were. In the early sixties, the only images most Blacks had of Africa were from Hollywood movies like *Tarzan* or textbooks that told of a "Dark Continent" of backward, uncivilized savages. Of course, back at Woodycrest, Mr. Harris had presented another view of Africa and I attempted to mediate the cultural tensions between John and our peers.

Tackling the misunderstandings and prejudices of an entire campus, faculty included, was a sizeable challenge. Corporal Jones had an impact on the handful of students enrolled in his course, "Emerging African Nations"; but beyond that small circle lay a vast body of ignorance concerning Africa. I explained to John that the American Negro simply didn't know any better.

Nathan K. Saziru, another of my Kenyan friends, tried to get his countryman to relax, but it was truly a case of miseducation on both sides. The students labeled John a savage; he called them barbarians. Sadly, relentless teasing tormented him throughout his years at North Carolina College. Nathan, on the other hand, was popular. A bit of a philosopher, he used Socratic-like questioning to shame ignorant, difficult classmates. He was as poor as John, but with wit and charm, thrived on the generosity of strangers.

Nathan and I spent hours comparing and contrasting the civil rights movement with the struggles of emerging African nations. We analyzed the ingenious strategies of Kwame Nkrumah who laid the blueprint for Africa's liberation from colonialism when he led Ghana to independence in 1957. We praised the leadership of Patrice Lumumba, who became the first Prime Minister of the Congo in 1960. Nathan was also brilliant in his own right. After college, I envisioned my friend returning to Kenya to take a top post in the government of Jomo

Kenyatta, who in 1963 was prime minister, but was positioning himself to become president of the country in 1964.

However, I was not trying to remake the world as I surveyed the list of my African friends in preparation for my second date with Bessie. I wanted to impress; so my choice was the moneyed Liberians or the Nigerians who threw lavish parties with plenty of food.

Among the Nigerians, my friend, Obina A. Ogueri, was a glaring exception. He was poor, but what he lacked in funds he had in brains. Actually, he and I had started as foes. In my sophomore year, I sat just above his shoulder in the small amphitheater classroom of one of the required courses for my chemistry major. On the day of the first exam, he rolled his eyes back at me and cupped his hand over his paper like I was going to cheat.

"What's your problem, man?" I asked.

"You don't look at my paper. Don't you copy my answers," he hunched his shoulders over his desk.

"Nobody wants to look at your paper." What I wanted to do was kick his behind.

Over the course of the semester, Obina and I resolved our spat and eventually enjoyed a close friendship full of laughter and, yes, arguments. But, Saturday night squabbles would not impress my date. Since Obina was closer to me than any of the Nigerians of means, the choice was clear. I went with the Liberians.

By the time Bessie and I arrived at Stan's off-campus house, a crowd had already gathered in the living room. We went straight to the kitchen, loaded our plates with spicy chicken, African red rice and a green salad. We ate heartily and, afterwards, stood along the wall gazing at other students who huddled in twos and threes or crowded onto the one small couch in the living room. The music was blasting and conversation was impossible. I wanted to get the party started but did not want Bessie to think I was rowdy. After ten minutes of shifting my weight from one foot to the other I shouted above the blare of Smokey Robinson's *Mickey's Monkey,* "I'm bored."

"You bored, do something about it!" Bessie snapped back. Her annoyance propelled me to the center of the floor where I started to "Waller." Everybody except her lined up beside me, wobbling and sliding back and forth to the beat. Though Bessie did not join in the dancing, she seemed to be having a good time.

Sunday was usually a quiet day reserved for church, the noon feast on the cafeteria's last meal of the day, and for preparation for the next week's classes. Determined to spend the entire weekend with Bessie, I ignored the routine and arranged a third date for the evening. Neither she nor I knew that a bombshell was about to drop.

I got lucky and borrowed enough money for a quiet nightclub. On Fayetteville Street a couple of blocks beyond the College Inn but on the opposite side of the street sat a little jazz spot. With four rapid knocks on the heavy wooden door, the rectangular peephole slid open. Searchlight eyeballs rolled slowly over us before the slot snapped shut. "Click, click, click" the locks rotated and the door cracked just enough for us to squeeze through.

"Hey man. Cool. Cool. Welcome to Birdland," greeted the proprietor—a dark silhouette against the hue of red bulbs that pulsated from dimly lit corners. Just like the famed Birdland jazz club in New York, a crystal ball rotated above the dance floor, casting a swirl of diamond lights around the room. We sat in an elevated booth overlooking the dance floor. I ordered a J&B Scotch with water and Bessie ordered a Coke.

Smooth jazz lured us to the dance floor where we shuffled around at arm's length. When I started to tremble, Bessie thought I was nervous. Actually, I was wrestling with my wolf instincts. I had sidelined my usual game which was to grab the girl and crush her body tight against mine. However, one vulgar move on my part and I knew she would be out the door. So, I quaked through the dance and quickly escorted her back to our booth.

Bessie disarmed me in every way. I had dated many women but had never really talked to them about anything that mattered. Painful slurs and ugly labels— "nut case," "psycho," "loony bug," and just plain "crazy"— had prevented me from discussing Mama's condition with anyone other than my sisters and brother. But that night, easy conversation with Bessie unleashed bottled up emotions that flowed like hot lava. I spoke, and she listened, not with judgment or pity but with understanding, like she felt my suffering. I told her when my mother jumped, that she was in a mental hospital, about the agony of growing up in institutions, and that I wanted to reunite my family. Funny, for the first time in three years I outlined my hopes and ambitions. In the process, Tilley's words came back to me: "You can do more for your family if you go to college."

Talking with Bessie reminded me that I was at North Carolina College to salvage something from the pain my family had suffered. When I fell silent hours later, a tremendous bond existed between the two of us. "It's called friendship," she offered. I knew it was something much deeper. A wholesome healing had begun within me.

After dropping Bessie off around ten that evening, I watched the full moon cast shadows over Chidley Hall and across the track field beneath the hill. I thanked God for looking out for me, for sending me a special person. Just maybe, my Heavenly Father was a God of love.

This new spiritual connection was a grace I didn't deserve. With Bessie, I had an opportunity and vowed not to let the whispering and teasing opinions of others change my destiny. The ability to express my true nature had surfaced, and, for the first time, I wanted to set boundaries, to mark off my personal life from petty social affairs. God had tapped me on the shoulder to say *I have a greater purpose for you.* Gazing at the moon, I whispered, "Welcome home, Jimmy," then stood for the longest, absorbing my blessing. Never had I felt so at peace.

"Jim, what's going on man?" a dorm mate broke my contemplation. I went inside and slept like a baby.

Starting the next morning, I stopped seeing all other women and devoted my efforts to endearing Bessie. Over the objection of staff, I walked out of the cafeteria with a tray, plucked a rose from a bush, braved the laughter of students and delivered the breakfast to her dorm mate, protesting "No, let her sleep; just give her this when she wakes up." I put out the word to the fellows on campus, "Stay away from my girl," and most of them gave in to my demand.

From October to December, Bessie and I were together every single day. Insisting that we were "just friends," she was unaware that she was falling in love, but I knew. Before I left for the holidays, I wrote a letter and as instructed, my roommate took it to the graduate dining room and dropped it in her lap exactly twenty-four hours after I departed for New York. It was the first day we had been apart in three months. Bessie read: "Aha! Thought you weren't going to miss me, didn't you?" Later she told me the tears flowed and that's when she knew that she loved me.

Carol was the farthest from my mind as I gazed out of
Gloria's living room window on Christmas Eve.

New York was adorned in celebratory splendor, not
just Manhattan but neighborhood streets shined
throughout the five boroughs. The fuzzy glow of plump
red, blue, and green bulbs danced in the cedar branches
and cast a warm radiance on the house across the street.
In contrast, our cheerless apartment had no decorative
lights, no presents for Eddie, very little heat, and no food.
When Donna, my girlfriend since high school, dropped by
for a visit, I figured on getting a couple of dollars to buy
something for dinner. Gloria joined in light chitchat
around the kitchen table. Just as I was easing up to the
question of money, six-year-old Eddie came in with an
ear-to-ear grin on his face and his hands behind his back.

"Donna," he called out.

We kept talking.

"Dooonna," he repeated, his eyes dancing and that
silly grin still plastered on his face. "This Uncle Jimmy's
girrrlfriend. Isn't she pretty?" he thrust an eight-by-eleven
photo of Bessie in her face.

I dropped my head. Gloria jumped up, hands on
her hips, she shot him an Eddie-stop-it glare; but, he
gleefully repeated, "Isn't she pretty?"

Squinting at me, Donna demanded, "Who is that?" I
looked around the room searching for a gentle way out,
but there was none. "That's the girl I'm going to marry," I
admitted. She grabbed her coat from the back of the chair
and raced out the door with our dinner money in her
pocketbook.

It was a bleak holiday season. Not only did I spend
much of my time scheming for food but Carol was having
a hard time of it. When Gloria brought me up to speed on
my younger sister's circumstances, I went and got her.

Throughout the holiday season, Carol and I pondered her time in placement. We recalled my junior and her freshman year in high school. It was the year she had entered what the child welfare system called a period of "gradual emancipation." It began with her taking the New York Central Railroad (today's Metro North) from Westchester County into Grand Central Station and hopping a subway down to Washington Irving High School. She was often late or absent due to train delays and bad weather. The transportation problems prompted the city welfare agency to transfer her from the upstate Hillcrest facility to the Girls Service League group home in the Gramercy Park area of the city.

I remembered the Girls Service League. At first, it had made sense for Carol. Absentees and tardiness no longer marred her high school attendance record and, for the first time, she had seemed genuinely happy. She had been assigned her own room instead of the barrack style sleeping to which she had grown accustomed. Her social worker had also been a big hit. She arranged theater nights, horseback riding and a variety of activities for the girls. When Olatunji, the master drummer with a superb African dance troupe, appeared on a local television show and mesmerized Carol, the social worker arranged for her to attend his 1957 groundbreaking concert at Radio City Music Hall. Meeting the rhythm king backstage after the show had been the high point of my sister's teens.

Even in high school, Daddy had continued to use me as a substitute father but it was okay. Carol and I had grabbed what little family life we could from one another. Over the course of those visits, I had discovered that, despite the wonderful array of social activities, the Girls Service League was lax with discipline. Some of the girls stayed out all night and one girl got pregnant, had a botched abortion and almost died. Within a year of the incident, the place lost its funding and shut down.

In Carol's sophomore and my senior year in high school, she had moved to her second group home: Barrett House, on East 12th Street, in lower Manhattan. She was even happier at the new location because every Sunday she went to dinner at Granny's house. After school she worked part-time at the Chock-full-of-Nuts on Wall Street. It was more like a social outing than a job. She gobbled down hotdogs and got a chance to meet the baseball great, Jackie Robinson, who was an executive of the chain of coffee house-restaurants. It was during this happy period of Carol's adolescence that frequent contact between the two of us slowed to occasional visits filled with her gleeful stories of Granny, Aunt Carrie Mae and our cousins. I was still living at Woodycrest at the time, and my moods were sullen. I had not wanted to live with relatives. No matter how fragile the arrangement, I had wanted Daddy back down the block at the garage where I could stop by and make a couple of bucks washing cars and Mama back in the kitchen frying chicken and baking biscuits.

After graduation, I left for college without the faintest anticipation of troubles that would engulf my sister. I had been too involved with my own life to fathom that all her support would evaporate instantly. After more than eight years of custodial care, toward the end of her senior year in high school, a counselor had simply said, "You got to go; you got to make room for somebody else." Secure with her own room, she had thought that she would live at Barrett House forever, but she was referred to an employment agency and given a one-month re-location deadline.

Carol found her first real job as a receptionist at an eyeglass store. Unlike the spending money earned at Chock-full-of-Nuts, her income from the new position was needed to survive. When she got her first check, one of the staff members at Barrett House showed her how to open a bank account. That had been the extent of her preparation before she was on her own.

One of her housemates also had to find a place. She and Carol pooled their money and managed to pay the monthly rent of fifty-six dollars and fifty cents for an apartment on Avenue D. It was no neighborhood for teenage girls but, with nobody to oversee their choice, cost was the only basis for their selection. The girls knew nothing about danger signs in neighborhoods or in associates, nor did they know about paying bills, buying food, and doing laundry or any of the basic tasks of daily living. They had been sheltered for so many years it was scary.

Like me, Carol would have been better off if the various children and group homes had taught her life skills like how to keep a budget, run a house, and most of all, how to judge people's character. Instead, the social welfare system had created aliens in a real world.

Without skills and lacking any planned transition, my sister was floundering when I found her Christmas 1963. I was shocked to see her surrounded by foul play and seedy characters on Manhattan's Avenue D. I had wanted to believe that her life would be different from thousands of children who had been wards of the state. Sadly, Carol's case mirrored the countless other "emancipated" youth whose success had been defined in terms of "healthy adjustments" to institutions when it should have been measured by their readiness to integrate into society at the end of placement. What was actually needed was training in life and job skills spread over the course of the institutional stay. As old people in the community always said, "Start like you want to finish."

Within days of my bringing Carol home to Gloria, she landed a job as a stock girl at Lord and Taylor's department store on Fifth Avenue. As the holiday season ended, she was preparing to move in with Aunt Carrie Mae. Our soul searching talks convinced me that she was well on her way to adjusting to life outside the walls of institutions. I promised myself never to lose contact with my sister again, and I didn't.

By fall 1964, Bessie and I were married with a child on the way. My parents' failings began to loosen their hold when I became a proud expectant father. Bessie had finished her graduate studies, but I would need a miracle.

After a long silence, Dr. Totten, a balding brown skin man of slight statue and the most conservative professor in the Chemistry Department, began stuttering, "You- you see Blake. You got these C- C- Cs and Ds here. Y- you not going to grrr-graduate."

Ignoring the smirk on his face, I pleaded, "But Dr. Totten let me take an overload of courses. I can do it. Look at my grades for last semester."

He shook his head and delivered the crushing news that I was missing Organic Chemistry, a requirement in my major offered only in the fall term. He added that I needed to earn an "A" in the course "when and if" I ever took it and then concluded, "You- you might as well lee-leave now."

Not since Woodycrest had my angry determination been so thoroughly roused. Only this time I was angry with myself. It was not Dr. Totten's fault. He was right: I was not "an exceptional student with exceptional circumstances." Though I had buckled down and studied in my senior year, his approval of a maximum load of five courses would still leave me one course short of graduation. Precious time and energy squandered on social activities in previous semesters had caught up with me. I wouldn't be marching with my class. I refused to give up.

During the summer I worked at the shelter and my wife and I lived on 107th Street with Uncle Willie, Aunt Agnes and their daughter, Lydia. Louis Armstrong's house was just two doors down the block, and Bessie wanted to meet him and Aunt Lucille, but my hours were inflexible. Daily, I worked from early morning to late evening in order to save enough money to cover rent and other expenses for when I would be back in school.

My dedication paid off; I met my financial goals. Yet, I worried about leaving Bessie with a family she barely knew. I thought it would be easier if she was with someone closer to her own age. So I rented a spacious room with Gloria, her husband Tyrone, and Eddie who had recently moved into a brand new three bedroom apartment on 111th Street. I also asked two trusted friends, Jackie Green and Carole Wooten, to help her get to know the neighborhood. Because she had just had a baby, I was especially relying on Carole to make sure my wife got back and forth to the prenatal clinic at the local health center. Despite introductions to friends, prepaid rent, and incidental expense money, I remained uneasy about leaving Bessie, but I had to go.

I had a single focus: earning an "A" in Organic Chemistry—taught by none other than Dr. Totten. What a situation! The most difficult professor was teaching the most difficult course in the department. I could not afford to panic. I tackled that course with the same energy I had pursued Bessie during our courtship. There was no partying or hanging out with the fellows. My idea of relaxation was short breaks from studying to watch television or to discuss approaching fatherhood with Nathan Saziru and Obina Ogueri, who competed over the naming of my baby.

"If it's a girl name her Kanari; it means star," offered Nathan. Obina stubbornly held out for "Muhanja." The name rolled off his tongue with a lyrical rhythm that made it my instant choice. On a weekend trip home, I sang to Bessie's belly to the tune of the Temptations' hot new single, *My Girl*: "Nothing you can do to take the place of Muhanja / Nothing you can do 'cause I'm stuck like glue to Muhanja." Bessie hated the name. April, her birth month, or Jamie after me were her top choices. We compromised and settled on Kanari. Though the pregnancy pre-dated sonograms that tell the gender before birth, neither of us considered a boy's name.

Near the end of October, Daddy made what was no doubt his first long distance phone call. "Little Jimmy!" he shouted down the miles from New York to North Carolina, "You a daddy! Yeah! It's a girl!" and for fear of running up his phone bill, he hung up.

I burst into the dormitory lounge, switched off the television and yelled to forty disgruntled guys, "I'm a daddy!"

Angry growls turned to cheers: "Get a cigar! Anybody got a cigar!"

Within minutes my buddy, Smooth, picked me up; and we rolled with a bottle of Kentucky bourbon from the ABC state-run liquor store. I got drunk and brawled with Charles Clinton. The next morning I took my battered face to the chemistry lab and finished up my experiments before bumming a ride to New York to see my daughter.

On the way from North Carolina, I rehearsed explanations for my black eye: *I walked into a door. No, too trite. I was shadowboxing with my roommate and he accidentally tagged me. Yeah, that's what I'll say.* It was a useless exercise; my composure was shattered by the alarm on Bessie's face when she opened the door. "I was drunk," I blurted. "It was a sucker punch. Charles Clinton jumped me when I was drunk," I added defensively.

"What a way to meet your daughter!" she said, and gave me a mercy hug.

Seeing Kanari in the crib that her Aunt Gloria had purchased filled me with awe. I wanted to snatch her into my arms but she was sleeping peacefully. I leaned over, inhaled the clean sweet smell of baby powder and watched her lips move in a sucking motion. My eyes soaked up the plumpness of her cheeks, the rosy glow of her skin, and the fuzz of black hair covering her head. Sleeping or not, I gently peeled back the layers of soft yellow and white flannel blankets. She was dressed in a pink flowered undershirt. Pink plastic Tweedy Bird safety pins fastened a snow white cotton diaper that peeked from the top of clear plastic panties that kept her dry.

Wow! She was barely the length of my arm from hand to elbow. She looked so fragile curled in a cuddly ball on her stomach. My hand felt massive as I slowly moved my thumb along the wrinkled softness of her arms and outlined the tiny frame of her body. I studied the redness surging beneath the tissue-paper skin covering the soles of her feet. "My baby," I whispered and closed my hand around one foot. This was reality. I was a father. I had to get my degree.

I returned to school, charged for the finish line. At the end of the semester I stood in Dr. Totten's office, fear pounding my chest. Unhurried, he reached for his folder, pulled my paper out, reared back in his seat and started stammering. "Y- y- you see, Blake, you- you'll never be more than a lab technician." His voice dripped with derision. "You cou- could have been one of my best st-

stu- students..." I stopped listening. Terrifying thoughts raced through my head: *I'm not going to graduate. I have a baby at home. I spent all those semesters partying. I've ruined my life.* Then, "...g-g- got an "A." exploded in my ear.

What! I snatched that paper from him and ran out of the science building, shouting like a wild man: "I got a degree! I can take care of my family!"

The **tightrope** that caseworkers walk trying to balance the injuries caused by parents against the injuries children suffer when separated from their parents is frightening. I experienced the problem first hand when Miss Corbett pulled together temporary sources of income to help me support my fledging family. She hired me as weekend supervisor at the shelter and arranged a paid internship at the Queens Society for the Prevention of Cruelty to Children, that I called the Society. We responded to complaints of abuse and neglect, initiated actions in family court to protect children and, if necessary, placed them in the shelter.

At the Society, I worked under Miss VanIyke, the social worker who had intervened in my life a decade earlier. Almost daily, she reminded everyone in earshot, "When I met Jimmy, his jaw sat out like a second head."

"Oh, really?" I tried to play it off.

"He growled like a little bulldog."

"Miss VanIyke, stop trying to tell people that stuff."

"Oh, it's in the record, Jimmy. It's in the record. You want me to go over to that file cabinet and pull the record?"

"Naaaw, don't get the record." Resigned to the badgering, I waved her away.

In taunting me, Miss VanIyke didn't mean to be cruel. Working with her revealed callousness brought on by tough cases of child abuse but it also allowed glimpses of her softer side. Our investigative work gave meaning to the moans and groans I had heard in the dark back in the days when I was a shelter child.

What happens to children behind closed doors is heartbreaking. They suffer unimaginable violence and abuses of every kind. At one home in South Ozone Park, Miss VanIyke and I discovered complete role reversals between a mother and daughter. The father had put the mother out and moved the daughter into the bedroom and given the fourteen-year-old full run of the house, including authority over the mother, who the girl ordered around like a two-year-old. Miss VanIyke swung into action but the judge could not send the father to jail. Mother and daughter refused to testify against him. However, Miss VanIyke's vigilant pursuit and my detailed report of filth in the house, of the lack of food in a refrigerator that was packed from top to bottom with beer, and of the girl's consistent absence from school was enough to remove the minor from the home.

The most horrendous case was a seven-year-old who nearly died and was brutally scarred on his face, neck and chest from burns suffered when his mother held him to a steaming radiator. Miss VanIyke found him alone in the living room, his body twisted in pain. She scooped the boy into her arms and rushed him to the hospital. He spent weeks in intensive care. His mother went to jail.

Miss VanIyke was crying the weekend she brought the boy to me at the shelter. "Take care of this one. I mean you look out for him," she ordered.

His first night in the shelter that little boy wailed, "I want my mama! I want my mama!" It brought me to tears. Most of the counselors were baffled, but I understood that his love for his mother was greater than the pain she had inflicted. The other children and I felt that little boy's agony and we watched over him. No one teased him about his disfigured face. He wore the outer scars of our inner pain.

As the supervisor of the shelter's weekend program, I interacted directly with the children, as well as worked to improve counselor sensitivity to children's needs. Some counselors did not understand that poor treatment by professional caregivers is the harshest form of cruelty to children in placement who have deep emotional wounds. I stopped all yelling and verbal lashings of kids; and I eliminated restrictions for small infractions. Whenever we went to the movies or the park, not a single child was left behind on punishment.

In staff meetings I gave illustrations of how to read a child's behavior. One youngster was constantly on restriction for hitting. I gathered the counselors in my office to watch at the window. Grinning from ear to ear, the boy would run up to a kid, punch him and, still grinning, race away like he was playing tag. "See," I told them, "he wants to play but doesn't know how to communicate it. Don't yell at him or punish him, sit him down and teach him." His counselor called the boy in and talked with him. The hitting stopped. A major overhaul of the system was not required; simple kindness made the difference. With compassion, communication and patience, counselors began to get greater results with less effort.

Working with hundreds of youngsters from broken families was like revisiting old haunts in Corona. My college degree had come too late to help Chino, Lucky, Torch and other guys from The Boulevard. When I bumped into them, the devastation of alcohol, drugs and incarceration was written on their faces. Yet, our brotherhood was strong; we were from the same social womb.

That bond I had with my lifelong buddies existed between the children at the shelter and me. I was a specialist with the toughest kids because I knew their world intimately. The hardness manifested outwardly did not reflect the soft inner-child crying to get out. Unable to escape, they built emotional walls to protect themselves from daily assaults and threats of harm. As Tilley had done with me, I talked openly to them about their pain, and like boilers with pressure valves, they released hurt in small gusts of emotions.

My first year of marriage was stressful. In addition to financial woes, we worried constantly about the draft. Under the Lyndon Johnson administration, the "Vietnam Conflict" grew into a full blown war. Eligibility status for drafting into the United States Army changed rapidly. Young men under twenty-five went off to fight or fled to Canada to avoid the draft. Though I registered for Selective Service as it was called, I was never drafted. First I was exempted because I was in school. When the army started conscripting students, I was married. Then, married men were called up, but not those with children. I managed to stay one step ahead of the draft. I was not afraid of fighting, but the thought of leaving Bessie alone a second time horrified me. I was grateful to be able to stay home and help her care for Kanari.

Meanwhile, making ends meet on an intern's salary was tough but Bessie was a trooper. She carefully calculated our weekly living expenses. In a meticulous weekly log, she accounted for every penny: rent - twenty dollars, food - fifteen dollars, diaper service - three dollars, transportation to work - two dollars and ten cents, a night at the movies - three dollars. After expenses, roughly one hundred dollars a month was put aside for a place of our own. Only twice did we dip into savings. First, I insisted on replacing her Louisiana wardrobe—a red cloth coat and cotton dresses—with heavier wear suitable for biting New York winters. Then, we made a sizeable withdrawal to return to North Carolina College for commencement.

On a beautiful day in May 1965, Bessie and I marched together. I received a Bachelor of Science in Chemistry, and she Master of Arts in English. Following the ceremony we ran into Corporal Jones. "I see you married a scholar," he said, referring to the gray and purple velvet trimmed Masters' hood that draped my wife's graduation gown.

"Indeed," I beamed. Silently, I pledged that Bessie would get the doctorate she had been planning when we married. Nobody would say she stopped moving ahead when she married Jimmy Blake.

Miss Corbett and Mr. Weismann, a caseworker at the Society, were impressed by my work with children. They constantly pointed me out as a shelter success story. After the end of my one-year internship, they used their contacts in the New York City Bureau of Child Welfare to launch my career. I was hired as a caseworker in the Division of Foster Care. The annual salary of nine thousand dollars was more than a decent income for my family of three in 1966.

I reported to work in February in the middle of the Social Service Employee Union's contract negotiations with the city. In addition to a salary increase, the union demanded reductions in worker caseloads that often exceeded sixty. The membership wanted the right to negotiate on any issue, including better benefits for welfare recipients. With the talks deadlocked, we voted to sit in at local welfare centers starting in June. The city retaliated by locking us out in the dead of winter.

Along with Sam Greene, a trainee with me in the intensive workshops that prepared us as caseworkers, I pounded the pavement for a grueling six weeks. The union relief check was less than what I had made as an intern at the Society. As if the decrease in pay was not enough, news reporters portrayed us as self-serving greedy workers looking for more money. Strangers threw pennies at us as we marched. Most articles failed to mention the struggle for better services for clients. Our effort was not lost, though, on the many welfare recipients who joined the fight for an increase in the Department of Welfare's basic living allowance. They wanted a check that actually covered the cost of food, housing and clothing.

It was revolutionary. Welfare recipients and workers battled for a common cause. Until then, mountains of paperwork had sharply divided caseworkers and clients. Strained relationships had hampered, and sometimes totally obstructed, the delivery of services. Clients compared their interactions with caseworkers to a patient bleeding to death in an emergency room while a clerk insisted on filling out insurance forms before calling a doctor. The parallel was a good one for a Welfare Department where human suffering had taken a back seat to bureaucratic rules and regulations. Insights gained on the picket line finally signaled a shift in caseworker and client attitudes. Both groups demanded to be treated with dignity.

In the highly spirited first days of the lockout, it was picket line by day and pep rallies at union headquarters at night. However, by the end of the second week, the financial pinch drove momentum down and hostilities up as workers crossed the picket line to shouts of "scabs" and "sell-outs." I became the shop steward at our welfare center on Lafayette Street. With Sam at my side, I mounted a desk in the center of the office pool and implored my colleagues to return to the picket line. Shirley Colvin and a handful of others followed us out into the cold streets. The next day, half of them returned to work.

On the bleakest days, Sam, Shirley and I spent hours weighing whether or not to continue the battle. Ultimately, we hung on with weary clients, but the decision to stick it out forced us to apply for welfare. We found ourselves on the other side of the desk with our colleagues asking us to fill out yellow and green eligibility forms. The meager welfare check did not begin to address the needs of our families. The real payoff was the knowledge we gained about client suffering. No other experience was capable of bonding us with welfare recipients like our being placed on the welfare rolls.

When the lockout ended after six weeks, bitter resentment remained between workers who stuck it out and those who crossed the picket line. Unfortunately, the split was along racial lines. Blacks felt that liberal Whites had led them into and then deserted them in a strike that was doomed to fail. Not only did worker caseloads remain at sixty, the right to negotiate on issues beyond wages was denied and the union dropped the demands pertaining to clients. Disillusionment with the Social Service Employees Union and commitment to continue the fight for improved benefits for welfare recipients led to the birth of the Association of Black Social Workers.

Despite the failures of the work action, I could see a measure of success. In addition to positive working relationships, the newfound unity between client and caseworkers spearheaded a grassroots welfare rights movement.   On a personal level, the struggle also cemented an unbreakable bond of brotherhood between Sam and me. He remained my friend, my confident, my "ace-boon-coon" until his untimely death ten years later. Shirley and I are still friends today. Whenever I see her, we recall the trials of getting our careers off the ground and how the strike helped to prepare us for the recurring nature of strife in the workplace.

A loving family wasn't enough to put my soul at ease. At the end of emotionally drained days of resolving conflicts between foster parents, foster children and natural parents, I listened to Symphony Sid, a popular jazz radio show; and, I learned about mothering.

Fantasies dissolved as I watched Bessie care for Kanari. The job demanded every ounce of her energy and every second of her time. She kept our baby spotless, played with her when she was awake, fed her when she was hungry, soothed her when she was sick and watched over her when she was asleep. The twenty-four-hour cocoon spun around Kanari made me realize what I had missed. Had God revealed the true meaning of mother when I was a child, it would have destroyed me. In His mercy He let the role unfold in an environment where I could enjoy it. Still, I couldn't let go of old pains.

Since the age of ten I had been on the streets or in dormitory-style settings. College, the fourth in a series of large institutions, had not been a big emotional adjustment. I was accustomed to living among strangers and lining up to eat in cafeterias. Sharing rooms, showers and television lounges in group settings was a well-established routine but marriage was a totally different institution. The intimacy of close household quarters stifled me. Frequently, my hands coiled involuntarily into tight fists. Bessie would walk over to the couch, sit beside me rattling on about nothing topics, gently uncurl my fingers and walk away as if it were the most natural thing in the world. Despite her kindness and my efforts to relax, I fled to my most consistent family—the guys in the streets.

I was already holding down two jobs—Foster Care on weekdays and the shelter on weekends—but by the summer of 1965 I had immersed myself in volunteer work. Evenings were spent at a youth program that my old friend and mentor, Lou Benson, had started as part of his ongoing effort to address gang problems that had rumbled from the fifties into the sixties. In an attempt to eradicate territorial claims of rival gangs and put an end to turf wars, The Elm-Cor (East Elmhurst – Corona) Youth Center brought together opposing gangs like the Chaplains, Viking Lords and Clovers. It was a risky undertaking.

One night, fifty teenagers stampeded the intersection at Astoria Boulevard and Kearney. Yelling and cursing, a stout rugged youngster snapped a radio antenna from a parked car. The domino effect erupted into swashbuckling Zorro style fencing that slashed faces, sliced arms, and spilled blood everywhere. In the heat of the fight, "Yo' Spade, duck!" rang out just as Lou stepped into the fray, grabbed the ringleader by the collar, slapped him around and ordered him to call off his boys. Then, he sat the lot of them down and made them negotiate a peace. That's where I came into the picture. I knew many of the guys. There was even a "Little Spade" in the group. The fellows listened to me because I was the dude from the streets who had made it.

I ripped pages from Mr. Harris' playbook. "Think with your minds," I challenged them in group sessions. "You cats are fighting and going to jail to restrict yourselves and your soul brothers to a few measly blocks while brothers and sisters in the south are fighting, going to jail and even dying to free our people to go anywhere we want in this country." I described my participation in civil rights protests and the time spent in jail. I read to them the article I had written in *The Campus Echo* about the visit of Dr. Martin Luther King, Jr. to North Carolina College. Then, we discussed Rev. King's "Letter from a Birmingham Jail," especially the section that stated: "We are caught in an inescapable network of mutuality, tied in a single garment of destiny. Whatever affects one directly, affects all indirectly. No longer can we afford to live with narrow, provincial 'outside agitator' ideas." After emphasizing our brotherly bonds, I informed the group, "One of the greatest freedom fighters, Malcolm X, walked these streets. He lived right here in East Elmhurst. Man, he was blown away this year fighting for your freedom." Most of all, I played on their love and respect for Lou: "This constant fighting is going to cause him to lose this center. Yeah, keep it up; they gon' close this place down."

The on-going rap sessions had a sobering effect on the guys and by the end of the summer they began to settle down. Conflicts continued to crop up but the youth center was orderly enough to deliver an array of recreational and educational activities. Eventually, operations were moved to a facility at the corner of 108th Street and Northern Boulevard that evolved into the stately building that is now named the Louis Armstrong Community Center. In addition to honoring Pops, the complex is a testament to the work of Helen Marshall, Cecil Watkins and my friend Lou Benson, who continued to serve as youth director for many years.

Working with the youth of Corona and East Elmhurst gave my life purpose. Though I didn't understand at the time that God was the driving force behind my involvement, I was conscious of how every facet of my life merged in my work at Elm-Cor. The pain of losing my family, of hungry days and cold nights in Corona, of years in children homes, of times in protest marches and on picket lines, combined in positive energy.

There had to be an unseen hand at work because I would have never chosen such a rough path to youth services. Though I no longer thought of the Father that I had dreamed would one day help me relieve the suffering of children, I knew that I was engaged in a work that took me beyond duty to fulfillment.

My work with foster children became a steady wind fanning flames of desire: I wanted Ruthie and Frances home. Bessie and I drove once a month to Wyandanch, Long Island to get my sisters for the weekend, but old cries rattled my spirit each time I carried them back to their foster home. "If only Mama was well," I'd lament.

My mother had been hospitalized for sixteen years. The boy inside of me held fast to the hope of her return. Every day at work, I watched the Division of Foster Care releasing children to parents whose situations had improved. It fed fantasies of Mama coming home and taking charge of her family.

"Let's do it," Bessie drew me out of my dream world. "I mean, why can't you and I bring your sisters home?"

I had no faith that we could do so. The agency didn't give children to brothers or sisters, or anyone our age. My wife was twenty-three and I was twenty-four; I doubted that we could get custody of two teenage girls. Eligibility for guardianship was restrictive. Children were not placed with single parents, homosexuals or with racially mixed couples; and on the rare occasion that a child went home to relatives, the financial help given to foster parents was denied. Placement with biological families, usually too poor to provide adequate food, clothing, medical and other living expenses, became revolving doors that shuttled children right back into the system. Experience told me that Bessie and I did not have a chance of getting my sisters.

"But, you know the foster care regulations," she pressed. "You know the people; there must be someone who can help." Ironically, that someone was Mrs. Couch, Ruthie and Frances' case manager at the Sheltering Arms children's agency and the former wife of Dr. William Couch, Bessie's thesis advisor at North Carolina College. Mrs. Couch worked against the odds and Bessie and I were certified as foster parents.

My sisters were home! For most of the summer of 1968, I walked around in a euphoric cloud, treating their presence like an extended vacation. In between sumptuous meals laid out by Granny and Aunt Carrie Mae, we went on picnics in Flushing Meadow Parks, on wild rides at Coney Island and on walking tours of Harlem, The Village, Times Square and Central Park. Meanwhile, Bessie worked out the practical arrangements of our more cramped living conditions. She identified a corner of the living room to store couch pillows when the sofa bed was pulled out at night. The closet was emptied in Kanari's room for the girl's belongings. In addition, Bessie kept me on track with health records and other paperwork necessary to enroll them in Bayside High School. Once my sisters were settled in school for the fall, she continued the search for a house in East Elmhurst.

Meanwhile, my family's case was helping to reshape foster care policy. We were among the first siblings or relatives granted benefits to assist with the financial obligations of caring for children reunited with their families. Today's growing trend in "kinship care" was not evident in the late sixties when Ruthie and Frances came to live with Bessie and me. We blazed a new trail.

Without a model to follow, I made many blunders. Because I saw my primary role as maintaining a roof over my sister's head, I continued to work two jobs—at the Bureau of Child Welfare and the weekend position at the shelter. I was out of the house almost all of the time.

Thank God, Bessie had a family model rooted in a Christian tradition built on a longsuffering kind of love. The extent of her day-to-day sacrifice and the source of her strength and patience was underrated because I was satisfied that I was doing far better than my father in providing food, clothing, and shelter. Her steadfast commitment to family unity got us through the trials that started immediately after my sisters came home.

Even though I was the biological brother, I was not spared the criticism leveled against foster parents. My wife and I were accused of bringing my sisters' home to improve our own living conditions. The charge against us was as unfair as it was for most foster parents. Sure, there were a few people who packed large numbers of children into their homes in an attempt to profit, but in my work at the Division of Foster Care, I found that the vast majority of people who opened their homes to children did so out of compassion. The welfare allowance for food, clothing, shelter, medical, recreational and incidental expenses was and still is insufficient.

In our case, household money closed the financial gap. Bessie's Master's Degree qualified her for a twelve-thousand-dollars-a-year beginning salary with the Board of Education. In 1967, she had gone to work as an English teacher at Intermediate School 61Q—the renamed, relocated in a new building, and restructured JHS 16 that I had attended as an adolescent. I continued to work at the Bureau of Child Welfare and at the shelter. Our combined income of nearly twenty-five-thousand dollars a year was a sizable income in the mid-sixties. It allowed us to contribute to the financial support of my sisters.

Bessie was a firm believer that paying rent was like throwing money out of the window. She had saved enough for a down payment on the purchase of a house and was searching for a place in East Elmhurst long before we considered bringing Ruthie and Frances to live with us. We did not need a welfare stipend to improve our lot; and, we could have certainly done without the aggravation of well-meaning but often inept caseworkers prying into our lives. Nevertheless, mean-spirited rumors persisted regarding our financial exploitation of my younger sisters.

I couldn't understand it then, but now I realize that family members had fallen victim to jealousy and guilt because of failures to fulfill long-held dreams that they would be the ones to bring Ruthie and Frances home. At the time, it really hurt that relatives, who should have been jubilant about my sisters' homecoming, raised their voices in a chorus of gossip. I didn't care that they whispered about me, but I did expect appreciation for Bessie's effort. It was particularly painful to watch my wife vilified, because she had suspended goals of assisting her widowed mother in caring for her own brother and sister who were the ages of Ruthie and Frances. I was grateful that Bessie ignored the gossip and remained firm in support of my desire for family unity.

Sadly, the loose talk reached Ruthie and Frances— two confused adolescents who had been in the throes of identity crises all of their lives. "In order to survive in foster care, I had to see the world as my family," Frances told me. Her world view had diminished her loneliness while in foster care, but once with us, she was still lost. For the longest time she looked at the ground whenever people spoke to her. "I had been missing so long that I choked up and couldn't express myself but inside I was happy to be home with my family," she eventually confessed. Though she and Ruthie took baby steps toward our family, it would be years before they truly came home.

Thanks to Tilley, I had a chance to care for my family my way. "You did it!" he shouted when I phoned to tell him my sisters were living with me. If he had not pushed me to accept the scholarship from Woodycrest I would not have met Bessie, and without her, I can't imagine how I would have brought them home.

Bessie thought that our meeting, her sharing my hopes for my sisters and her connection to their caseworker through her thesis advisor was all coincidence. I knew they were ordered steps. God had put into motion according to His timing the answer to my many years of sincere prayer. Mama's friend, Jesus, had not brought her home but just maybe it was Him who sent my wife's help with my sisters.

Sharing the news of Ruthie and Frances' homecoming was among my last communications with Tilley. In our very last conversation, he called my office to ask for help in getting a job. He was drunk and sounded like he was down and out. Promising to do what I could, I asked him to send me a resume, but he never did. Even so, I promised myself to follow up with him. Next I heard he was dead and buried. Sorrow washed over me. I should have been there for Tilley. I comforted myself with the thought that he died knowing that, thanks to him, I had succeeded in bringing my sisters home.

Tilley left a good legacy. Because of him I understand that one person can have a far-reaching impact on another's life and that suffering can be molded into good deeds. Without Tilley, only God knows what would have happened to me; because of him I have helped thousands. Starting with my internship at the Society and continuing until today, every troubled person who comes into my office is a Jimmy Blake sitting across from a Tom Tilley. Modeling his approach has made me effective in addressing the severest problems. I reach beneath superficial stereotypes of age, economic class, social status, race, gender and sexual orientation in attempts to transform pain into power. My epitaph to him is, "God wrought a good work in Tom Tilley."

"I can't say who I am without my parents getting upset," foster children on my caseload complained.

"Ain't I enough? Why can't they let that go?" foster mothers grieved openly about biological parents.

This rift between parents and children caused me to initiate group sessions at the Division of Foster Care in the summer of 1968. Knowing too well the deep and lasting wounds inflicted by silence, I decided to bring together foster parents and children to talk about their anguish. Two things happened. First, the children confessed that they were afraid to speak about their biological parents for fear of ridicule or revenge or both. Second, foster mothers agonized over the inability to soothe the children's aching desire for their birth mothers. All sides were trapped in a system that bred uncertainty. In a hell where children lost their natural parents, temporary custody arrangements dragged on for years. With the support of the new group sessions, foster parents began to deal effectively with the reality of uncertainty and gradually they encouraged the children in their care to talk about and in some cases to visit their biological parents under the supervision of the agency. Slowly, levels of tension dropped in the foster homes on my caseload.

The emotionally charged group sessions had a surprising but significant personal outcome. Before the group conferences, I saw myself solely as big brother to Ruthie and Frances, but over the course of the sessions I became aware of my additional role as foster parent. Like with foster children at work, I started talking to my sisters about our parents. We spent many loving hours reliving bits of family history. I hoped the stories would draw us closer together, but their deepest emotional attachments remained sister to sister. I did not understand that my approach was doomed to fail; that my sisters' needs were opposite of most foster children. They wanted the freedom to talk about the foster parents that they had recently lost.

My family needed professional support to work through the problems we faced in our unique foster home. Ruthie and Frances wanted to talk about Mrs. Washington, the woman who had mothered them for as long as they could remember. However, she was a complete mystery to me. For the ten years my sisters had been in her home, I could not recall ever seeing her. I knew nothing about her personality or character.

It took years for Ruthie and Frances to open up to me about their foster care experience. I would discover over time that they were not the first foster children in the Washington home but their placement was the longest. Clearly, money was not the motivation for the Washingtons. Besides Ruthie and Frances they had taken in only two other children who had stayed for only a few months. So, my sisters had been the center of attention in the household until they were ages nine and ten, and Mrs. Washington gave birth to a daughter, Debbie.

A kind-hearted, hardworking man of few words, Mr. Washington was often at work and left the running of the house to his wife. Mrs. Washington had a definite set of rules: speak when spoken to, behave in school, and obey in public. If Ruthie or Frances misbehaved in public, they got a mother-look that said, *straighten up or you are going to get a beating.* Once, Ruthie had acted out in school and the foster mother showed up and whipped her on the spot.

Like most Black mothers of the fifties, Mrs. Washington believed in tough love, but her role as disciplinarian was balanced by a contrasting tender side that was always present. She let the girls bring a stray dog home and keep it for years. Her tenderness was obvious as she looked after Ruthie who suffered from eczema, an itchy sometimes painful skin rash. Mrs. Washington patiently gave oatmeal baths; then, gently rubbed Vaseline over my sister's inflamed neck, arms and knees; and, as a preventive measure, carefully monitored her diet.

Despite the genuine love and care of a good mother, Ruthie and Frances learned to be on guard. They were acutely aware of their status as foster children. Sessions with social workers and trips to the agency to visit with me left no doubt that they had another family. In addition, firmly planted in their minds were the two children who came and disappeared quickly from the Washington home. My sisters did not want to risk the same fate; so, they were careful, very careful.

Long after becoming an adult, Ruthie would explain that Mrs. Washington was happy to see Frances and her reunite with our family. Mrs. Washington was also sad and a little hurt, but this loving mother sacrificed any visible expression of her feeling. She was not the kind of person to say, *I did a good job and now you are leaving me.*

However, back when the girls came to live with Bessie and me, knowledge of Mrs. Washington's motherly ways remained cloaked in mystery. Without any real acquaintance with the foster family, I relied on impressions formed as an adolescent on the outskirts of Ruthie and Frances' lives. In my mind, their foster mother was the woman who had relegated meetings with my sisters to child welfare offices and train platforms.

As a caseworker, I became aware of agency regulations that determined the frequency, quality, and location of meetings between foster parents, foster children and the biological family. Yet, I was emotionally unable to acknowledge that limited access to my sisters during my teen years had not been Mrs. Washington's doing. The barriers erected to protect foster parents and children had unwittingly erected a wall of resentment that blocked an easier transition for my sisters into my household. Avenues of communication between the two families would have freed Ruthie and Frances to express feelings about the dramatic changes taking place in their lives. Sadly, it would be forty years before I met Mrs. Washington and discovered a really fine human being.

Meanwhile, Ruthie and Frances were happy to be with me but afraid to talk about their foster mother. For them, the emotional vacuum between the Washington and Blake families fueled yet another cycle of being very careful. They viewed their homecoming as an experiment that could go wrong and cause the agency to take them back to foster care. They tiptoed around me.

They were my blood sisters, but our childhoods were so very different. Once I was placed in Woodycrest I knew I had left home for good. As bad as my experience had been, it could not be compared to the limbo Ruthie and Frances suffered. For them, foster care was ten years of hoping that our parents would come. Instead, Bessie and I showed up—a couple in our early twenties feeling our way as adults. Though I was biological family, I could not replace Daddy nor could my wife substitute for Mama. So we were the best big brother and sister that we could possibly be.   It was not enough.   Ruthie and Frances harbored anger and sadness and fears that were hard to penetrate. Despite my attempts to touch the core of their beings, they frequently shut themselves in their room, and clung to one another. The homecoming that answered my prayers suspended them between the long-lost family that was found and the loving foster family that was lost.

———•———

"**A** natural! You are a natural!" Dr. Schwartz exclaimed. He compared my group work skills to a good piano player who could not read music. I related to his comment because I was just that sort of piano player.

"Come to Columbia, Jim, and learn to read the notes. You got to know the theory behind what you are doing."

"I can't afford to go to Columbia. I have a family to support." I told him, but he was excited.

"I'll discuss it with Mrs. Gutman," he said and walked away leaving me confused.

By the time of Dr. Schwartz's conversation with Rose Gutman, the Director of the Division of Foster Care, had already seen my case reports. My supervisor, Ivy Hayward, had scribbled in the file, "Improved relationships between foster parents and children." Impressed by my performance, Mrs. Gutman called me to her office. "The agency is moving toward Group Work and I want you to help in the pilot project," she announced. "You will have the privilege of working directly with our consultant, Dr. William Schwartz of Columbia University. He is one of the foremost authorities on Group Work."

Dr. Schwartz's lobbying on my behalf paid off. In fall 1968, I enrolled in Columbia University's School of Social Work on a fellowship from the New York City Department of Welfare. My entire salary continued and all tuition and educational expenses were covered. In exchange, I agreed to work at the Bureau of Child Welfare for at least two years after receiving my Master's Degree.

On my first day of graduate school, Carol Irizarry, my field supervisor at St. Luke Hospital's Division of Community Psychiatry, sent me to work with teens on 103rd Street. Very little traffic entered the stand-alone block. It was bound by Central Park West on one end and the towering Frederick Douglass Housing Projects on the Manhattan Avenue end. The housing project ran a community center based on the Mobilization for Youth philosophy of reducing juvenile delinquency by removing barriers to opportunities. Despite the close proximity, the youth on 103rd Street did not participate in the available activities. My job was to link them to the resources of the community center.

When I arrived on the block for the first time, I did a surface evaluation of social conditions. Rusty fire escapes hung off the front of five-story pre-World War I tenements. The contents of garbage cans spilled onto the sidewalks and into the gutters. Cracks and crevices in the stoops mirrored the potholes in the streets. In nearby huddles, young men smoked reefer and old men laughed and joked and turned up to their lips bottles inside brown paper bags. An army of children—mostly twelve and thirteen year-olds—chased one another, shadowboxed, batted balls with broken sticks, stood on top of parked cars, and cursed loudly. There had to be an underlying organization to the apparent chaos. After observing for a while, I approached the likely leader of the rowdy bunch.

"Hey man, how you doing? What's your name?"

A lanky coffee brown boy around fourteen studied me with suspicion, mumbled "William," and walked away.

I followed him, "Hey, wait a minute, man. I'm talking to you."

"Yeah? About what?" he said with unmistakable hostility.

"I'm a youth worker, assigned to this block."

"What the hell is a youth worker?"

"I'm here to help you guys get a group together and do some things that maybe you don't do, like go to the movies or go on trips. We'll all sit down as a group and make...."

"Who dat? Who dat?" another kid ran up to us.

"I don't know. He say he a worker... a youth worker," William answered.

"He a police! He a police, William! You going to jaaail."

"No, I'm not the police," I declared. William started inching away. My tone grew defensive. "Wait a minute! I'm not the police! I'm here to try to do some things with you guys. I'm here to help! Where do you live? Maybe I can talk to your mother."

He pointed to one of the buildings.

Past the men on the stoop, up the steps, through the unhinged door, beyond open mailboxes, beneath dislodged light bulb sockets, through a cold, dark and urine-stenched hallway, I maneuvered to the stairs and climbed to the fifth floor. When I introduced myself to William's mother, Tassie, the first words out of her mouth were, "What did William do now?" Relieved that he was not in trouble, she listened and welcomed the idea of someone working with the young people.

Overcoming the group's resistance to change was a challenge. Except for school, which they rarely attended, the youth never left the block. Central Park was a few steps across the street but it was a world away. Whenever I tried to take them there, they picked fights and pouted, "We don't want to go to no park." It did not take long to figure out that they were terrified of leaving the haven of predictable routines on their block. It took several weeks to convince them to take a small step to broaden their horizon.

"You guys listen," I told them beforehand, "We are going to walk down to the corner and take the train to 42nd Street. I have a subway token for each of you. Now, I don't want you guys clowning around."

A fuss stirred in the group: "Man you hear that; he talking to you; you the clown." "No, you the clown." "Who you calling a clown?" "Man, I'll..."

"Stop it!" I scolded. "You see, that's exactly what I'm talking about. You guys want to go or not?"

Silence.

"Alright then, we're going to have a good time at the movies."

They slipped the subway tokens into their pockets and, on a sunny fall afternoon, the twelve of us ambled down the block to the subway on the corner of Central Park West. Then, at the top of the steps they stampeded as if on cue. Shoving people aside, they jumped the turnstiles and left me yelling at their backs. I paid my fare and caught up with them on the platform as the train rumbled into the station. When the doors of the subway car slid open, they pushed their way inside, cursing and hooting and howling to the top of their lungs. Other passengers pulled themselves tight against their seats and avoided eye contact with the rowdy group of Black boys who acted like they were ready to attack. The ten-minute ride to 42nd Street was dreadful.

As soon as we came up out of the subway, the group quieted. At the theater when I presented our tickets, the clerk got the manager. A balding, stocky man came out to the lobby, "Look we don't want any trouble," he said nervously.

"Trouble? We're here to see a movie," I asserted as my group waited silently.

"Well, yes, I'm going to let you in but I'm just saying we want it orderly. We don't want to spoil it for other moviegoers."

"Do you see any disorderliness?" I asked.

The guys calmly observed the exchange. When the manager stepped aside, they lined up for popcorn and sodas and streamed methodically into their seats. The lights went down and, "Eeeeeek!" trumpeted above the bellowing preview that flashed across the screen.

"Man, what you doing?" William's deep voice rang out. "What you doing?" "Gimme some of that popcorn." "Don't throw popcorn on me!" "What's wrong with you?" All I could see were shadows in motion, then the manager's flashlight beckoning to me. We were evicted.

On the way back to 103rd Street, not one squeak came from the bunch. I cursed the whole time. I vowed never to return to that block.

I was mad, mad, but my field supervisor had a good laugh before insisting that I go back. My academic schedule required three days a week of field placement and two days in class at Columbia. Despite Carol Irizarry's instruction, I took a week off before trudging back to the block because I needed the field credits for my degree.

The guys shocked me, "Jimmy is back! Jimmy is back."

"Let's go to Central Park and talk," I suggested, and surprisingly, they followed without resistance. Shivering on cold benches at the edge of the park, we held our first formal group meeting.

"You guys upset me because I care about you. I want you to get better out of life than what you're getting." I pointed to the high-rise Frederick Douglass Houses standing at the head of 103rd Street. "They got activities in there that you would love: basketball, table tennis, music, dancing, movie passes and refreshments. You know how you guys like to eat." After I finished, they confided that they felt unwanted by the center because the children in the projects made fun of them.

"Well, the director wants you," I assured them. "He talks all the time about you joining in the fun." They took a vote and decided to go to the Frederick Douglass Community Center for our next meeting.

I was glad Carol forced me to continue with William and his friends. They reminded me that it takes time and patience to build trust. During the movie outing they had tested my sincerity, but mostly they had been blocking any potential pain of rejection. Those guys were trying to get a jump on the world before the world jumped on them. So, they rebuffed me before I could rebuff them. The fact that I returned after they had done everything to get rid of me proved to them that I cared. Once trust was established between us, they were ready to take risks with other people.

True to their word, William and his crew crossed a vast psychological terrain, joined the community center's youth program, and literally came in from the cold. Our subsequent group sessions were held in the warmth of a room that the center director provided,

The real work began. We tackled problems of adjustment to program regulations, of alienation from the project children and of conflict resolution when tempers flared. Over time, two or three of the fellows dropped out but William and the others settled down—especially after the staff began to understand that, to survive, the center needed the children as much as the children needed it. Once that fact was established, laying down the law with the order, "Get over here!" shifted to the encouraging invitation, "Please, won't you join us?"

Tassie approached me on a raw day in February. An infant had died in the freezing cold of her building. Pleased with my positive influence on William, she wondered if I would talk to Charley, the building superintendent, about sending up some heat. Charley lived on the first floor just above the furnace. When he raised the thermostat, his place became a sweltering sauna. He had a choice: roast or let the rest of the building freeze. He acted with self-interest. I agreed to talk to him but insisted that Tassie come with me. She wanted to enlist the support of the other tenants. So we set a meeting date.

The evening of the meeting, Tassie's apartment was packed with women and two middle-age men. They were all dressed in heavy coats, caps, gloves and wool scarves. On the stove, steam rose a foot above four pots of boiling water, and then disappeared. Drafts of heat bounced out of the open oven door and back in again. In a losing battle against arctic winds that whistled through broken windowpanes and loose plaster, the indoor temperature dropped below ten degrees. I was horrified. Conditions at our haunted house back on 97th Street had not been as deplorable.

Carrie, the mother of another of the boys in the youth group, gave an impassioned talk about the poor precious baby losing her life because nobody cared. Other residents chimed in with a litany of complaints. They wanted Charley to do his job and make repairs, starting with the broken windowpanes. They whipped up a heady anger and decided not to wait another minute; they were taking action then and there. As the appointed spokesman, I led the charge to Charley's apartment. On the strength of one hundred percent unity, we would not leave until he raised that thermostat.

During our descent, I noticed the two men disappear between the fourth and third floors, but Tassie, Carrie and the women were on my heels. When I reached the first floor, I gave Charley's door a forceful banging.

"Yeah, what you want?" he squawked.

"It's Mr. Blake. The tenants and I want to talk to you." Charley opened the door with a confused stare and I pressed our point. "We got babies and children in this building and we demand that you put the heat up now!"

"We? We, who?"

"We, the tenants!" I announced with a sweeping gesture and a glance over my shoulder. Not a soul was behind me! They had peeled away floor by floor and left me to face Charlie alone.

"Man, you ain't no tenant. You better get the hell out of here before I call the cops!" I left fuming.

Next time I saw Tassie she apologized and said the tenants really wanted to do something about the heat. She begged me to please try again. I agreed to another meeting but not with Charley; it would have to be with the landlord, Mr. Katz.

For the second meeting, Tassie's apartment was again packed. While we waited for the landlord, all the talk was about getting him told. He finally showed up an hour late with a broad smile on his face and a paper bag in his hand. He greeted, "Hey, Joe. John, good to see you. How you doing, Carrie? Brought something for you, Tassie," then slid a fifth of scotch out of the bag and sat it in the middle of the table.

Everybody started grinning, "Ah, thank you, Mr. Katz." "This sho' is nice." "Tassie, git some glasses over her." "Pour one for Mr. Katz." The landlord pulled up a chair.

"Wait a minute, don't drink that!" I ordered.

"Ah Jimmy, just a little taste."

"No!" I protested. They drank anyway. I tried to outline the purpose of the meeting. They talked gibberish. Pretty soon, Mr. Katz was saying, "See you later." I shook my head and walked out too.

After that, Tassie avoided me but I could not bear the thought of children suffering and dying in the cold. Finally, I went to her, "Tassie, what's going on?"

"Mr. Blake, all of them have arrangements with Charley. They give him gifts and he fix little things for them. Nobody wanna give up their side deals." She paused a few seconds, "You see, you have a place to go when you leave here. If we lose our apartments, we have no place to go."

The stinging truth of her words ended my attempt at organizing the tenants. For the first time, I realized that the leader's risk for change must equal that of the people. To address the dangers posed to the children in Tassie's building, I went to a welfare-rights organization. One of the lawyers wrote to Mr. Katz threatening a rent strike. The landlord acted in a hurry—changing the boiler, putting lights in the hallways, placing locks on the mailboxes. At the end of my field placement on 103rd Street, he was patching up holes in the apartments.

When I left the block for the last time, I noticed that the dilapidated building on the corner of Central Park West and 103rd Street was draped with a huge banner announcing "Luxury Units." Renovation of the building was already under way. It seemed the biggest threat to Tassie and her neighbors would come in the form of gentrification. Sometimes this transfer of apartments from the poor to the middle and upper middle classes is camouflaged as "Urban Renewal" or "Empowerment Zones," but that time it was more accurately labeled, "Luxury Units."

Theory and analysis in Bill Schwartz's classes provided valuable insights into my work on 103rd Street as well as fresh perspectives on my personal life. As he had predicted, graduate school transformed me into a "piano player who read the notes." His 1969 publication *Private Troubles and Public Issues* sounded the most powerful note: for every private problem there is a public policy issue. On 103rd Street, public policy issues abounded. Among them were the need for decent housing, child services, welfare reform, jobs programs, health care, quality education and other concerns too numerous to name. Constantly, I found myself asking, "What is the public issue behind this problem?"

A more theoretical way of thinking led me to lobby for changes aimed at uplifting the poor. Influenced by the work of Dr. Richard A. Cloward, my social policy professor, and his co-worker Dr. Frances Fox Piven, I joined the rising grassroots Welfare Rights Movement of the late sixties. The live-on-a-welfare-budget campaign received notoriety for its effort to heighten policymakers' awareness of the suffering of the poor. Most rewarding for me, though, was the involvement of poor people in shaping policies and practices that impacted their lives. Together, professionals and welfare recipients organized rent strikes, drafted letters, and circulated petitions aimed at landlords and elected officials.

My coursework at Columbia stimulated an activism untainted by the smear of rabble-rousing demonstrations. It was an activism that went beyond protest to the creation of meaningful programs for the needy.

Policy perspectives also helped me to see my childhood in a larger societal context. No longer would I bemoan my family's predicament as entirely personal. I understood that my sisters, brother and I were not alone in our suffering. We inhabited a vast limbo that stretched beyond foster care and children's homes. An entire underclass of poor people resided within our borders. Unfortunately, this new intellectual understanding did not soothe my soul. While I talked more intelligently about my past experiences, empty spiritless spaces in my heart widened.

"**W**hat's wrong?" I rushed over to my wife who had sunk to the floor the minute she poured ammonia into a bucket of water on cleaning day at our new house.

"I'm pregnant," she whispered.

"Pregnant? How you know that?"

"I know the feeling."

"Go ahead, Brother Blake, she'll be alright." My mother-in-law, a youthful forty-four-year-old, dropped to her knees and rubbed her daughter's forehead. She had arrived from Louisiana with Bessie's adolescent sister and brother on the eve of moving day. Her church family addressed her as Evangelist Tommie Waites, but she was MamMaw to five-year-old Kanari. I called her MamMaw too.

"Shouldn't we take her to the doctor," I asked.

"Awww, that won't be necessary," MamMaw smiled calmly. "You and I have to get this cleaning done."

I obeyed though I was uneasy about Bessie's condition.

The packing was completed back at the apartment in East Elmhurst. Once the cleaning was done, Big Jimmy and I moved the little furniture we owned into our new home. Next day, MamMaw unpacked while I took Bessie to the doctor. The pregnancy was confirmed.

Thank God for MamMaw. Every day she searched the eight-block stretch of the Laurelton business district on Merrick Boulevard. She looked for just the right foods to settle Bessie's stomach. Rounding the corner at 226th

Street, she strolled by Zuckerman's Hardware Store, pass the shoemaker's shop, across from the movie theater, beyond Martin's Paint and down to the Everything Store. Along the way, Italian and Jewish delicatessens, restaurants with linen-draped tables, corner grocers, meat markets, bakeries, the fish house loaded with fresh catches and several vegetable stands offered a variety of choices. For two weeks MamMaw weaved in and out of the local shops and purchased food that she cooked with delicate flavors to soothe the stomach. She also kept up with the cleaning and made sure that Bessie rested peacefully.

The house was quiet. Ruthie and Frances left home early for summer jobs. Bessie's younger sister and brother, Honorene and Stanford, went on daily sightseeing ventures with my nephew, Eddie, who was thirteen but wise beyond his years. Since age six, he had been able to find his way on the streets of Corona. He and his dog, Lindy, would explore the two blocks between Gloria and Daddy's apartments and perform what Eddie called his "good-deed-of-the-day." One afternoon he would carry for his elderly neighbor heavy bags of groceries that threatened to crush his bony frame. The next day he and Lindy would drag a discarded refrigerator carton from the middle of the road to prevent a car crash. Over the years, Eddie had grown even more street savvy. I placed Honorene and Stanford in his hands with the utmost confidence. They would not get lost and I knew they would have a good time because Eddie had a crush on Honorene, a really pretty brown skin girl with hair to her waist.

With an empty house during the day and Bessie out of commission, I had a chance to really get to know my mother-in-law. I had met her on a trip to Louisiana but we developed a real relationship on her first visit to New

York in August 1969. I learned that Mam-Maw had also grown up without a mother. Knowledge of our common bond erased barriers of age and cultural differences rooted in her southern and my northern background.

With MamMaw there was no need to force emotions into words. Yet, I talked incessantly. In an atmosphere of complete trust, I spoke candidly about my innermost feelings. "You know how painful it is not to have your mother to talk to?" I brooded.

"Oh yes, Brother Blake." Being a minister, she addressed me as a fellow child of God.

"I feel naked and I want my mother to clothe me. You know what I mean?"

"Oh, I know what you mean." She rubbed her hands together and gently patted her knees.

"Did Bessie tell you I was in a children's home?" She nodded. "Well, the children in the shelter cried and sucked their thumbs and yelled out in their sleep. I wanted to jump out of bed and make it better for all of them. I wanted..."

"Brother Blake," she interrupted, "God's been with you since you were a little boy. Because you care for others, God cares for you. In times of great trial, He is ordering your steps even when you think you don't have direction."

We were two orphans missing our mothers, but unlike me, through scripture and prayer, Mam-Maw had found peace. Calm surrounded her as she recounted her mother's death when she was three years old. She spoke of how God sustained her during a motherless childhood. "God is touching you too, Brother Blake. So, be anxious for nothing."

MamMaw was the first person to talk to me about God in a way that had meaning for my life. However, I was so happy to be speaking to an elder with whom I had a common experience that I rattled on.

"Mam-Maw this world is so crazy; sometimes I wonder why God puts us through horrible things. Do you ever wish you had your mother or money—you know, things other people have?"

"No, Brother Blake, I'm thankful for what God has given me. I'm not looking for anything else because His grace is sufficient."

"What's grace?"

"Grace is when you are given a reward, a favor you haven't earned."

As an example of God's grace, she launched into her beautiful testimony. She said she was not living right. In fact she was thinking about killing her husband when she fell sick at twenty-two years of age. God sent his word and healed her after she read in the Bible that she could move mountains through faith. God spared her life though she was planning to take her husband's life. Her healing was a blessing she had not earned.

At the end of her testimony, she urged me to believe that God would give me the strength to accomplish great and mighty things even though my mother was not with me. "Everybody is going to know that God has his hands on you. Oooooooo! Brother Blake, people are going to read about you!" she exclaimed with an enthusiasm that excited me though what she foretold about my future was a mystery at the time.

I was fascinated by MamMaw's story, but it was not until I witnessed her effect on casual acquaintances and total strangers that I discovered her spiritual power. On one of her later visits to New York, I strolled down Merrick Boulevard with her on my arm. In front of the barbershop I waved but kept moving because the owner had a reputation for being unflappable. He never stopped clipping hair to witness an accident, a fire, a fight or any happenings on the street; however, that day he laid his instruments down and ran outside.

Startled by his quickness, I began, "Oh, Roy, this is..."

"You don' have to tell me who this is," he cut me off and bowed his head like a little boy. "Pray for me mother!"

Standing in the middle of the sidewalk on busy Merrick Boulevard, Mam-Maw placed her hand on Roy's head, "Lord, you know my brother's needs. Bless him from the crown of his head to the soles of his feet. I ask in the Name of Jesus." The prayer was quiet and unpretentious. Calm fell on me, and Roy was downright jubilant.

"Thank you, mother! Thank you," he beamed and danced back into the barbershop. I was flabbergasted. It all happened so quickly and seemed so natural. Over time I repeatedly witnessed this kind of reaction to my mother-in-law and felt even more blessed by our kinship.

I didn't know the fullness of MamMaw's spiritual wisdom back in summer 1969, but I knew enough to press her for answers.

As her first visit to New York was nearing its end, I asked her opinion about my standing up against injustice regardless of personal consequences. "People tell me self-preservation should come first," I told her.

"Brother Blake, she responded, "your heart is just like His Son's heart. When you act, you don't care what happens to you; you care what happens to others. That's what Jesus did. He cared for others without concern for His own life. Even though you don't confess to be a Christian, you are doing the work of Christ. He helped the despised, the rejected, the downtrodden, the ones nobody else paid any attention. You know," she looked at me and winked, "you don't have to wear the biggest hat on Sunday to be a soldier for Christ." Bessie later elaborated on her mother's meaning: "While it is important to be in the church it is more important for the church to be in us. Wherever we find ourselves, we should be transforming the world the way Jesus did."

MamMaw was the first to discern the depth of my heart's longing to ease human suffering. I told her people labeled me a troublemaker when I intervened on behalf of others. She answered that Jesus was considered a troublemaker by the established order of his times. "It's okay to be a bad boy, if you're God's bad boy," she said with a smile.

I missed my talks with MamMaw after she returned to Louisiana at the end of August. Never had I met a woman as warm and encouraging. With her I had a sense of being clothed with mother love. Also, I felt an exciting spark of spiritual awakening. Without pressuring me to go to church, she had made me see the relevance of my work in terms of church principles.

April 1970, Bessie was nearing full term. Her thoughts were on her birthday, but six days into the month she delivered a healthy baby boy. On his first day home from the hospital, I thrust him toward the living room ceiling and bellowed in total rapture, "I can die now; I have a son!"

"No you can't," Bessie chuckled. "You have to help me raise him; and then, you can die."

Ruthie and Frances were dancing in Harlem with Olatunji, the famed Nigerian drummer. They were caught up in the cultural awakening and African pride of the early seventies and proudly named their nephew, Shango—god of thunder, god of war.

Shango's birth forecasted a season of change in our family. That spring Kanari was a kindergartener at P. S. 132 Q where the staffing pattern of the school did not yet reflect the racial composition of the community. The student body was predominantly Black and the virtually all White staff griped openly about the days when the school had "good"—meaning White—students.

The level of insensitivity to the children was alarming. I entered Kanari's classroom one morning to drop off her forgotten lunchbox and got jolted into reality. My daughter was sitting right up against the blackboard breathing in chalk dusk. When I asked why, the teacher arrogantly stated that Kanari was "a spoiled brat always complaining she can't see. She wants attention. So, I've placed her where she can be seen. Maybe now she'll shut up."

"You'd better get my daughter's desk away from that board and move it fast!" I grabbed Kanari by the hand and marched behind that teacher like a fire-breathing dragon as she scrambled to fit Kanari's desk in among the others. Then I called her into the hallway, "And, I better not hear any complaints from my daughter. I'll be watching you," I said, spun around and headed for the principal's office and warned, "If you don't fix this situation, I'll throw a one-man picket around this building!"

The incident highlighted the importance of my involvement and presence in the school. Not only did Bessie and I attend all meetings called by the principal or PTA, I made frequent spot-check visits. We also discovered that Kanari needed glasses, something that her pediatrician had missed. Since the school did not screen for hearing and vision problems like when I was growing up, with our children to follow we made sure their doctors conducted these examinations.

In the spring of 1970, Frances graduated from Bayside High School and was accepted at Texas Southern University, a historically Black college in Houston. Ruthie, poised to enter her senior year at Bayside, had her eye on Howard University. I was finishing up my last year at Columbia, where the campus was charged with student unrest about government and university policies. Home life was stable, but I was in for a rocky semester at school.

Part Four:

Fire in my soul

Upset about Columbia University's Kent State memorial, I dropped by Dr. Schwartz's office on the eve of the program.

"Look Bill, we got to change the agenda," I stated.

"We can't do that," he replied hastily.

"Well, students at Jackson State down in Mississippi were killed last night and we have to let the agenda reflect that."

"Oh no, people are already coming; we can't change. One thing about group work, when people are coming to a meeting, they need to know the agenda ahead of time so they can buy into it or not. It would be wrong for us to split the agenda."

"There is no split agenda here. Students died at Kent State; students died at Jackson State. The only difference is one student body is White and the other is Black, but it's the same agenda: students died." I was growing impatient and Bill's anger was creeping up his neck in a red blush. "So, you're not going to change the agenda?"

"No, we can't do that."

"Bill, you're showing indifference to the suffering of Black students. It's wrong. We should be concerned about loss of life regardless of skin color. We need to include Blacks!" By now we're shouting.

"I'm not changing!"

"It's gonna change!"

"Jim, you can't make me change!"

"Okay! You have it your way!" I stormed out of his office.

Bill was a tough and demanding professional who frequently agitated students in an effort to get us to be more sensitive to the needs of our clients. In his class and in review of field placement activities, he was also unyielding about the need for group leaders to establish a clear and concise purpose for the group's existence. His experience and his research told him that any departure from the stated group purpose would make the group dysfunctional. His refusal to change the Kent State memorial agenda was rooted in this theory.

In my view, Bill's theory did not allow flexibility during a time of rapid change. He couldn't see that the broader student agenda had already changed. In 1968, Mark Rudd had led the occupation of five buildings on the Columbia University campus in protest against the Vietnam War. In the two years that followed, the campus was constantly rocked by protests, but Bill held to his theory.

I wouldn't have been as upset with anyone else as I was with him. He had fought to get me into Columbia. In fact, he had threatened to resign his position if the university didn't admit me into its Graduate School of Social Work. I was known around the campus as "Bill's protégé." That's why our disagreement really got under my skin. Someone dear and close to me could not see the importance of changing a historical pattern where the pain and suffering of Black people was treated differently from that of Whites. The students at Jackson State University had integrated the anti-war movement into their struggle for civil rights. In their May 15, 1970 protest against rising racial tensions in Mississippi, they had remembered the loss of life at Kent State. Brute police force had killed student protestors at both Jackson and Kent State

Universities. I couldn't see how memorializing their deaths in a single ceremony blurred the lines.

I was out of Bill's office and thought I had cooled down on my walk over to the library to finish an assignment. However, near the front of the reading room, a couple of radical students I had seen around campus were preparing for the Kent State memorial. One was trying on a black academic robe because he was scheduled to introduce a speaker at the service. Watching him was a skinny fellow with shoulder length hair. I walked over to them.

"Hey man, I'm boycotting the Kent State memorial," I addressed my robed comrade.

"Why?" he asked.

"No! We need you man! We need you," his friend pleaded. I knew they wanted the memorial to have the appearance of unity between White and Black students and they knew that I could sway Black students not to attend. Both of them had heard about the students mowed down at Jackson State; it was all over the news. I got right into an account of my conversation with Dr. Schwartz.

"As a Black student, I'm offended by his refusal to expand the agenda to include the victims at Jackson State," I concluded the summary of the exchange between Bill and me.

"That's wrong! That's absolutely wrong! He won't budge?" asked the robed radical.

"He won't budge," I answered.

The longhaired fellow, who had been listening intently, spoke in a quiet soft tone: "You know what we should do? We should re-enact the Jackson State killings as a drama to wake them up from their stupor."

"What do you mean?" I puzzled over how we could pull it off. It was after seven in the evening and the memorial was scheduled for ten o'clock the next morning. He explained that his brother was a police officer about his size and he could get his uniform. Firing a pistol full of blanks, he would chase a Black student into the auditorium during the proceedings for Kent State.

"Oh, man that sounds cool." "That's a winner," we laughed and slapped one another five.

"But, what if this thing seems so real, we get a backlash? What if someone in the audience has a bad heart?" the robed radical hesitated.

"Yes, Irving Miller has a bad heart," I offered. "He just got out of the hospital but I tell you what, I'll go speak to him." With that promise our plans were set. We gave no thought to anyone else who might have had a bad heart or an equally grave condition.

I found Dr. Miller in his office. Despite his constant teasing about my being Bill's protégé, he and I had developed a good relationship. Irv was legally blind, and after one of his class sessions in "Social Welfare and Social Policy in America," I had walked him ten blocks along 5th Avenue from the Carnegie Mansion to a meeting down on 81st Street. We fell naturally into a conversation about the history of social programs and policies in the Black community. He admitted that he had never really thought about the subject and suggested I do research on the topic. As I worked on the project, an ease of communication about racially charged subjects evolved between us. Therefore, I headed to Irv's office confident he would hear me out on the Jackson State matter.

"Dr. Miller," I greeted to get his attention. "There was an incident at Jackson State."

"Yeah, I heard about it: terrible, terrible. What's going on with this country?"

"Well, we want to do something about it. I don't want to get into the details, I simply want to let you know,

Dr. Miller, that between ten and ten-thirty you should not come to the auditorium. We're having a protest."

Protests were so commonplace on the campus that he was not disturbed by the news. He simply asked, "What time should I get there, then?"

"Get there after eleven."

"Okay Jim Blake, if that's what you say."

I reported back to my fellow protestors, "Everything is cool with Dr. Miller."

Next morning, the memorial for Kent State started with great solemnity. We stayed in the background for about fifteen minutes of the program, then the doors to the auditorium burst open. A Black student in a ketchup-stained shirt raced down the aisle chased by what appeared to be a White policeman firing, "Bang! Bang! Bang!" and shouting, "Stop Nigger! Stop!"

Pandemonium broke loose! People screamed, ducked between seats, and stampeded toward the doors while Bill crouched behind the podium.

"No!" "Stop!" "Wait!" we shouted. "This is a protest against the Jackson State killings!" "This is a protest!" "Remember Jackson State!"

"Order! Order! Order!" Bill yelled when he realized it was a staged disruption.

"You are out of order, Dr. Schwartz!" I yelled back. "You are responsible for this! You are out of order!"

Bill was furious. He slammed the gavel on the podium and walked out.

"This is just a drama to convince Columbia School of Social Work that Black people's lives are valuable too!" I attempted to address the crowd that franticly rushed for the exits. It was too late. After the auditorium all but emptied, the dozen or so students who remained had a frank discussion about Kent State, Jackson State, race relations in America and the Vietnam War. All things considered, the protest was not a total disaster. We shed light on an issue that was begging for attention and no one was injured, killed or arrested for impersonating a police officer and posing a threat to public safety. Glad to get our point across, we failed to realize the extent of our recklessness. Today, I would still protest for the same principle, but I would do so without endangering the lives of innocent, unsuspecting people.

Bill did not forgive me. Mutual friends brought news of his hurt. "He likes you, Jim," they'd say. "He didn't think you'd turn on him like that." Dr. Mary Funyae, my field instructor my last semester at Columbia, tried to bridge the gap between Bill and me, but neither of us budged. My attitude at the time was *I'm dancing to a different tune.*

I stood on the brink of 1970s America—after a decade splintered by unrest. The racial divide was definite: two Americas—one Black one White, separate and unequal. On a parallel course, the generation gap widened; parents and children glared at one another from opposing sides of questions surrounding the Vietnam War. Inspired by the civil rights movement, women, gay and Chicano rights issues erupted. In December 1969, Caesar Chavez was jailed after organizing a boycott against grapes and rallying in Sacramento, California to call attention to the plight of migrant farm workers. The following summer, the Stonewall uprising powered the gay rights movement. In the 1970s, persons with disabilities pushed for and got the first laws promising barrier free access. The American Indian Movement (A.I.M.) agitated to reclaim the sovereign rights of Native Americans and seized the town of Wounded Knee. The list was endless. Passion for justice and equality crept into every tight corner of American society and boiled in the streets. In such a climate, it was easy to say, *Forget Bill; I'm moving on.*

Dr. Preston Wilcox, the only Black male on the faculty of the School of Social Work, had observed at a distance the rift between Bill and me. Finally, he pulled me aside and said: "Blake, make your anger functional. Do something positive. Join with others who feel the way you do and make a difference. Otherwise, your anger will tear you apart." I heeded Dr. Wilcox's advice. In an effort to make relevant change, I reconnected to the Association of Black Social Workers.

I graduated and drifted away from any involvement at Columbia University. Years later I heard about Bill's death. With a heavy heart over a breached relationship never repaired, I took a train to Westchester County to the funeral and grieved the loss of my friend.

Until this day, tremors of regret mock my inability to have reached beyond our differences to the countless things about which Bill and I agreed. We shared a passion for helping others and we both felt that a person could be helped no matter the form or size of the problem. I admired Bill for the standard of excellence he maintained in rendering service to the poor. He applied it himself and required it of others. He often admonished his students, "Get past what you see; go deep! You can touch that person and empower him to take control of his life." He shaped skilled social workers and counselors who were not afraid to get messy in their quest to help others become self-reliant. "Don't be wooden!" he would snap. "You have to feel for people. You have the capacity to help. It's in there but you've got to reach for it!" The irony is my life as a counselor and a community worker is still governed in large measures by principles I shared with Bill Schwartz.

Discontent best describes my attitude after I returned to work at the Bureau of Child Welfare. I had been promised a supervisory position once I graduated from Columbia with my Masters of Social Work degree but the New York City hiring freeze of the early seventies blocked the promotion. I was stuck as a caseworker in the Division of Foster Care with no foreseeable upgrade in job title. My life was ripe for change.

On a hot muggy Manhattan afternoon, I came up from the subway on Broadway and walked along 51st toward Rockefeller Center in search of a place to grab a light lunch. A few doors from the old Taft Hotel, among the coffee shops and entrances to office towers one sign stood out: "Borough of Manhattan Community College." Intrigued by the discovery of a college in the hustle and bustle of midtown, I decided to check it out. At the top of the stairs on the second floor a security guard directed me down a narrow hallway. A stocky, deeply tanned man with a blond beard sat behind the desk in the first office on the right.

"Is this the counseling department?" I smiled down at him.

"Yes." He sounded flat, disinterested.

"Who are you?" I asked.

"I'm Dr. Manasse, the head of counseling."

"You're the one who hires people?"

"Yes..." he paused. "Yes, I do that."

"Well, this is your lucky day!" I announced with an even broader smile.

A frown crossed his face. "Why do you say that?"

"Because you are going to be remembered as the guy who hired Jim Blake."

He chuckled, "And, who is Jim Blake?"

"That's a good question; here's the answer." I pulled from my briefcase the resume I had been carrying around.

He surveyed my credentials. "Oh, I see you're a recent graduate of Columbia."

"Yes and, if you read on, you'll see I have extensive background in counseling."

"I see. I see," he nodded. "You know it just so happens we're going to be hiring four people. I'll submit your resume to the committee. If they are interested, I'll give you a call." I sensed his attraction to my personality and I knew my resume was strong. I felt good about my prospects and, indeed, a few weeks later Gus Manasse called.

When I went for the interview, I was greeted by a tall, dark skin man with a bowtie. He introduced himself as Dr. Sam Pittman. Though he chaired the search committee, the other members (Professors Vernell Garnett, Margaret Moreland, Frances Fascetta and Sidney King) did most of the questioning. My answers were engaging and informative and the interview went smoothly until Dr. Pittman, the only one around the table with a skeptical look on his face, interrupted the flow. "Young man, what would you do if a group of students came to you with a legitimate grievance against the administration and enlisted your support in a protest against the college? How would you respond?"

I thought he asked the question because I had a big Afro. To him Afros and dashikis probably marked so-called militants the way do-rags and oversized clothing profile the hip-hop generation. However, rather than consider the prejudice embedded in his question, I framed an answer based on the mediation model for which Bill Schwartz was famous. The model defined the symbiotic relationship between people and institutions: that is to say, they need one another though there are times when the lines of interdependence are blurred because of conflict. At critical junctures of conflict, an effective group leader does not join sides but works instead as a mediator to bring the two sides together to resolve the dispute and restore a healthy functioning relationship. With that answer, I clenched the job.

Though the City of New York was still my employer, I had to repay every penny spent on my education because I did not remain at the Bureau of Child Welfare. To satisfy the obligation, I signed a payroll deduction agreement that extended over a three-year period. It cleared the way for me to start on November 1, 1970 as a counselor for the Borough of Manhattan Community College, known within the City University system as BMCC.

In my new job, I had every intention of fulfilling the counselor-mediator role and was actually successful for a couple of years. Students complained that the college was totally separated from the community. I told them, "You put 'community' back in this community college." I helped them organize a community service club and we brought elementary school children from Harlem to the college, fed them, tutored them in math and reading and provided cultural enrichment experiences beyond their cramped blocks.

The Community Service Club flourished but its sponsor, the Student Government Association, remained disgruntled. The school had no real home. Clusters of classes and counseling services were housed in dingy rented quarters at several locations in mid-town Manhattan, while the President was perched high in a plush executive suite of a modern office tower on the corner of Broadway and 51st Street. The obvious disparity in facilities caused unrest among students but I deflected the frustration with a beautification program. Students sewed curtains to cover dirty windows, bought plants for offices and painted bright posters to liven up dreary hallways. A protest to tie up traffic in mid-town Manhattan was averted.

The pacification of students enabled the university, the city and the State of New York to continue to drag their feet. In the end, agitation for a home for BMCC was necessary. As the point man of the college administration's political action committee, I made countless trips to Albany to lobby for funding for a building. Simultaneously, I supported and even led student protests for decent classrooms and learning resources. In the process, my role wobbled and boundary lines collapsed between my commitment to students and my obligation to the administration.

Troubled by Joseph's living condition, in 1970 Bessie and I had started to visit him more frequently. We took food and toys to his family on holidays and brought his children to spend weekends with us on a regular basis. All the while I searched for keys to unlock his prison of despair. I saw the danger that surrounded him and was not surprised when I received a late night call in February 1971.

"Jimmy, you better come see 'bout your brother. I been pleading and pleading but he won't go to the doctor." I hung up from Mattie Mae and woke Bessie for the drive to Brooklyn. When we got to Joseph's apartment around eleven thirty that evening, he was sitting in the dark.

"What you doing here?" he grumbled.

I ignored his annoyance and got to the point: "Joseph, you need to go to the doctor?"

"I'm alright."

"You alright? Then, put the light on; let me see."

"I don't need no light."

Mattie Mae knew he was angry with her for making the call; so she remained in the background while I fumbled around the room for the switch. I clicked on the light and froze at the sight of my brother. Burnt and puffy, the right side of his face, back around his ear and down his neck, looked like a piece of charred beef.

"It ain't nothing, man," he managed a distorted grin.

"Come on Joseph, cut the crap."

"I told you ain't going to the doctor."

"Look, it's late; stop the crap!"

My fists clenched at the precise moment that Bessie snapped, "This is ridiculous! You know you need to go to the doctor!"

"Okay, don't get worked up. I'll go." He usually met fire with fire but he stood up, slipped into his coat, and within seconds, we were outside pressing against a bitter February wind.

I had never seen Joseph open up to anyone the way he did to Bessie. On the day they met he had told her of deep aspirations never shared with me. They discussed his dream of becoming a writer and he later gave her one of his stories to critique. The piece, "One Night in Hell," was much like the February night we were experiencing. As we hurried down the block to the car, the last two lines of his narrative popped into my head: "I only hope that someone will try to do something before it is too late. There is something howling and tearing at my door." I wondered if the tale was Joseph's way of asking for help with his troubled life but I quickly dismissed the thought as overdramatic. It was probably a mere exchange between two would-be writers.

Joseph climbed into the back seat of the car like it was a taxi and ordered Bessie to take him to St. Mary's Hospital ten blocks up the street. Then, despite obviously excruciating pain, he started teasing her: "Where's that pretty smile? Ooo-wee, you pretty! Jimmy ever mistreat you, I'll kick his butt."

When Bessie parked in front of St. Mary's Hospital, she and I jumped out of the car but Joseph did not budge. "No. I don't want to go to this dump. Take me to Booth Memorial in Flushing!" We hopped back in the car and, on the Brooklyn-Queens Expressway, he changed his mind again. I was about to curse him out but Bessie patted me on the knee. When we pulled in front of St. Mary's the second time and Joseph had another change of heart, she spoke up, "Joseph, I'm getting a little tired. Can we go here?"

"That's what you want, sweetheart? You got it," and out of the car he bounced. With an appreciative nod from Bessie, he marched heroically into the hospital. Giddy from the attention of family, he was relishing every moment of his boyish stubbornness.

St. Mary's had a sorry emergency room. Little more than a grimy hallway, it was packed with bleeding, groaning poor people who had not sought medical care until their situations were desperate. During the two-hour wait, the skin on the side of Joseph's face began to split and though he never dropped his playful demeanor, I could tell he was in a lot of pain. I tried to get someone to take a look at him but detached nurses and doctors rudely brushed me aside. *Get back over there and sit down; we'll get to you when we get to you* was the prevailing attitude.

Doing all that she could to keep me calm and to salvage the agreement wrangled from Joseph to get medical attention, Bessie suggested we go back to Queens. On the drive I remembered that Dr. Lopez's office was attached to his home in East Elmhurst. Unable to bear another emergency-room ordeal, I banged on his door at two in the morning.

"An acid burn," the doctor informed us. He cleaned up the wound, rubbed Joseph's face gently with a lotion, gave him an injection of antibiotics along with a prescription for more pills, and handed him the bottle of lotion to continue to apply at home. Before we left the doctor scheduled a follow-up visit for the next week. Joseph nodded but, unaccustomed as he was to doctors, I knew he would not keep the appointment.

On the way back to Brooklyn I learned who had thrown acid on my brother. Outside a check-cashing place a female friend had been smacked by her boyfriend for refusing his demand for money. Joseph never could stand for a man to punch a woman. He grabbed the guy, who gestured like he was striking back, then fled, leaving Joseph's face on fire. Thank God it was a surface wound that healed without noticeable scarring. A more lasting effect was my worry about enemies that lurked around my brother.

The downward spiral of his life had accelerated back in his late teens. Defiant against the system, he had done everything I wanted to do. He walked away from the Hebrew Children's Home. Later, while I lamented my fate in the shelter and in Woodycrest, he roamed the streets freely. Though only a year older than me, he had been considered too old for foster care and too set in his ways for private agencies that admitted "easy-to-handle" children. I hated growing up in institutions but, watching my brother that night in Brooklyn, I realized that his plight had become a daily struggle for survival.

It turned out that institutions had given me something I could never have gotten at home. Despite my resistance, the shelter and Woodycrest had provided rules, regulations and a discipline that was good for me though I couldn't see the benefit of structure while in those institutions. In the heat of adolescence, my definition of freedom was a life without controls. I wanted to run up and down The Boulevard, hang out with the fellows, drink wine, listen to do-wop harmonies, eat fish and chips, and groove at basement grind-'em-up parties. I didn't want to slow down and think about the impact of my actions or to prepare myself through study and discipline for real freedom of choices. I had wanted Joseph and Gloria's brand of freedom because nobody told them when to come and when to go.

I had resented my older sister and brother because they hadn't spent long years in the child welfare system like Carol, Frances, Ruthie, and me. However, that night in Brooklyn with Joseph, it finally hit me: neither he nor Gloria had been free and they weren't having fun on the streets of Corona. The truth was they had lived anguished lives with no structure, no guidance, and none of the basic necessities that I took for granted. Life for them had been a constant search for food, clothes and a warm bed.

When our family fell apart none of us children were spared hardship but we all did better than Joseph. Even Gloria, wounded by the nightmare of being left pregnant and alone, had done better. She had struggled for Eddie's sake, become a nurse and she and Tyrone had purchased a house in Roosevelt, Long Island.

The social agencies that I hated had rescued my younger sisters and me. I was a college professor with two wonderful children and a schoolteacher wife. Ruthie had embarked on a career in Special Education for the Washington D.C. school system and Frances was flying all over the world as a TWA flight attendant. Married to Ricardo Patterson of Pittsburgh, Carol was the mom of three beautiful daughters: Kenja, Shamika and Rashida.

Joseph's plight was vastly different from the rest of ours. While his siblings moved forward, his life remained virtually unchanged. Convinced that he was worthless, he had given up early. As a teen, he had been treated like an adult who could take care of himself. In his twenties he never held a job. Heavy drinking that started in his adolescence fueled the swift journey to the stay-at-home dad of seven children that he had become the night Bessie and I came to his aid. His life centered on caring for Little Joseph, Carol and Virginia—the children he fathered with Mattie Mae—as well as for her four sons. He had seemed strong enough to handle the web of danger spinning around him and his family. However, that cold February night zipping back and forth between Brooklyn and

Queens, I detected in my brother vulnerabilities not previously exposed. I had taken my eye off him. I wouldn't let it happen again.

Despite regular contact between Joseph and me, it was evident that we lived distinctly different lives. He was wedded to a tight little street crowd in Brooklyn and I lived the life of a young urban male just entering the middle class. Weekdays, I groomed my bushy Afro, slipped into bellbottom pants and a velvet blazer and headed off to work. Mornings were strictly business in the office; lunch was a two-martini-cocktail affair; and, evenings were spent drinking with buddies. Weekends, Harold Fowler—who had moved to New York after college—hung out with me up in the Bronx at the parties of one of our NCCU buddies, Pete "the DJ" Jones. When I surfaced on Sunday mornings, Bessie complained that the dark circles under my eyes looked like rotten meat. "You're dying, Jimmy!" she once burst into tears.

She accused me of treating life like one big fun-loving party; said she wanted joy in her life. I invited her to hang out with me but she refused. Her reaction frightened me. My mind returned to the long conversations I had had with MamMaw. Without speaking of our marriage, I phoned to ask, "What's the difference between fun and joy?" The simplicity of her response shook me: "Brother Blake, fun is on the outside and joy is on the inside. Fun is all those activities we chase after trying to make ourselves feel better but joy is an excitement deep within. When we know that we are doing the right thing, peace flows from our very souls." MamMaw"s answer ignited a desire for joy, but fun kept winning out and my marriage continued to crumble.

Distressed by the state of my affairs, I showed up at Joseph's door unannounced.

"What's going on?" he asked.

"I've had it with that woman! I'm moving to Atlanta," I unloaded without saying hello.

The stunned look on his face toned me down. "I'm upset," I said. "I just want to talk to my big brother."

"Big brother? Man, what you talking about? You've accomplished more than I have. You graduated from college. You a professor. I never done anything with my life. I'm a failure. You my big brother; I'm the little brother," he squinted through half-closed eyes.

It made me hot to hear him talk like that. "I don't care if you're lying in the gutter and I'm the head of a corporation making millions of dollars, you'll always be my big brother. Nothing can ever change that."

His eyes softened, and a little half smile curled his lips: "Man, what's wrong with you talking about leaving your wife? That's a good woman. You need to go home and get your stuff straight because you know you're the one screwing up! You ridiculous!"

I wanted to air my side of the marital dispute but no support or comfort came from Joseph. I headed for the car and he followed. Just as I was about to slide under the steering wheel, he grabbed me in an awkward embrace, "Little Jimmy, I love you, man." I clung to him. It was our most tender moment ever and I did not want to let go.

"You alright, man? You straight, huh?" I attempted a joke then got in the car and looked up, studying his face. "I love you too," I said. On the drive home I contemplated his advice regarding my marriage and resolved to work things out with Bessie.

A week later I got a pre-dawn call from Mattie Mae. "Jimmy! Your brother won't wake up! He won't wake up!" Somehow, I knew he was dead.

By the time Bessie and I arrived at his apartment, the coroner had already removed Joseph's body. Mattie Mae fell into my arms weeping. "I found him in the chair this morning," she repeated over and over. Unable to calm her, I gently loosened her grip on me and headed to Kings County Hospital to identify the body. The task went to me because my father was sick. Instantly, I had become the big brother of the family.

Bessie waited in the car while I went inside the hospital. A staff person led me down sterile and impersonal corridors, onto an elevator to the basement and placed me in front of a window. Without warning Joseph rolled before me on a gurney. In his street clothes, a trace of blood at the corner of his mouth, my brother lay there with a tag dangling from his big toe. Flaming arrows flew from the pit of my stomach to the center of my brain. I staggered away from the window and out of the building. Bessie rushed to my side to keep me from falling.

That week, she helped me plan Joseph's funeral. All the while, I drank to cover the drunkenness that death had wrought. "He Ain't Heavy, He's My Brother" were the only words to penetrate my grief. I played the song over and over, and later at the funeral.

After we buried Joseph, the family gathered at Aunt Carrie Mae's apartment. Bessie tried to stop me from drinking. Failing every attempt, she decided to take me home but I got out of the car at 37th Avenue. Unable to persuade me to come with her, she left me hanging on the cyclone fence at P.S. 143Q. With arms stretched outward like Jesus on the cross, I wailed. Only, I berated God. I wanted to know why He had taken my brother. Minutes dissolved into hours before I stumbled up to Northern Boulevard and revisited haunts where Joseph had hung out as a ditty-bop.

For weeks, I contacted the hospital for an autopsy report. Finally, Mattie Mae told me Joseph choked to death. Without my knowing it, he had suffered from seizures since his teens. She was accustomed to the attacks and at the onset of labored breathing would call for an ambulance. The morning she found him slumped in the sofa chair in the living room, she had called several times begging for an ambulance but one never showed up. The account of his last night unleashed tidal waves of fury: *Damn! They let my brother die. His life as a Black man wasn't worth much.*

"The System" had failed Joseph. The child welfare agencies that deemed him too old for help, the educational system that was blind to his bright mind, the juvenile justice system that destroyed instead of rehabilitated him, and callous medical institutions unconcerned about his health, had all failed. Together the network of institutions and agencies—The System—had considered my brother just another piece of garbage for the heap. I thought back to our time at the Hebrew Children's Home and realized that my brother had been the victim of a great lie: that some children are worth saving and others are not. It is the lie that eventually killed him.

Joseph had thought he was a burden to everybody. He was never heavy to me; he was, simply, my brother. I always thought I would die at thirty. Instead, God took him and spared me. My survival had to count for something.

Still wounded over Joseph's death, I cursed Gloria until I
was emotionally spent, and then slammed the phone back
down on the receiver. It took an hour for me to settle
down and call her back.

"I'm sorry, Gloria, what's this about Eddie?"

"He has cancer."

"Where is he now?"

"Here with his girlfriend."

"Okay, I'll come out there on the weekend."

Eddie was a happy sixteen-year old living in
Roosevelt, Long Island with his mother, stepfather and
their German shepherd, Jumbo. He was an excellent
student, witty, charming and extremely athletic, but
people loved him most for his good nature. Never in any
trouble, he could be found at home studying, playing with
Jumbo, hanging out with his girl or on the basketball
court with his buddies. Matter of fact, he was playing
basketball the day he collapsed.

Gloria was crushed by the doctor's report but, being
a nurse, she hid her anguish behind medical jargon.
"Melanoma, malignancy, metastasized" crept into her
description of Eddie's condition.

"Speak plain English," I told her.

"Well, Jimmy, the doctor said the disease hit him
when he was in a growth spurt and spread like wild fire.
It's in all his major organs. Nothing can be done," she
finally wept.

I could not accept it; neither could Eddie. He called
me at work one afternoon and asked for a set of barbells.
He wanted to do weight training. "This is going to work,"
he said. I promised to get them, but Gloria called back to
say that he was not strong enough to handle barbells; the
exercise would accelerate the spread of the cancer. So, I
went empty-handed on my next visit. When I arrived at

the house, Eddie was walking around shirtless, flexing his muscles for his girlfriend.

"Where are they? I'm ready," he beamed.

"Oh, I didn't bring them this time. Next week," I lied, but he saw through me.

Crestfallen, he begged, "Pleeease, Uncle Jimmy, get the barbells. I'm getting stronger. See," he extended an arm of skin and bones.

It was hard to say no in the face of his enthusiasm. "Yeah man, I think you can handle it. I'll get them." I thought to myself, *What harm can it do? Maybe it'll do him good if they just lay in the corner of his room.*

I didn't keep my promise. In two days, Eddie was admitted to Mercy Hospital on Long Island. I visited him often. Most times the pain was severe but the injections were unbearable. One evening, I stood holding his hand when the nurse came in with a needle that looked to be three inches long. He squeezed my hand. I leaned my ear to his mouth. He whispered, "Uncle Jimmy, don't let them give me another needle, please."

The nurse chimed in a perky tone, "I have to give him something for the pain." Never taking his pleading eyes off me, he screamed a raspy hiss: "Get her out of here!"

"No more!" My hand flew up in a stop sign. "Don't give him that! That's it!" The nurse backed out of the room. "She's gone, Eddie. She's gone."

"Thank you, Uncle Jimmy." He slumped onto his pillow and closed his eyes. That night, he died.

Eddie's death splintered me into tiny pieces. *Don't go over the top, Jimmy* I cautioned. Determined not to collapse like I had at Joseph's funeral, I braced for raw emotions from relatives and youthful friends, but the ceremony eulogizing my nephew was dignified. The saddest scene at the service was groups of teenagers quietly sobbing on the viewing line. In the era just prior to the wholesale slaughter of urban youth due to drug violence, those young people in the mid-seventies were stunned by the brutal realization that someone their own age could actually die.

Seeing Eddie lying peacefully in the casket, took me back to the day I first saw him—a newborn in a makeshift dresser-draw bassinet. Maybe Gloria's tradition of buying cribs for her nieces and nephews was her way of purchasing the one she hadn't been able to afford for Eddie. Thoughts of his beginning reminded me of things denied in his short life. Hard times had come early but suffering had not bred bitterness. He was a happy child who delighted in small gifts and family. Joyful remembrance was the most fitting tribute to this wonderful man-child, but I was hurt that such a good kid had died.

No matter how hard I struggled against it, sorrow over my nephew's passing threatened to drown me. For weeks I churned in agony as I sought solace along the boardwalk at Long Beach. I watched the water rush to shore then recede to the ocean. Lost in the alternation of the waves, my mind floated back and forth until finally I caught sight of a tiny wondrous window of eternity. A wave dashed against the shore and in a violent splash, a single drop of water separated from the swell and was suspended in the air for a split second before dropping back to the surf and sailing back out to sea. The repeated nature of this occurrence reminded me of a verse I had read in the Book of Daniel: "How great are the signs, and how mighty are his wonders! His kingdom is an everlasting kingdom, and his dominion is from generation to generation."

When I observed the wonder of a tiny drop of water rejoining the vastness of the ocean, I realized that Eddie—

the hope of a new generation in our family—had rejoined an everlasting generation in time without end. I knew that my nephew was in the hands of a mighty God who had shared him with my family for a split second. In the smallest fraction of time, standing on a windy beach, I chose life over loss. I began to count the many ways that Eddie had enriched my life. My heart opened in thanksgiving for the gift of Gloria's funny, generous, truly loving man-child. In doing so, I began my journey from grief to gratitude.

Like he had done with Joseph's death, my fifty-seven-year old father said goodbye to Eddie at a distance. Weak from diabetes, he stood behind the living room curtain of his house on 112th Street and watched the hearse roll by carrying his grandson to rest.

Daddy had been hospitalized with several episodes of insulin shock. Everybody in the family had been sure he would be the first to go, but my father continued to alternately enrich and make our lives miserable. We saw him through many a crisis, rushed him to the hospital in the middle of the night, cried when he went on dialysis, and comforted him when he cried because he could no longer hold on to his woman. Beating the odds, he ate butterscotch candy against our will and ordered Bessie to drive him to Harlem to purchase collard greens from the back of a truck that he swore had "just come up from Florida." He insisted that I move him back to Florida; said that was where he wanted to spend the rest of his life. As soon as I transferred all his medical records and social security benefits to the sunshine state, he demanded that I bring him back to New York. A thousand goodbyes were wrapped in the energy we spent on Daddy but he outlived his son and grandson.

Joseph and Eddie were gone but God's grace sustained me. Within the next two years, Bessie and I had another daughter and son—RiShana and Takbir— who were born fourteen months apart. For the birth of my son, I was in the delivery room. He was my last child but the first birth that I witnessed. The doctor passed him to me all wrinkled and speckled with blood. I whispered in his ear, "Takbir," meaning God is the greatest.

My father spent seven joyful years with my two youngest children. At her birth, he had cooed to RiShana and cut an eye at me, "Watch out, Little Jimmy; she a beauty." With Takbir, Daddy had folded his tiny newborn hand into a ball and declared, "He got a big fist; he gon' be a boxer." By the time Takbir was six years old, thumb wrestling had become their regular method of dueling. With seven-year-old RiShana he danced while holding onto his walker. He spoiled both of them with sweets and other goodies. "Dr. Bessie," he proudly addressed my wife after she received her doctorate, "Come to the house; I got a watermelon. Yeah. Pecans too. Come get 'em for the children."

When Daddy died at age sixty-seven, I was saddened but not distraught like with Joseph and Eddie. I was again called to identify the body. Thankfully, there was no trip to the morgue. When I arrived at the hospital, he lay on a stretcher behind a curtain in the emergency room. I lingered a while, pondered my life and told him, "I love you, Daddy. I know you did all you could. I can't believe you're gone but I know you're with your 'buddy,' Jesus. I'm here for you. I'm here for Mama too."

Indeed, it was an honor to handle my father's burial arrangements for my mother who was still hospitalized. In the process of planning his funeral, I grew closer to my brother, Kenneth—affectionately called Kenny. It was not that he was new in my life. In fact, he was the only one of my siblings who lived Daddy from birth to adulthood. Kenny was twelve years younger than me, and I thought of him as a member of my children's generation. He had been a little boy playing around the house when Kanari was a baby, a big brother wrestling with Shango, and a teenager gobbling down his mother's coconut cake with RiShana and Takbir. But, in the last days of Daddy's illness, he emerged as a young adult caregiver who attended to our father's daily needs. When Daddy died, Kenny stepped forward to help with the final rites. The boy had become a man and I still had a brother to call on.

Daddy was buried alongside Eddie and Joseph at a gravesite on Long Island. "Death comes in threes," older people in the community offered comfort. "Your season of grief has ended." They spoke of loss. I focused on the gain of three ever-present watchmen. I envisioned my father, brother and nephew watching over me and cheering me on in my efforts to help our family. I wouldn't let them down.

I **tried to change** but couldn't. In the seventies I had a good job, a beautiful wife and two wonderful children, but I was killing myself. Two of my childhood friends—Cody, renamed Elias Muhammad, and George, with a 43X behind his name—had overcome the negative elements of a childhood in Corona. They were clean-shaven, suited up in bowties and sounded intelligent when they analyzed the plight of the Black man in America. In contrast, with my two college degrees and a wild Afro, I spouted the rhetoric of Black power but my life was in shambles.

Harold kept reminding me, "Jim, I know who Bessie is; she's an angel sent to you from God." He was right. She was an anchor in the midst of my madness. When I was distraught over Joseph's death, she was a comfort, and she had been unflappable in helping me raise my teenage sisters. Despite her steady support, I neglected her.

Finally, with a troubling quiet that said it was not a vain threat, Bessie asked for a divorce. "You're never here anyway. It'll free me to move on with my life, and get somebody else," she added after a pause.

Her words were bombs exploding in my head. "Are you out of your damn mind? What kind of chump you take me for?" Rarely did I curse. I had heard so much filthy talk growing up that I absolutely loathed vulgar language, but vile words heaved up from my gut at the thought of my wife with someone else.

"So you want somebody else?" my ranting ended in an exasperated flurry of emotions. After an awkward, confused silence, I confessed, "I never considered being with anyone but you."

"Of course not! Alcohol is your lady friend. You always talk about dying by age thirty. Well, you just passed your thirtieth birthday but you're still a man in search of a tragic end and I'm not going there with you!"

Bessie dropped the conversation and left the thought of our breakup hanging in the air. Whether she raised such a radical solution to shock me or had serious intent was unimportant. A major transition was underway. I pondered Joseph's last words about my wife: *"That's a good woman. You need to go home and get your stuff straight."* His words rang true but I didn't know where to turn.

In search of a solution, my mind settled on my friends, Elias and George. Perhaps religion could turn my life around as it had done for them. The Muslims emphasized strong family values such as sexual morality, the protection of women and children, fathers as financial providers and abstinence from drugs, cigarettes, alcohol and the avoidance of unhealthy foods. In one of their popular publications, *How to Eat to Live,* they encouraged a diet of beans, fish, whole grains, fresh vegetables, fruit, and juices. It was exactly the kind of discipline I needed to get my life on track.

I went to the temple and joined. Energy previously wasted on partying was channeled into the organization's social agenda of "Freedom, Justice and Equality for the Blackman in America." Enterprises supporting the group's goals included: farms, restaurants, schools, bakeries, barbershops, health food stores, food cooperatives, and an emerging international fish import business. I worked sixteen hours a day with no pay but the serious discipline required by the schedule saved my life. At age thirty I had been dying like my brother.

However, after I became a Muslim, I stopped drinking for the first time since I was fourteen.

In addition to taking on the social justice agenda, I enjoyed the wholesome lifestyle of the Muslims and the strong comradeship among the brothers. We always greeted one another in peace and encouraged one another with the often repeated saying: "I want for my brother what I want for myself." At the same time, we believed in fighting with those outside of the temple who fought with us. I actually thought it was okay to love my Muslim brothers and despise others—especially those who had mistreated me.

Forgiveness was not a practiced principle for me but Bessie had a Biblical response: Do good to those who despitefully use you. She said, "It takes love to remake the world. Isn't that what you're trying to do—change the world with the goodness you bring to others?" Her question left me pondering.

When the Honorable Elijah Muhammad's son, Imam Warith D. Muhammad, converted the Nation of Islam into the American Muslim Mission after his father's death, I began to understand what Bessie was saying. The Imam taught that man's relationship with God is not dependent on skin color. He lectured: "What makes men brothers is our belief in One Creator. You call him God and I call him Allah but we are still brothers. The same God you pray to, I pray to. None of us is above the other. Praise no man; all praise belongs to God. When giving praise for inspiration that comes from a person, say 'Takbir'; it's an utterance that recognizes the greatness of God and the brotherhood of men." The Imam's message made me want to be a better person—to reconnect to my brothers and sisters of different religious and ethnic backgrounds.

As I grew spiritually, the prejudice and injustice of the world grieved me more than ever. I continued to address flawed systems, but my greatest challenge was addressing my own flaws. My quest for self-love left little room for ill feelings or resentment regarding past wrongs done to me. Rather than wallowing in hurt, I addressed societal and personal problems with a renewed compassion for the other fellow.

Bessie took note of the shifts in my attitude and the monumental changes in my behavior. She even explored Islam as a way of life for herself. In addition to their alternative educational system (Muhammad's University of Islam), she was attracted to the dietary discipline outlined in *How to Eat to Live.* She studied the Muslim publication on healthy eating along with Jethro Kloss' *Back to Eden.* It was a popular whole-food, natural healing book written back in 1939 but updated and sold in the Muslim bookstore.

I already considered my wife a health-nut because of our family diet of mostly fruits, vegetables, fish and occasionally chicken. However, after I became a Muslim, her vigilance kicked to another level. She taught the children to read the labels of their snacks for the ingredients and nutritional content, while she further reduced our intake of animal products.

The first time she placed one of her peculiar looking dishes in front of me, I asked: "What's this?"

"Tastes like chicken," she answered.

"But... is it chicken?"

"Well, it's wheat gluten, but it tastes like chicken." She stood over me smiling while I took a bite.

Damn! I said to myself.

"How is it?" she asked.

"Ummmm," I smacked my lips and played it off. Soon as her back was turned I went out and got me some real chicken.

Thankfully, as time passed, she moved away from wheat gluten and vegetable textured proteins to delicious, nutritionally balanced whole food meals.

Though my wife returned to her Christian faith, she continued the discipline of healthy eating, regular exercise and eight hours of sleep a day. When people asked how she kept her skin so beautiful, she'd give the short answer: "I drink plenty of water." They also asked how I reconciled the fact that I was a Muslim married to a Christian. "That's easy," I would say. "We both love God and we respect one another." I now know that my answer was grossly oversimplified. I didn't really hear the import of what my wife had been saying to me about Christ. I was years away from understanding her faith that the "...unbelieving husband is sanctified by the believing wife."

Despite differences in religious persuasions, the spirituality and sobriety I found in Islam contributed greatly to the mending our marriage. Still, I had to pursue Bessie like when we first met. Over a seven-year period, our wounded relationship healed. Joseph would have been proud to see that I "got my stuff together."

Friends and colleagues failed to see spirituality in my quest to better the lives of broken and oppressed people.

My wife kept urging, "Read James. He is your namesake. Seems you'd want to know what he has to say."

The more I read the Book of James, the more I understood that the truly religious person is required to do good for others. He states:

> *Suppose a brother or a sister is without clothes and daily food. If one of you says to them, 'Go in peace; keep warm and well fed,' but does nothing about their physical needs, what good is it? In the same way faith by itself, if it is not accompanied by action, is dead.*

Finally, words from the Bible (NIV version) explained the spiritual nature of my passion for helping others. Lessons from James filtered into every aspect of my life and reminded me that it is not enough to will change; you have to act to create change.

On my job I had a new confidence, a boldness that altered my course. I could no longer sit on the fence between students and the administration. It's not that I had lost faith in Bill Schwartz's mediation model; I had gained a yardstick that measured when to attempt reconciliation of opposing sides and when to act. In the struggle over the creation of a Black Studies Department at BMCC, I decided to act with students.

The study of the history of my people had had a profound impact on me in Corporal Jones' classes at North Carolina College and back in Woodycrest when Mr. Harris first told me about my ancestors. In fact, it was this knowledge that had caused me to seek the higher education that allowed me to feed and clothe my family. I believed that self-knowledge would make the same difference in the lives of students.

The handful of Black Studies courses offered at BMCC had the potential to foster positive self-esteem in Black students and provide a more balanced education for students of all backgrounds. Splintered by disagreement, the program failed on both counts.

An African, with whom students were dissatisfied, ran BMCC's Black Studies program. He championed aspects of colonization such as the building of much needed roads in Africa. Sonia and John were faculty in the program and advocated for a leveling of the curriculum by including perspectives on the destructive forces of colonization. They agreed that building roads was a positive development but argued that those roads were also used to rob the continent of gold, rubber, copper, diamonds and other natural resources.

The College President, a conservative Black Republican, was adamantly opposed to the shift toward an African perspective in the Black Studies program. To add to the controversy, students pressed for a full-fledged Black Studies Department and wanted Sonia as the chair. After countless meetings and no progress, they felt pushed against a brick wall. Deciding to force the issue, they staged a sit-in in the President's Office. Black faculty lent verbal support to the cause but Sonia, John and I were the only ones to join the protest.

The College was still spread out in several buildings in midtown. We assembled at the "A" Building on 51st Street and Seventh Avenue around two o'clock in the afternoon. We three faculty members marched with eighty students one block to the College's executive offices on Broadway. Chanting, "Students united will never be defeated!" we swarmed sidewalks already crowded with pedestrians and marched around honking yellow cabs and trucks.

We entered the office tower, took the elevators to the eighth floor, pressed past the secretary and into the office where the President sat behind his desk. "What's going on here?" he asked.

Oba, the student spokesperson declared, "We are staying until you address our Black Studies issues."

The President got up and walked out. Shortly afterwards his Dean of Administration, the same Dr. Sam

Pittman who had been leery about hiring me, showed up and announced in a nonchalant tone, "The police will be here in five minutes. Whoever is in this office will be arrested. That includes faculty," and then he exited.

I advised the students: "If there is anyone here with a prior record, or you have child care responsibilities, or challenging illnesses, or other extenuating circumstances, don't feel bad about leaving. This is what we did in the civil rights movement. Those who cannot make the sacrifice should not be looked upon as sellouts or cowards. You can play a role by spreading the word to the student body regarding our plight." Fifteen students left. Within the hour, the rest of us were handcuffed and hustled out of the building, past hundreds of cheering students from the "A" building who had been alerted by fellow protestors. We were marched back up 51st Street and into a line of waiting police vans.

Unlike my arrest as a student protester in North Carolina, the police separated me from the group and placed me in a cell with inmates charged with felonies, while John and Sonia remained with the students. I supposed Pittman had fingered me for special treatment because by participating in student protests, I had broken the mediation contract that I had outlined in my job interview

A big muscular dude in my cell pranced back and forth cursing, "They say I stabbed him; that's what they accuse me of; they say I killed that so and so." Then he walked over to me, "What they got you in here for?" I looked into his twisted face, and around at seven other beat-up guys who looked angry enough to fight.

Don't look like you afraid, Daddy's voice tunneled through time. "I was sitting-in at the President's Office!" I blustered in the boldest voice I could muster.

"Doing what!" Muscleman seemed offended.

274

"I was sitting-in at the President's Office!" I repeated and squared my shoulders in an attempt to show strength.

He flashed a look at the other prisoners as if to say, *What they got this wimp in here with us for?* "Man, that's all you have to do with your time?" he bristled. His contempt made it clear that I was definitely not a part of his group.

Pretending to be tough, I shot back, "Man, I'm fighting for Black Studies!" Because I knew that Muslims were protected in prisons, I added, "The Honorable Elijah Muhammad teaches us, 'We die from a lack of knowledge!'"

With that single sentence the tension in the cell vanished. I passed the night telling the inmates how they could change the course of their lives with self-knowledge. When Conrad Lynn, a well-known civil rights attorney and our lawyer, bailed me out, Muscleman bade, "As-Salaam-Alaikum, my brother."

At the arraignment, the courtroom was packed with supporters. Pointing at me, Pittman testified, "Your Honor this man is the ring leader. An example should be made of him for misleading these students."

"What is your job at the school?" the judge asked.

"I'm a counselor."

"What were you doing with the students in the President's office?"

"I was counseling them." Everybody laughed.

"Case dismissed," the judge cleared all protestors.

Pittman was furious. Not satisfied to let it rest, the next day he came to my office and informed me that he was going to put my name on a "blacklist" at the University's central office at 80th Street. I thought to myself, *Dark as I am, I'm already on the blacklist. I was on the blacklist when I came out of the womb.*

"Young man," he addressed me like I was thirteen instead of a man in my mid-thirties. "Why would you risk your professional career for these students?"

I had expected repercussions so I talked frankly about my motivation. "I believe in this fight for a Black Studies Department. Self-knowledge helps students become self-reliant. Black people will never take control of their own destiny if they know nothing about who they are and what their people have already achieved."

Pittman was a Texas boy who believed that a person should pull up by his own bootstraps. He liked what I had to say about self-reliance. That day marked the beginning of a sustained dialogue regarding conditions in the Black community. From adversity sprang a friendship that caused him to sigh, "Forget about 80th Street; you can do any damn thing you want at this college." He also credited me with inspiring an interest in history that would eventually distinguish him as one of the foremost collectors of African American memorabilia.

My arrest protesting for Black Studies coincided with a series of well-publicized indictments. Huey Newton, Bobby Seale, Eldridge Cleaver and other Black Panther Party members, including some from the Corona chapter, were either jailed or exiled by the threat of jail, while Fred Hampton and Mark Clark had been killed. Left in disarray were services for youth like breakfast programs, tutoring and cultural activities. An explosion of these high-profile cases helped me to see that I could do more for young people on the outside of prison walls than in a cell. I decided never again to go to jail for a cause. I had a new outlook on sacrifice: I would live and, like a dripping faucet, tap away at problems day after day.

Major changes in my personal life continued in the eighties. I prized myself on being a good husband who responded admirably to family life. Bessie slept late while I cooked breakfast, dressed the children and drove them to school, but not before placing a hot cup of tea on her bedside table. When I returned, invariably, I found her weeping.

"What's the matter?" I would ask.

"I don't know," she would blow her nose and wave me away.

Almost daily, I left for work defeated. At the end of my morning chores, again and again I returned to a cup of warm tea spiked with tears. "What's the matter?" the exchange would start again.

After endless tearful episodes she finally cried, "You're not helping me enough!"

"Not helping you enough? But, I'm helping you, Bessie." Gut-wrenching sobs hammered my brain, while I defensively listed tasks of which she was already well aware.

Friends told her: "Girl you better get yourself together." "I wish my husband helped me like that." "You got yourself a good man." She cried even harder. Somewhere in the downpour of tears, Bessie found a stream of clarity. "Jimmy, I know what it is," she said. "I want you to stop helping me..."

"Oh, you won't make it if I don't help you," I interrupted, pointing to her responsibilities as a college dean, overseeing seven urban campuses.

"I'm not finished, Jimmy. I want you to take over and let me help you."

It was like being hit by a stray bullet. "Me? Take over?"

"Yes, I'll be your 'go-for.' You make the grocery list and I will do the shopping. You plan the menus and I will cook. You schedule the doctor's appointments and I will take the children for their checkups. You review their homework and I will attend the teacher conferences."

I was speechless.

"Okay? Jimmy, you hear me?"

"Let me think about it," I mumbled and got the heck out of there. I hoped she would forget the whole thing. Three days later, she raised the proposition again.

"It won't be the way you do things," I took a last stab at changing her mind.

"That's okay."

"I'll try but you know you're a perfectionist."

"I'll adjust," she said with a hint of sarcasm.

Hesitant and confused about how Bessie had roped me into the new domestic arrangement, I embarked on one of the most difficult periods of fatherhood. For the first few months I wiped my brows, "Whew, this is a major operation. Do you know this is a major operation?" I asked her.

"Yes," Bessie replied, and continued on her merry way.

At the end of most days, I was mentally drained and physically exhausted, but all hard work should be as satisfying as the tasks I performed serving the needs of my children. They teased me harder, were more competitive in their games, and most of all, they confided their secrets. In getting to know my children better, I became the dad that I thought I had been all along. Thanks to Bessie, our children had two fully involved parents.

Despite the closeness I felt to the children, I wanted to escape the unending demands of running the house. When I sought another marital contract negotiation, Bessie was not hearing it. The household duty scale had tilted ninety-to-ten in her favor, with me doing ninety percent of the work. No way was she returning to the old arrangement. My best shot at change was to ease into a fifty-fifty deal.

After the infamous first contract negotiation, several distinct marriages followed. "I've been married seven times," Bessie used to shock people until she added, "to the same man." As circumstances changed, the marital partnership evolved to accommodate our individual needs. Bessie and I continually reworked our relationship and, in doing so, we kept our marriage vibrant.

After twenty years of gloom, Bessie overhauled the sorry state of our affairs once again. Mother's Day 1984 she stormed into our bedroom and declared, "Enough!"

Mother's Day was unfolding in unbearable sorrow as it had every year. I brooded in one corner of the house while Bessie alternated between tearful flare-ups and attempts to present a cheerful face to RiShana and Takbir who showered her with bouquets of wilting dandelions. Overpowered and paralyzed by thoughts of my mother, I made no attempt to orchestrate a celebration for my wife. Instead, a mood of separation and loss weighed heavily on the entire family.

"We're going to see your mother," Bessie roared into the room.

"I'm not going out there," I dismissed her outburst.

"Yes you are!" "No I'm not!" We argued like two kids.

"Well, I'm going with or without you," she ended the exchange and dressed while I sulked behind the Sunday paper.

The sound of footsteps descending the stairs ceased, but calling her bluff, I sat stubbornly in my chair for a moment before peering out of the upstairs bedroom window. Bessie was headed for the car with nine-year-old RiShana and eight-year-old Takbir trailing behind her. Shango, a student at Cardoza High School and Kanari a junior in college, watched from the porch. "You don't know how to get to the hospital," I shouted down to the driveway.

"I'll find it somehow." She cranked the motor and the children's heads jerked upward in unison. You-better-not-let-Mommy-get-lost daggers sailed toward the window.

"Wait a minute, Bessie!" I hollered down to her. She turned the engine off. "Damn it!" I mumbled.

In a clenched-jaw one-hour ride from Laurelton to Central Islip, not one word did I utter. The thought of seeing Mama overwhelmed me. I had seen her in 1973 when Gloria brought her home for Thanksgiving but I could not recall ever spending a Mother's Day with her. Matter of fact, I remembered only two visits to the hospital: once as a child and again to introduce Bessie as my bride.

Both visits had been depressing, but the visit that crippled me occurred when I was ten. Uncle Esau had driven Granny, Carol and me out to see Mama at Pilgrim State Hospital in Brentwood, Long Island. The day started pleasant enough. I sat on the picnic bench beside her and we gobbled down her favorite foods: macaroni and cheese, potato salad, collard greens, glazed ham and fried chicken.

"I want to go home," she said the minute she swallowed her last bite. Everybody got quiet. "Now!" she demanded. When no one responded, Mama started cursing. In the tirade, she called her brother, Big Jimmy, "a bastard child!" It was the first time I had seen Granny angry with my mother.

"Shut up, Nettie!" she shouted, throwing leftover food and dirty containers into brown paper bags.

The mounting tension erupted into the frenzied

goodbye that had tormented me for years. Mama cursed above the noise of the buzzer that signaled our re-entry into the building; louder than the clanging bundle of keys that locked the metal door behind her; and, above the hysterical screams of patients whose glazed eyes signaled they were unaware of their surroundings. But, Mama knew where she was and where she wanted to be. "I want to go hooome!" she shrieked. The more she cursed, the louder the other patients roared until her voice sank in bedlam.

Doors slammed shut in far corners of my heart when I left Mama in that place. With tears streaming down my face, I held onto Uncle Esau's hand and muttered over and over, "Ain't coming back." That simple oath of a ten-year-old had kept me away for thirty years; and now, Bessie was dragging me back. She was playing with fire.

We rolled onto the grounds of Central Islip State Hospital. Some years earlier, Mama had been transferred there from Pilgrim State. We parked in front of a red brick building with a bold black "4" tacked on one corner. The dreaded procedure started: ring the bell to the building, summon the elevator to the third floor and listen for the clanging keys. I walked onto the floor wondering if I could bear the encounter. Struggling to keep my balance, I leaned my head against the metal door and peered through the tiny square window that allowed a straight-line view down a long empty corridor. A quiet calm rested on the ward.

Maybe the patients are in the cafeteria; it's getting close to noon, I thought. *No, wait.* A dumpy nurse emerged from a door on the left of the hallway asking if she could help me. Unable to mask her surprise and pleasure over my mother having a visitor, "Nettie, your son is here," she sang out cheerily.

A tall blueberry-black woman with thick braids rushed from the first room on the right. Clapping her hands, she leaped and bowed like an African dancer, and shouted, "Jimmy! Jimmy! Jimmy!" in blissful glee. When the door swung open, she fell into my arms. That was it! We reconnected and I knew the bond would never break again. Finally, I understood that a mother's love had sustained me through a childhood of children's homes.

When I was too young to remember, Mama had somehow communicated to me a sense of well-being—that I was somebody. Though I lost her at an early age, I had always felt special. A mother and baby I observed on a New York City subway conveyed the mother-son feeling I am trying to describe. When the baby pulled on the mother's necklace, she would take it from his hand with kisses: smack, smack, smack. His eyes glued to his mother's face, the baby would break into a grin—his entire body jerking and trembling with each kiss. The woman had rough hands, like she had been scrubbing floors, but those hands were softness to her baby. That is the kind of love and security my mother had deposited in me. However, deep recesses of my soul had felt empty for so long that I thought Mama's love had died, but it was alive again when she fell into my arms.

All the money and education in the world are not as valuable as a mother's love. That's why it hurts me to see women abuse their children. I shudder when I hear a woman say to her toddler, "Come here stupid; sit your dumb self-down!" What will that child have to hold onto in life when inevitable hard times arrive? I don't recall what my mother had done or said, but early on she imparted love that had taken me through rough waters.

Our 1984 Mother's Day reunion occurred in a small room just outside the locked door of the hospital ward. Those tight quarters held the tranquility of Eden. I thought Mama would not remember me, but she did; that she would explode when it was time to leave but she didn't. Years of needless fear had kept me from her but mercy had brought me back to the mother I had been desperately yearning. Our reunion taught me how to move beyond fear—that to conquer fear I must act even when I am afraid.

Once I faced my fear, there was no stopping me. Bessie and I established a new Mother's Day tradition of visiting Central Islip. By two o'clock I was home honoring Bessie, the remarkable mother of my children and a woman of insight and compassion who transformed Mother's Day into a holiday.

Soon, I was visiting Mama throughout the year. Sometime the children joined us, but mostly the two of us took home-cooked meals to Mama, spread picnics on the hospital grounds, and drove her around the little suburban village to purchase flowers and snacks for her room. We laughed and sang and tiny slithers of recollections from South Carolina and Corona slipped from her lips to create precious memories. After three hours, we said our good-byes in joyful anticipation of the next visit.

"**C**harity begins at home and spreads abroad," Bessie chimed. She was not asking; she was making the case for moving my volunteer work closer to home. The crack epidemic of the mid-eighties was sweeping through urban communities nationwide and Laurelton was not spared. For safety reasons, she wanted me nearby rather than volunteering on political action committees and community organizing projects in Manhattan. "Take advantage of your new free time and work on local problems that affect your family's daily life," she summed up.

Ha! I have no free time, I thought but said nothing. It had been nearly two years since my removal as Assistant Dean of Students at BMCC because of my involvement in student protests. I was still fighting to regain the position I had held for five years. I was determined to keep on fighting but decided to do enough small projects in the community to get my wife off my back.

Starting slowly, I called the sanitation department and had illegally dumped trash and garbage removed from the alleyway adjacent to our backyard. The trimming of tree branches that obstructed the stop sign two blocks down from the house and the filling of potholes along 133rd Avenue followed. Next, I got a bullhorn and rallied my neighbors to shut down a makeshift auto repair shop that had opened on a nearby side street. Then, to inspire pride in the neighborhood and to show determination against blight, I patrolled the streets armed with the bullhorn that fast became a trademark. My amplified voice called people out of their houses at sunrise, "Your children tore up the place last night with Fourth of July fireworks. Come on out and clean up behind them." I was hooked. Work in my own neighborhood became my new passion.

The echo of the bullhorn chased young people off street corners after midnight, but during the day I took a closer look at the wounded youth hanging out in the community.

"Brothers, brothers," I walked right up to five guys in their late teens loafing in front of the store across from the Long Island Railroad. "What has happened in your life that you are here at ten in the morning sharing a 'forty'?" Baffled by the question, they froze and I knew from street experience to keep talking. "You see that train." All eyes lifted to the platform where the train slowly pulled away. "I'm supposed to be on it but I came back down here because I love you and I want to find out what happened to you. I know you don't want to live like this. What do you need? Is it a job? See me, I'm your man." Scribbling my work number on a piece of paper from my briefcase, I continued, "A place to live? I'm the man. A GED—you know, General Education or High School Equivalency Diploma? I'm the man."

One of the guys had a definite I-don't-want-to-hear-this-crap look on his face, but four of them warmed up to me. Shifting the forty-ounce bottle of beer behind his back, one of them asked, "Yo man, where you work?"

"Borough of Manhattan Community College. I take this train every day. You can stop me anytime," I told him and went on my way.

When I returned home at ten that evening, the Laurelton Station was deserted and dark but I recognized the sullen fellow from the morning. He said nothing. So, I started the desolate walk beneath the overhanging tree branches of 225th Street. Three blocks into my stride, I realized I was being stalked. My body grew rigid as I weighed my options: *I don't have a knife or a gun but I'm not going down like this. When he attacks, I'm going to try to take him out.* At the darkest spot of the street, he yelled, "Yo, Professor Blake!" I spun around with fists clenched.

"No! It's not like that! It's not like that," he backed up.

"Then, what is it?" I growled, still jumpy.

"I just want to ask you about that GED."

"Well, man, don't walk behind me; walk beside me."

We strode toward Merrick Boulevard. I learned that he had kept quiet earlier in the day because he didn't want his boys to think he was copping out. He had waited all day for me to get off the train; that's how bad he wanted to change his life. Next day, I took him to the GED program at BMCC where he eventually earned his diploma and an associate's degree.

Word got around among the fellows on the street: "Professor Blake is real. He cares about us." Walking up to so-called "negative elements" in the community became routine. I would say, "You don't know me but I love you," and their tough-guy attitudes dissolved. My instinct coupled with training as a social worker told me that teenagers who drugged and drank on street corners were fleeing some serious issues at home. Like the rest of us, they sought wholeness. I referred them to literacy programs, took them to rehabilitation centers and helped some of them get into college. People think it takes an enormous amount of effort to reach young people, but most times it takes a kind word and a little of our time.

Spots in the neighborhood where most adults refused to go, I was greeted, "Yo, Mr. Blake," and given a pound, a high five or a handshake. They knew I loved them but they also knew that I would blast them with my bullhorn.

My portable loudspeaker bellowed chants at rallies to close down strip joints and peep shows that opened when longstanding businesses on Merrick Boulevard moved to the suburbs. However, I left my bullhorn at home when I challenged complacency at meetings of parent groups, block associations, garden clubs, civic organizations and churches. My central theme was: words plus action equal results. "If we are to save ourselves from the plague of drugs and violence destroying young people and our community," I urged, "stop settling for the rhetoric of powerless leaders and unresponsive elected officials. We can't sit on the sidelines; we need to get up and do something about our plight!"

Before long I had a reputation as a "community activist." Bessie called it "charity," and then added "It's loving your neighbor as yourself."

With an understanding of my actions as loving my neighbor, I responded to the call to serve when the 218th Street Area Association sent for me to help shut down a crack house. We demonstrated and demonstrated. Nothing happened. Then, on my way to one of our strategy meetings at the local Catholic Church, I made a detour.

Boom! Boom! Boom! I acted like I was going to knock down the front door of the drug den. An emaciated wild looking junkie appeared. I pointed at him and in a near whisper, said, "Brother, don't you tell anybody I came here! Look, they coming down on y'all. This is serious! In twenty-four hours all y'all gon' be in jail. I'm telling you as a brother; this is it—no play! They been demonstrating but now everything is lined up. If you don't get out of here, ya'll gon' be sitting in jail this time tomorrow."

The junkie studied my face and I looked him straight in the eyes without flinching. After a long pause he mumbled, "Appreciate it, man."

"Peace, brother!" I saluted him.

He and his buddies cleared out of that house in a hurry. I went on to the meeting and reported that the problem had been solved. The organizers of the demonstrations were amazed, but it was simple. Guilt had weakened any resolve the addicts might have had. Because their wrongdoing undercut their firm footing, they were left defenseless.

Of course people do not always know that they are wrong; in which case, other tactics are needed. On the heels of the success of shutting down the crack house, the 218th Street Area Association called again. This time they needed help with a woman who gave loud parties in her backyard and sold booze out of her garage. Calls to the police had turned into cat-and-mouse games. When officers arrived, the music would go down. As soon as they left, it would go back up.

"Did you speak to her?" I asked.

"No, she's crazy," the leader of the association assured me.

"Set up a meeting and I'll invite her."

"She won't come," he stated, but reluctantly scheduled a meeting.

I knocked on the woman's door, "I'm Professor Blake from the community. Your block association has a problem with you."

"Whaaat?" Her eyes widened and her smooth round face folded into a frown. "What's the problem?"

"They are having a meeting tomorrow; come find out. I'll pick you up."

When she and I arrived at the meeting, people started right in: "Last weekend, you gave another one of those parties and the music was loud." "It kept me awake." "Cars were double parked and blocked driveways." "People stepped on my flowers." "They threw whiskey bottles all over the block." "People came to your house from all over the place and they didn't leave until three and four in the morning."

"Yeaaah," she proudly bobbed her head up and down. "It was a nice party, wasn't it!" Absolutely clueless to the disturbance she had caused, she looked back and forth for approval.

"Nice party to you," I interjected, "but your neighbors are saying you are destroying their property."

"Oh," she looked hurt.

Feeling sorry for her, I proposed a solution: "You know what? We need somebody like you to be the block watcher."

"Block watcher, what's that?"

"Somebody who looks out for anything suspicious. You know, they let the block association know about anybody being loud or out of order."

"I can do that?" she asked. I nodded and she gladly accepted the job. A good-hearted person, who simply did not understand the culture of the neighborhood found her place in the community. She was vigilant in her new role. I often imagined her telling her friends: *I can't have no parties 'cause I'm the block watcher.*

Following the successful resolution of a couple of problems for the 218th Street Area Association, David Jefferies, Gene Upshaw, Lamar Gilmore, Glinton Coleman and I teamed up in a campaign for clean blocks, safe streets and healthy youth. Our multi-faceted approach included closing cracks houses and targeting illicit businesses on Merrick Boulevard. In near blizzard conditions, the five of us demonstrated against a "grocer" who protested that he was not selling drugs and alcohol to youth though his store was stocked with nothing but beer. Not even a loaf of bread was visible. We weren't able to shut him down completely but our constant spotlight made it difficult for him to do business.

Within the first year of my community involvement, the number of projects quadrupled. As part of an anti-drug initiative, I conducted a series of sensitivity training workshops for the local precinct that were aimed at improving police-community relations. Around the same time, at the invitation of Iris Petiford Cox, a longtime Laurelton resident, I organized groups of young people to clear weeds and debris from the center malls of Merrick Boulevard. The latter undertaking led to the revitalization of the Laurelton-Springfield Gardens Chamber of Commerce. With me as President and Iris as Executive Director, the Chamber monitored new businesses that came into the area. We also sponsored a variety of activities like Community Pride Day that showcased youth talent and brought local merchants together with the young people they had previously viewed as the riffraff who blocked the entrances to their stores.

In the process of bridging the gap between youth and merchants, the Chamber identified issues facing small business owners. In an attempt to attract customers that flocked from Laurelton to the Green Acres Mall in suburban Nassau County, the store owners sought protection from robberies, and eligibility for loans to upgrade products and services. To address these problems, Hutchinson, the owner of the computer store, helped me organize The Laurelton Merchants Association. He was elected the founding president of the group.

Together, the Merchants Association and the Chamber of Commerce began a beautification program. We established a patrol to make sure shopkeepers swept sidewalks and curbs in front of their stores. Through joint efforts with the Laurelton Garden Club, individual businesses sponsored flower bins on the center mall. They strung holiday lights for Christmas. In the summer, they draped decorative flags on light poles that announced "Laurelton Business District."

Bessie had coaxed me into local volunteer projects with the expectation that I would be around to help her, but my involvement in community activities kept me in the streets more than ever. The household duty scale had tilted again in her direction. Though she was Dean of the School of New Resources at the College of New Rochelle and was responsible for seven campuses in the New York metropolitan area, at the end of an exhausting workday she was cook, maid and primary parent.

To add to her burden, whenever I was home, people showed up at all hours: "Tell Mr. Blake, my neighbors are playing their music too loud." "Those kids on the corner all hours are keeping me awake." "My basement is flooded again. The city needs to do something about the drainage."

One day a middle-aged woman banged on the door at eight-thirty in the morning, "Where is he?" she demanded.

"He's gone to work," Bessie answered.

"He's not home?"

"No, he's gone to work."

"Well, I got this garbage in the alleyway that needs to be removed."

"Wellll, he's not here right now."

"These elected officials are never here when you need them!"

"He's not an elected official; he just helps the..."

"You mean he ain't nothing."

"He's something to me!" Bessie slammed the door shut and left the woman on the front porch mumbling.

When I heard the story, I laughed in an effort to ease my wife's exasperation, but on a deeper level I contemplated ways of pulling the community traffic away from my front door. I thought about Helen Marshall. Back in the mid-sixties when I worked with Lou Benson at the Elm-Cor Youth Center, I watched her busily doing things for others in the community. At that time, I thought she was quirky, but by the mid-eighties she had become one of the most respected elected officials in Queens. In doing so, she had brought great resources to Corona to support projects such as the Manpower Center, The Langston Hughes Library, the Louis Armstrong School and Elm-Cor Youth and Adult Activities, Inc.

Helen tried to do something about the guys that wasted away on the corner of Northern Boulevard and 104th Street—a place she called "Vietnam." Proud that I had escaped that environment and gotten a college education, she always introduced me with a chuckle, "This is Professor Blake; he has a PhD from the School of Hard Knocks."

Helen Marshall felt the pain of the community and shaped effective programs to address the needs. She was my political role model. Like her, I wanted to formalize duties that I had already assumed as a volunteer.

As an elected official, I would have resources at my fingertips for better city services and much needed youth programs for the Laurelton community. Also, people could reach me at my office rather than my home. With the idea of reforming the system from within, I jumped into the fray of local Queens County politics.

The cry of "Blake in '88" set off my campaign for membership on the District 29 Community School Board.

The Ocean Hill-Brownsville struggle for community control of New York City schools, in which Bessie had played a role twenty years earlier, had resulted in shared powers between the central board of education and new local boards. Decisions such as hiring and promotion of teachers and staff, along with selecting and purchasing educational equipment and materials were delegated to the community school boards.

Because of my devotion to addressing the needs of young people, the school board was a natural point of entry into politics. Everybody gave verbal support to the idea that children are our future but whenever I asked politicians for help in establishing youth programs, the typical response was: "Blake, kids don't vote." In the eighties, poor children were sacrificed to drugs and violence while many elected officials turned a deaf ear.

I wanted to usher in a new era. By running for membership on the school board, I hoped to change the justice equation for young people. As I weighed what I had to offer them, the God of justice that I clutched to my chest began to merge with the God of love in ways I had not previously experienced. Through the eyes of neglected children, I began to see the oneness of love and justice. Both demand that we do right by our fellow man; and, I planned to do right by children.

Not only was the School Board the right place but 1988 was the right time for me to enter politics. Blacks of southeast Queens had their first opportunity to capture a majority on the nine-member local school board of District 29. With the aid of Assemblywoman Cynthia Jenkins and Al Mack, a keen political strategist, I ran a successful campaign but the Board of Election confirmed my opponent, a Black female, the winner of the race. In a recount, two citizens of Rosedale discovered that I had garnered the majority vote and tried to persuade me to challenge the results.

Rosedale was a community that burned crosses on the lawns of the first Blacks to purchase homes in that neighborhood. Reopening the election would have given them a chance to regain control of the schools. I knew I could defeat the declared winner but I did not want to risk losing the newly gained majority on the board by splitting the Black vote in a runoff election. I conceded. The sacrifice brought respect from my community and pride to my family. Privately, we celebrated the fact that I had actually won the vote in the regular election.

The victory was infectious. After my first venture in politics, I ran for office every time the campaign season opened. As an insurgent, I bumped heads against county bosses who tied me up in bogus court challenges to keep me off the ballot. They removed legitimate signatures from my petitions and refused to certify and pay my poll workers. It did not matter that the people wanted me; the political machine was against me. Every other year I suffered defeat in races for District Leader, the State Assembly or the City Council. All was not lost though. In each campaign, I raised the important issues, kept the elected officials on their toes and, indirectly, brought improved services to the community because they never knew which one of them I would choose to run against.

On off years, when there were no political races, I continued to war against drugs and for youth services. The two efforts merged in 1990 when Assemblywoman Cynthia Jenkins invited Governor Mario Cuomo to Laurelton to speak about the drug epidemic. It was a time when children dodged bullets if their parents dared let them go to the store. Crack addicts lit up on people's stoops, and homeowners closed off their yards with what Bessie called "chicken wire fences." It was to no avail. The flimsy barricades were no match for police who chased suspected dealers over the chain links and through the precious flowerbeds that neighbors were trying to protect.

The Governor challenged the community to come up with innovative strategies to combat drugs. He spoke of growing up in Queens and keeping off the streets and out of trouble by working in his father's store after school. The moving account of his teen years evoked Bill Schwartz's mediation model—especially the part of the model that describes how institutions and people are dependent on one another. In a flash, I envisioned the merchants, the youth and government agencies engaged in a common struggle for healthier communities.

Using my office as President of the Laurelton-Springfield Gardens Chamber of Commerce, I set out to meet the Governor's challenge. First, I brainstormed with Bessie about a possible youth program. She listened intently and pressed for details. Piece by piece she pulled concrete parts of the project from my broader vision.

"What?" she asked.

"Internships," I replied.

"Where?"

"In the businesses along Merrick Boulevard."

"What businesses?"

"The different businesses on Merrick"

"You mean varied internships?"

"Yes, VIP," I said.

"VIP? Very important people?"

"No, Varied Internship Program."

In this manner of questioning, a proposal took shape. Bessie wrote it up and Charlotte Jefferson, a staff member of Lt. Governor Stan Lundine, put it in his hand.

In 1991, the Varied Internship Program (VIP) received funding from the New York State Office of Alcohol and Substance Abuse Services to run an after school employment, mentoring, anti-drug initiative for youth, ages fourteen to eighteen. It's newly formed governing board named me as chair and hired Nettie Burgess as the program director.

The VIP was, and remains today, a paid work experience that also provides seminars and workshops on job awareness, career exploration, and self-esteem. From its inception, the program was unique. It enrolled youth from diverse social and economic backgrounds; emphasized local business-youth partnerships and ran parenting workshops. To paint clear pictures of their options, VIP youngsters journeyed to historic sites, national monuments and corporate headquarters as well as to city jails to talk with prisoners about pitfalls to avoid.

In twenty-one years, the VIP has not lost a single youth to drugs and many former participants are college graduates. Among its thousands of alumni are doctors, lawyers, teachers, business executives and youth workers who give back to their communities. The VIP formalized my commitment to youth in ways that freed me to apply skills gained from personal experience as well as from my professional training.

"**B**rother, brother, brother," jumbo loudspeakers blasted, "we don't need to escalate/ War is not the answer/ Only love can conquer hate. What's going on?" The timeless Marvin Gaye song captured perfectly the goal of stopping the unprecedented Black on Black violence driven by the crack epidemic.

October 16, 1995 was Mama's 81st birthday. In gratitude for time spent with her, I headed to the Capitol Mall for five o'clock prayer. Not many men were visible in the dark, but I heard the tramping of feet and whispers of, "Hey, brother" and "As-Salaam-Alaikum." Darting past me in the dark, I glimpsed men dressed in suits and ties, shirts and sweaters, kufis and robes, dashikis, fraternity sweaters and an array of sweatshirts and hats stenciled "Million Man March." They reminded me of the Adhan: "Rush to prayer."

The music stopped at exactly five o'clock. A Muslim imam and a Christian minister recited prayers. Dawn slipped gradually into day. Suddenly, a luminous red sun flashed over a sea of Black men that rolled to the horizon. I saw before me a non-violent unified brotherhood. The Million Man March called by Minister Louis Farrakhan and denounced by critics as a crazy pipe dream was a spectacular success.

From every direction crowds gathered and busloads of men, including my group from Queens, had not yet arrived. Security was tight. Young clean-cut uniformed Fruit of Islam handled crowd control in a polite but firm manner. Contrary to good judgment, I pushed against the flow back to my hotel when I should have been picking up the pass that would allow me access to the area near the stage that was reserved for organizing committee members. I was excited to phone New York and give Bessie a blow by blow account of history in the making.

"Jimmy," she said without giving me a chance to utter a word beyond hello, "I want you to go over to the Watergate Hotel and see how you can help Mrs. Parks and Elaine."

"But that's away from the Mall. You don't understand; this place is packed, and most of the people aren't here yet."

"Jimmy, Mrs. Parks is elderly. They might need your help with all those people around. Go over there and see what they need. "

I hung up and was about to head downstairs to hail a cab when the phone rang. It was Shango, twenty-five and married with a son. In my absence he had taken charge of the fleet of sixty buses from Queens. "Times Square, Dad, Times Square! Men were everywhere!" He described the usually quiet midnight scene on Merrick Boulevard and concluded his report, "They're all rolling." I told him that he could reach me at the Watergate if needed, and then he headed to Penn Station to catch a train.

Around eight o'clock, I grabbed a taxi to the hotel. I intended to get over there, do what I needed to do, get back by noon and pick up my pass to the stage area, but the cab crawled through heavy D.C. traffic. As we crept along, I thought back to my first Rosa Parks mission. In late May 1986, my office phone had rung. "Parks who?" I wanted to know.

"Rosa Parks, the Mother of the Civil Rights Movement." It was Bessie asking me to pick up Mrs. Parks and escort her to Sunday commencement to receive an honorary doctorate at the College of New Rochelle.

"Come on, you're joking."

"No, I'm not." She assured me.

"You bet I'll pick her up!" I was beside myself with joy and so was Bessie, who would have picked Mrs. Parks up herself, but as Dean of the College's largest school, she was busy clearing students for graduation and preparing to read five hundred names at the ceremony.

The next day, I hired a stretch limousine and headed to LaGuardia Airport an hour early. Standing alongside the driver, I waited anxiously with a single long-stem red rose in my hand. The moment I saw the Mother of the Modern Day Civil Rights Movement, "A rose for Rosa," I said and introduced myself. She, in turn, introduced her traveling companion, as her "dear friend, Elaine Steele."

Once we were settled comfortably in the limousine and on our way, I said, "Mrs. Parks, tell me something that happened on that bus that most people don't know."

"Well..."

"No, wait. You are answering too fast. Take your time and think about it."

She smiled warmly and started again, "You don't..."

"Stop, Mrs. Parks. I want this to be a special story. One day, I'm going to tell it to my grandchildren."

A hint of amusement crossed her face and she started a third time, "Professor Blake, I don't know about most people, but I will tell you something YOU don't know. The name of the bus driver who had me arrested is James Blake."

A student of Black history taken by surprise! She had certainly put me in my place but I made a swift come back. "Well Mrs. Parks," I told her, "that James Blake refused you a bus ride but this James Blake is going to put you in a limousine when you come to New York City."

Bessie heard the story and made good on my promise. When she could free herself from the demands of her job, she drove Mrs. Parks and Ms. Steele to their engagements whenever they were in town. Other times, she entrusted their care to family members. First, Frances' husband, Larry Williams, was a regular host; and then, Kanari's husband, Charles Smith. Over the years a friendship developed between Mrs. Parks, Ms. Steele, and our families.

"The Watergate!" the cab driver jolted me out of my reverie back to Bessie's marching orders on the day of the Million Man March. The code she had given me provided immediate clearance to the Presidential Suite where Ms. Steele had left the door ajar. The television in the living room announced, "More buses are arriving."

Look at the size of that crowd; I might not even get onto the Mall, I was thinking when I heard rustling behind me. It was Mrs. Parks in her housecoat and slippers.

"Is that you Professor Blake?"

"Yes." I turned and placed a light kiss on her soft cheek.

"Is Bessie here?" It was the inevitable question whenever I showed up without my wife.

"No, Mrs. Parks, Bessie decided to obey the organizers' request that just the men come; she sent all the men in the family."

Mrs. Parks was eighty-two years old, but spry and I liked teasing her. The knowing smile said: *I know Bessie stayed home because she doesn't like crowds.*

She sat down on the couch and stared at the television, "Look at all those men. Are those men at the march?"

"Sure are, and it's still early," I answered and then asked, "What would your husband think about this march? Would he be here?"

"Oh he would be here. He would like this."

"Yeah, he was a rebel rouser, wasn't he?"

She chuckled, "Raymond liked to do things. He liked to get things done. He stood for human rights."

"Mrs. Parks, get up and make me a cup of coffee!" It was a laugh-out-loud moment for her.

"Oh, I don't drink coffee. I don't know how to make coffee," she said.

"All you have to do is go in the kitchen and run some hot water over the grinds. That's all you have to do. I want to tell my grandchildren..." I paused, poked my chest out and mimicked a pompous version of myself, "Mrs. Parks served coffee to me on the day of the Million Man March."

We both laughed but she surprised me, got up and was headed toward the kitchen when Ms. Steele came out to the living room. "Lady we got to get dressed," she said and aborted my royal cup of coffee. Then, she turned to me, "Professor Blake, a number of people are coming up; will you receive them for us?"

"Okay," I said and watched television until people started piling into the suite. The first to arrive was a delegation of brothers and sisters from the Nation of Islam to escort Mrs. Parks to the march. Following them were volunteers from the Rosa and Raymond Parks Institute, a youth services organization co-founded by Mrs. Parks and Ms. Steele in 1987. I chatted with Institute staff about details of the programs designed to fulfill their mission of "helping young people live up to their full potential." The organization provided an impressive array of tutorials, as well as banking and other youth services in Detroit where Mrs. Parks lived. I was most touched, however, by the volunteers' accounts of Pathways to Freedom tours where young people retraced the routes of the Underground Railroad and the Civil Rights Movement, as they visited historical sites and talked with eyewitnesses to history along the way.

Though I was familiar with Pathways to Freedom (named so by Bessie in her volunteer work with the Institute), hearing the stories of people who had traveled the country on the tours made me see my presence at the Million Man March in terms of the work I did with youth in my neighborhood. The exchange of ideas with Institute volunteers stimulated a broader vision of services for young people in New York. I was uncertain about the form my organizing would take when I returned home but any new endeavors would definitely incorporate an emphasis on education.

As I talked to Institute volunteers, people continued to file into the suite. Mark Kerrin, who often made security arrangements for Mrs. Parks, was followed by a host of friends and dignitaries—all charged with anticipation. The masses of men shown on television fueled speculations that the numbers at the march would exceed a million. Reports circled the room that trains were jammed and buses were being diverted from Washington to parking areas in surrounding Maryland and Virginia.

I wondered whether our buses from Queens had gotten through the traffic to the mall. When Shango finally called, he wasn't able to provide any information on the fleet's progress but he assured me that sixteen-year-old Takbir had boarded one of the buses to D. C. along with their cousin, Mustafa Whiteside from California and my son-in-law, Charles. Then, he launched into an account of his powerful journey:

"New York Penn Station was packed with Black men, the women cheering them on. At stops along the way—Newark, Trenton, Camden, Philadelphia—the scene is the same. Hundreds of women clap and wave as more and more men get on the train. The brotherhood is fierce; those of us already on board are the welcoming committee for each new group of men that load into our car. There's laughter, embracing, and the sounds of palms slapping high five as we greet one another, 'Going to D.C. brother!'"

Shango was having the ride of his life. I wanted the same for the sixty busloads of men who had departed from Laurelton. Meanwhile, I studied the television screen for possible close-up shots of faces from Queens.

Chatter swirled around the room until the bedroom door opened and Mrs. Parks stepped out followed by Ms. Steele. They spent a few minutes greeting their guests before Ms. Steele outlined transportation arrangements to the Mall: "We have three cars," she began, "In the first car will be the escorts from the Nation..."

I had fulfilled my mission from Bessie and in the process had expanded my vision for youth services. I needed to work my way back through the crowded city to the march. Slowly, I eased towards the door and was quietly saying my good-byes when I heard, "...and in the second car, I will be in the front seat with the driver. Mrs. Parks will be in the back seat. Sitting next to her directly behind the driver will be Mr. Mark Kerrin and directly behind me, on Mrs. Parks' right, will be Professor Blake."

Whoa! I turned as Ms. Steele ended her comments, "In the third car will be Mrs. Parks' family. Thank you for coming." Signaling to me, she instructed, "Professor Blake, help Mrs. Parks to the elevator." I stepped forward and proudly took charge of my post.

In the lobby, people recognized Mrs. Parks. She smiled and nodded. They moved forward trying to touch her. Mark had her by one elbow and I the other. "Mrs. Parks keep moving," I said because I knew how warm and accessible she was with people. Outside the hotel was another crush but I held her close and we moved swiftly to one of the black town cars waiting at the curb. Trailing a police escort, the cars zipped toward the Mall. On the way, Ms. Steele continued to give instructions.

"Mark, you and Professor Blake are going to help Mrs. Parks up the steps to the stage—only you, no one else. It's going to be your responsibility to stay with her."

The closer we got to the site, hundreds of Black men flooded in one direction: toward the Capitol Mall. In the rush I spotted Percy Sutton, former Manhattan Borough President and head of Inner City Broadcasting in New York. Seeing someone of his stature huffing and puffing down the sidewalk underscored the blessed ride that had been bestowed on me.

When the cars turned off the street into the Mall area the brothers in the front car got out and cleared a path for us to roll through. "Who's in that car? Who's in the car?" the men yelled as we slowly made our way through the crowd. Somebody recognized her and shouted, "It's Rosa Parks!" Brothers respectfully fell back to make way for the queen's passage. A thunderous, "Roosa! Roosa! Roosa!" swept over us. Mrs. Parks smiled and waved in her humble fashion.

We crept through the never-ending throng of men, and she waved for so long that I said, "Mrs. Parks, put your hand down. They're not waving at you; they're waving because they saw me on the Donahue Show the other day." The car shook with laughter at the reference to my fifteen seconds of fame when I had spoken from the audience of the show in support of the march. Mrs. Parks quietly folded her hands in her lap and I happily waved all the way to the stage.

Mark and I helped her and Ms. Steele up the steps to seats on stage with Coretta Scott King, Betty Shabazz, C. Delores Tucker, Dorothy Height, Merle E. Evers, Maya Angelou and other women of the movement. In close proximity were Dick Gregory, Jessie Jackson, Al Sharpton and a huge congressional delegation. I took a position in the aisle at the end of the row where Mrs. Parks and Ms. Steele were seated.

The sight from the stage was incredible. Flags waved in sunny greetings from Jamaica, Puerto Rico, Ghana, Nigeria and the United States. Crescents, crosses and fraternity emblems bobbed up and down among an array of indistinguishable symbols. Placards and posters proclaimed "Million Man March," "Atonement," "Unity," "One God, One Nation, One People." As far as the eye could see men stood in peaceful harmony. I was drinking deep when the piercing command, "Brother!" spun me around to the stern face of a young Fruit of Islam. "We got to clear this area!"

"I'm part of Mrs. Rosa Parks' security."

"Brother, the minister is coming. We have to clear this aisle."

"Brother, I'm on security for Mrs. Parks," I repeated more emphatically.

"Brother, we have that covered. We'll secure her. You have to move out of this area."

"Brother, I'm not going to abandon my post." The subtle reference to language used in the Nation of Islam, *Don't abandon your post until you are properly relieved*, caused him to go get one of the captains.

Flanked by four brothers, the captain told me in quiet but certain terms, "Brother, you have to get off this stage. If you don't, we will remove you."

The "brotherly" conversation continued in deadly monotone.

"Brother Captain, I'm on security. I can't leave my post."

"Brother, we're going to secure Mrs. Parks."

"Brother, that's like me saying to you, I'm going to

secure the minister after you have been given the assignment. Would you relieve yourself of your post?"

"Brother, if you don't move, we are going to remove you."

"Brother, you see those television cameras; you touch me and there is going to be a fight on this stage for the whole world to see." He froze momentarily. Up to that point the march had been peaceful.

While he weighed his next move Minister Akbar strolled over to chat with me. Previously known as Minister Larry 7X of Temple #7B in Corona, he was at that time Minister Farrakhan's top aide. I had not seen him in years. We chatted about the time I helped the Nation of Islam purchase the Woodycrest property in the Bronx back in the seventies when Bilal Salaam had informed me that the children's home was moving all of its operations to upstate New York. The buildings had been slated for demolition to make way for luxury housing, but to his credit Mr. Merrill, the Executive Director, sold the facility below market rate in order to preserve an important piece of social services history. The Muslims had purchased the complex and held it for several years before selling it to a South Bronx organization that ran an AIDS hospice. Akbar wanted to know what had happened to the facility. I told him that the main building on the site was listed as a historical landmark and would stand as a monument to the children who had entered its doors.

As Akbar and I talked, out of the corner of my eye I watched the captain dismiss his backup crew. When my conversation with Akbar ended, the captain extended his hand, "As-Salaam-Alaikum, brother," and I stayed on my post.

From an exalted vantage point, I bathed in prayers, songs, speeches and the glorious sight of united Black men until Ms. Steele came over. Her instructions were clear: "They'll be calling Mrs. Parks shortly. When you hear her name, you and Mark will escort her to the podium. I want you to stand right behind her, Professor Blake." I heard and obeyed, and my picture ended up in *Ebony Magazine* standing with the Mother of the Civil Rights Movement as she addressed a million men and me.

When I met Bessie back in college, I had told her, "Stick with me baby and you'll go places." Instead, she took me to the edge of a world stage of luminaries and dignitaries. Because of her I befriended Rosa Parks; served on panels with Bishop Desmond Tutu of South Africa; got to know photographer, poet, filmmaker, writer, composer, Gordon Parks and his talented daughter, Toni. I also met President Clinton and Vice President Gore. Bessie took me to corners of this country I never dreamed of visiting and then carried me home to Africa. The Million Man March was just one of many experiences enriched because of my wife.

At the Million Man March, Minister Farrakhan challenged Black men to take responsibility for our roles in destroying one another and to build coalitions that benefit our communities regardless of religious and political persuasions. I took seriously the pledge to work collaboratively and returned from Washington to reach across lines that divided my community. Life had prepared me for the job. I was known on a first name basis as Spade to the guys on the streets, Takbir to members of the American Muslim Mission, James 2C37X to the Nation of Islam, Brother Blake to Christians, Professor Blake or Jim by colleagues and students, and Jimmy to close friends and family. I appealed to Christians and Muslims, men and women, youth and seniors, elected and civic leaders, businessmen and corporate heads.

Members of these various groups came together to form the Million Man March Coordinating Council of Queens. I was the Chair and Sister Nzingha Abena was the Executive Director of the new organization. Sister Betty Dopson and Dr. James Macintosh, co-chairs of CEMOTAP (Committee to Eliminate Media Offensive to African People), were solid supporters. Dr. Macintosh was also co-chair of the Coordinating Council during its formation. Dave Reeves consistently provided a meeting space in his bookstore. Our activities were channeled through four standing committees and their chairs: Youth and Education – Shango Blake; Economic Development – Joe Jones; Political Action-William Nelson; and, Fund Raising - Sister Rosena Pou.

In addition to its impact on local communities, The Million Man March of 1995 was the march that begot million-marches. It was followed by the Million Woman March, the Million Youth March, the Million Family March, the Million Mother March and the Million More March. Not long after the Million Woman March of 1997 we renamed our group the Million Man/Woman March Coordinating Council of Queens and Sister Nzingha and I shared the leadership as co-chairs.

By the time the owner of Karri EDGE Dance Studio of Laurelton walked into the headquarters of the Million Man/Woman March Coordinating Council, it was firmly established in the basement of Dave Reeves' D&J Bookstore on Merrick Boulevard. Familiar with our youth committee, Karri had persuaded a group of angry young brothers who were planning to avenge the death of a friend to wait and speak to me.

Sister Nzingha, my nineteen-year-old daughter RiShana, Shango and other Youth and Education

Committee members went with me to the meeting at the dance studio. The grieving Herriott family sat in heavy silence near the door. Twenty-five males—late teens to early twenties—were scattered around the room. Clad in bandannas, baggie pants and oversized shirts, they slumped on folding chairs, leaned against the walls and brooded in crumpled heaps on the floor. Some of them were rappers and musicians connected to the dance studio, others were friends of friends angered by what they had heard, but five were present that night.

It was a raw session. The atmosphere was thick with pain and I wanted to be real with those young people. Not wanting to promise them something that could not be delivered, I began, "I know you lost your friend, but who wants to tell me what happened so we can all be on the same page?"

A stocky dark skin brother with shoulder length braids stood up and recounted events the evening of the tragedy: "We were happy to see John because he had been away at school. We all went to junior high and high school together, but John was the one who made it. He went to college. The night he came home for a visit, some of us got together and we talked until it was too late to go to Manhattan. He...," the speaker pointed to a fellow seated on the floor with his back against the wall and his knees pulled up to his chin. "He suggested this all-night spot up on Supthin Boulevard. Except for him, none of us had been there before. Right away we saw it was a strip club but we thought we could get a corner table and continue to talk. When a half-naked girl came over and started shaking her behind in our faces. 'We not here for that,' I said. 'We just want to get some drinks.' We laughed her off. She musta got offended and told one of the bouncers 'cause this big dude came over, 'Ya'll gotta go,' he said. We protested, you know? 'Why we gotta leave?' we asked. 'We haven't finished our drinks.' 'You can't stay. Get out!' he ordered. Words got heated. The bouncer exploded and a fistfight followed. We all jumped in. A gun went off and John fell to the floor."

The young brother ended his report and slid to the floor sobbing uncontrollably. It hurt to look at the pained faces of John Herriott's parents. The young man who suggested the club for a gathering place wrung his hands in guilt. Others cursed under their breaths, groaned softly, stoically clenched their fists or wept openly. Shango, an assistant principal accustomed to working with teens, circled the room along with the other youth committee members. They were superb in helping the guys express their grief. "Get it out." "It's okay to cry." "It's okay to be angry," they consoled the group.

Everybody in the room was a victim. The Herriotts had lost a son; innocent young lives had been altered; and, all were caught up in the fiery grip of grief. I wanted to pull something good from the bowels of our anguish.

"Listen," I said, "I understand your loss. I understand that you want revenge but retaliation with violence is not the way. If you really want to honor the life of John Herriott, let's close down that club. Spots like that have no place in our community. Let's shut it down. I'm going to be straight with you; I'm suggesting something that is really hard to do. It's easy to go up there and shoot up the place and get yourselves killed, but it takes commitment to honor John and his family." The young men took heed and a resolve for justice straightened their shoulders.

The first day of protest, one of the guys on the line warned, "They crack heads first and talk later."

Looked like he knew what he was talking about. From half a block away, I read defiance in the stance of three six-foot tall bruisers guarding the entrance to the club. As I came closer, the most muscular one exclaimed, "Oh Shoot! That's Professor Blake. He ain't no joke!" It took a second to recognize my former BMCC student of the seventies.

"Batman, what are you doing here?" I asked.

"I work here, Professor Blake. I'm one of the bouncers."

"Get yourself another job, Batman! We gon' close this place."

"Ahhh man! But, Professor Blake I was there that night the young boy was killed and there is a lot..."

"Batman, I don't want to hear it. Get yourself another job 'cause you right: I don't play!" He looked worried and the attitudes of the guys with him changed. We proceeded with our demonstration without interference.

It took over six months of organizing and vigilant protest, but we shut that club down.

John's friends had wanted revenge for his death. Instead, they got justice and a measure of comfort for the Herriotts. A note from John's aunt underscored their appreciation. "February 23, 1997 was the day John Herriott was killed," she wrote. "Shortly thereafter, Professor Blake helped the Herriott family bring justice for their son's death. Professor Blake contacted Mayor Guillani's office and Deputy Mayor Rudy Washington along with Professor Blake attended many meetings and showed us how to go about requesting permits to picket. Letters to the politicians and the criminal justice system closed down the strip club where John was killed. I publicly salute Professor Blake and his son, Shango, for their support." Any small comfort to the Herriott family humbled me; for the loss of a child brings unutterable sorrow.

The success of closing down the strip club had a ripple effect in the Youth and Education Committee. Discussions about alternatives to violence had a huge impact on our youngest member, eight-year-old Kiara Kennedy, whose grandmother, Miss Maggie Hyman, religiously brought her to meetings. Kiara wrote an anti-bully proposal called "Let's be Friends" and presented it to the Committee for review. Her program asked classmates to make friends with children who were alone or being bullied. Feedback from older youth committee members helped her implement the plan at school and she received encouragement during her weekly progress reports.

Motivated by the power of worthy sacrifice, fifteen-year-old Jimmy Virgus joined the Coordinating Council's Political Action Committee and used organizing strategies learned in the Youth and Education Committee. No job was too big or too small for Jimmy. He stuffed envelops for bulk mailings, went door to door passing out leaflets, hung posters for our candidates and doubled his efforts when opponents tore them down. Because he reminded me so much of myself at that age, I fondly referred to him as "Little Jimmy."

Of all the lessons learned by members of the Youth and Education Committee, the most important one was an understanding of the power of a unified community. Those young people brought a new collaborative zeal to youth day productions, talent shows, and to the year-round workshops that addressed teen violence, pregnancy, substance abuse, self-esteem, job readiness and college preparation.

To help other young people obtain the education John Herriott had been pursuing when he was killed, the Black College Tour—started by Shango a year earlier—was inaugurated as an annual event. Under the leadership of Sister Lois Simpkin-Douse and with the help of Sister Nzingha, RiShana and Shango, the tour linked urban adolescents to the history of southern Blacks. Students returned from the trips testifying about a spiritual journey. Their visits to college and university campuses that were established right after slavery became walks through the history of Black people's struggle for empowerment through education. Hip-hop teens from New York discovered that the majority of America's Black doctors and lawyers had graduated from historically Black colleges. It caused the youth to set college goals for themselves. Through the countless young people that benefited from the Black College Tours, John Herriott lives.

A creeping remorse crawled into my spirit. I had bathed in the intimacy of Mama's love for nine years before a social worker that I will call Miss Brown approached me for a "little chat" during one of my hospital visits.

"You know your mother has been institutionalized for more than thirty-five years."

Thirty-five years is a lifetime, I reflected.

Miss Brown continued, "She's getting up in age and I want to discuss alternative arrangements."

"Different arrangements? What kind of arrangements?" I wanted to know, but it was not convenient for her to get into details on the spot. We set an appointment for mid-week.

Boarding the westbound Long Island Railroad in Laurelton, I transferred at Jamaica Station for an eastbound connection out to the hospital. Every five to ten minutes the train lurched and stopped in little townships remarkably the same. Alternately, clusters of flowers or shrubs encircled flagpoles in parking lots where rows of cars waited for owners who had fled the suburbs to work or to relax in the city for the day. The train trip nearly doubled the forty-minute car ride to which I was accustomed, and it underscored the distance between my mother and me.

When I entered the social worker's office, a thick file lay in the middle of an otherwise cleared desk. The whole of my mother's life was crammed between those covers. I wanted to grab the folder and run. Instead, I took a seat and Miss Brown began to describe my mother's frail health.

"She had her breasts removed, you know?"

"No, I didn't know," I answered but thought, *How am I supposed to know?*

"You were probably too young," she answered the angry question as if reading my mind.

"Was it cancer?" I asked.

"No. The breasts were draining and she had to wear pads all the time. The doctors didn't want her to develop sores from the moisture."

Lazy bastards! Was it too much to keep her dry? I raged inwardly. My stomach tightened.

Miss Brown rambled on: "Because of her condition, we feel a nursing home will be best. There is no need to keep her locked up. She hasn't been violent since her lobotomy..."

Lobotomy! The word ripped through my brain like a tornado scattering debris. Fragments of a buried conversation, *"They don' operated on Nettie's head,"* swirled from decades past. Still reeling from the news of the breast surgery, I didn't question Miss Brown about the lobotomy. Those details surfaced a few months later from a doctor, who probed, "Why did they do a lobotomy on her?"

"I don't know why they operated," I muttered. I had not yet seen the PBS television documentary about the numerous experimental lobotomies done back in the fifties at Pilgrim State Hospital where my mother had been a patient; nor had I stumbled, in an internet search, on the shocking sketch of a Black female in restraints that was the very image of Mama. So I mumbled, "I don't know" to the doctor's question.

"That's a shame," he proceeded. "Lobotomy is not the treatment for schizophrenia; shock treatment maybe, but not lobotomy." He paused, waiting for my response. I was mute. He continued, "It amazes me that Nettie is so feisty. Most patients become listless after that procedure. Your mother is a remarkable woman."

"Yes she is. She certainly is!" Pride in Mama's strength rallied my spirit. From years of visiting her, I had come to know her loving heart and lively, sometimes defiant attitude.

Mama was a survivor. However, back in the social worker's office at Central Islip Hospital, I was unable to focus on her positive attributes. I sat in a fog—my body rigid from news of her several surgeries. Oblivious to the emotional punches she was landing, Miss Brown rattled on about Social Security, Medicaid, Medicare and comparative institutional costs. Then, like a seagull drifting through mist to the shoreline, a phrase fluttered at my ear, "...a place near where you live."

"What? Repeat that."

"I was thinking you might want to bring your mother to a facility close to where you live. The decision is up to you."

Miss Brown finally had my undivided attention. "You don't have to decide today. Look these over." She handed me a bundle of brochures. "They are nursing homes in your general vicinity or you can choose another area. In any case, go check the places out; interview the staff."

Mama is coming home! It was what I had waited for all my life. It did not matter that she was being transferred to another institution. For the first time, I would have a measure of control over her destiny. I determined right there in that social worker's office to find the best place—something as close to Corona as possible. Vowing to put my social work skills to work for Mama, I shook hands with Miss Brown and floated out of the hospital. The train could not go fast enough. I was impatient to get home and share the good news with Bessie.

Over the next few weeks, Miss Brown filed the necessary medical forms and drew up the papers that transferred the guardianship of my mother from the State of New York to me. Meanwhile, I was on a crusade. I explored nursing homes in East Elmhurst, Flushing, and other neighborhoods adjacent to Corona. The horror of what I witnessed was sickening. Smiling faces beamed on lobby bulletin boards while upstairs the ghosts of those once vibrant people stared at walls, lay in their own filth, or sat idly in so-called recreation rooms with blaring televisions that nobody watched. It pained me to see our elderly set out like garbage on pick up day. The "Hard Knocks" Nursing Home was the worst. Foul odors greeted me at the door. Patients were naked, the bed linen was dirty and nurses were yelling at men and women old enough to be their grandparents. Determined that my mother would not be victimized by another callous system, I searched to find the right place. Woodcrest Nursing Home in the Whitestone section of Queens satisfied my requirements.

At first I was reluctant about a place with a name almost identical to Woodycrest, but the facility was clean and the staff was friendly. Visiting hours were flexible and a full schedule of activities was posted in the corridors. On the day I visited, residents were exercising in the recreation room, reading in the lounge or watching television in their own rooms. They looked well cared for. An air of dignity filled the place. My own experience with residential institutions told me that Woodcrest was the home for Mama.

The staff left me alone "to get a feel for" a fourth floor room that overlooked Flushing Bay across to East

Elmhurst-Corona. I stood a long while gazing out the window at the bay Mama had taken flight toward more than three decades earlier. In less than a week, she would return.

In the late eighties and early nineties, newspapers were filled with reports of New York State's move to downsize mental health institutions. Large hospitals like Pilgrim State and Central Islip were closing. Their patients were relocated to community-based facilities—nursing homes for the elderly and small group homes for younger patients. The new policy got mixed reviews. Intended reduction in State expenses for mental health care created an economic boom for nursing homes. However, an unanticipated consequence was an explosion of homelessness caused, in part, by patients discharged to outpatient care without appropriate and sufficient supervision. In my mother's case, I became the buffer in the new system. Through regular contact, Bessie and I integrated ourselves into the team of aides, nurses, doctors, and social workers that made decisions regarding Mama's care.

Familiar feelings of dread and shame had surged when Miss Brown chronicled Mama's life as a mental patient. When I was a young boy, only buddies on 108th Street who saw my mother jump knew that she was sick but we never talked about that fateful day. Over the years, my closest friends remained clueless about who or where my mother was or what I suffered in her absence. At an early age I learned to shield myself from names hurled at the mentally ill. Had I revealed my mother's condition she would have been branded crazy, insane, deranged, or a loony bug in the loony bin. Afraid that her dreaded stigma would stain me, I carried my secret through childhood and into my forties before I reconnected with my mother and replaced negative images with portraits of bravery, strength, and love.

The true knowledge of Mama gained during my visits at Central Islip Hospital, had stripped away biases harbored regarding mental illness. By the time we started the transfer process to Woodcrest Nursing Home, I openly shared stories of my mother's suffering and extoled her virtues to personal friends, to audiences in public speeches, and on television shows. No longer ashamed and ashamed of being ashamed, at every chance I broadcasted her beauty despite persistent societal prejudices. Reactions to my speeches varied. A few sympathetic souls patted me on the back; some shied away from me; others made small talk as if I had not spoken on the topic; and, all were afraid. They left an unspoken but tacit question hanging in the air: *Could it happen to me?*

The phobia about mental illness was made painfully clear when one of my nephews was hospitalized with schizophrenia. The nurse was shocked to see a teenager her son's age unraveled by the disorder.

"Why?" she asked.

I shook my head.

"Drugs?" she pressed.

"No," I answered.

"Jail?"

"No, my nephew is an all-around good kid."

"Alcohol?" I was growing impatient but had to satisfy the nurse's desperate need for a comforting answer before she could get on with her job.

To get her moving, I said, "Heredity."

"Oh." She paused and I supposed she was searching a family lineage file in her head. Finding no apparent instances of mental illness in her bloodline, she relaxed, administered the medication in a crisp methodical fashion and moved quickly away. Like with most people, fear demanded a simple answer to a complex problem.

There is no conclusive evidence regarding the causes of different types of disorders of the mind. Promising recent research points to a web of biological factors, as well as environmental stresses that trigger chemical imbalances in the brain that are not yet fully understood. Still, the treatment of mental disorders has made great strides since my mother's hospitalization in the fifties. You only have to watch television to hear about the latest breakthroughs reported on the news; to see ads by drug companies touting the newest pill; or to get information about research projects that invite suffering patients to participate. Clearly, more effective drugs and therapies have been discovered. Unfortunately, today's advances were not available for Mama.

Until her discharge from Central Islip Hospital, the prevailing question of my life had been, "What caused Mama to lose her mind?" I learned the answer the hard way. Through support of a close family member and the counseling of a host of students with mental disorders, I gained painful insights that dispelled previously held spooky notions of spells, trances and insane asylums like the ones pictured in the movie, *Snake Pit* that I had watched as a child at The Dumps in Corona.

As a counselor and a student of chemistry, it fascinated me to read about the biological roots of mental illness. I discovered that an imbalance in chemicals like serotonin and dopamine in the brain can, to some degree, be regulated by medications. At the same time, there is no magic pill. Each medication has to be tailored to the individual; it is not one-size-fits all. Not only do patients require different medications for the same disorder but depending on their body metabolism, their social stresses, their support systems or the lack of support, different dosages are required according to different schedules. Therefore, it can take weeks or sometimes months to stabilize a mood. The good news is most of my students avoid hospitalizations when they stay on a medication regimen once it is set. The bad news is maintaining the schedule is so very difficult. Patients complain: "The medication makes me gain weight." "It makes my senses dull." "The drug kills my creativity." "I don't want to be ruled by a pill."

Medication by itself is not enough. The recovery of mental patients is also dependent on positive connections to friends and family. Involvement in significant relationships helps to restore self-worth and to strengthen patients as they fight to rebuild shattered lives. However, all too often the battle is waged in isolation. With debilitating and potentially fatal illnesses such as cancer, diabetes, and strokes people reach out with compassion; but mental patients are avoided when they most need caring companions. I know that people don't mean to be cruel. They operate out of fear and are mostly unaware of chemical imbalances or of the daily clinging-to-life struggles of persons with mental disorders.

Frequently, people who suffer from depression, bipolar disorder and schizophrenia are treated like they have character flaws. Much of the time they are blamed for their ailments. I have heard friends and families of sufferers comment: "They should stop it." "They could help themselves if they wanted to." "She stressed herself out; now look at her." "If he hadn't been so in love, it wouldn't have happened." "Ain't nothing wrong with him; he's just plain mean." The level of denial is amazing. Sadly, these negative attitudes can also be found within the medical profession where a more enlightened perspective should prevail.

On one occasion, I had dinner with a friend, a surgery resident at a major New York hospital. He said he started out studying psychiatry but switched to surgery because he did not have the patience to wait for "those people," meaning the mentally ill, "to decide they want to get better." I have also discovered similar attitudes among psychologists on my job. Therefore, I appreciated my friend's decision to switch his specialty. Once he realized he was not suited for healing of the mind, he had the decency to get out of the profession.

Don't get me wrong, I have also been blessed to work with exceptionally kind-hearted, skillful, dedicated mental health professionals. When I connect with these angels who respect and believe in their patients, I stick with them.

Television shows like *Oprah* or *Charlie Rose* or the PBS series, *Healthy Minds,* attempt to educate the public regarding why mental disorders are physical illnesses. However, much work remains to change a largely one-dimensional societal view: He is bipolar; she is schizophrenic is still the prevailing public perspective. Nobody says: He is cancer; she is stroke. Yet, unfair labels persist for patients with chemical imbalances or brain injuries.

The healthy progress of any patient depends on a holistic strategy that strengthens frailties and appreciates abilities. In my work with students with mental disorders, I have seen them create paintings of spectacular brilliance. I have heard gibberish flower into poetry. I have also witnessed class and racial lines dissolve into friendships that rarely exist in the "sane" world where people's hatred for one another fester way beyond the boundaries of reason. I have learned that the richness of a person's life far exceeds the limitations of disease. In my mother's case, the social worker at Central Islip Hospital outlined her infirmities, but thank God, she also positioned me to get to know her strengths.

In 1989 when the ambulance attendants rolled Mama on a stretcher into the small lobby at Woodcrest Nursing Home, her face was terror-stricken. When she caught sight of Bessie and me, she flashed an immediate smile of relief. "Welcome home Mama," I kissed her cheek. We went with her to her room, got her settled, and had a leisurely visit before returning downstairs to complete the battery of forms to be signed.

Just as we concluded the paperwork, Aunt Carrie Mae arrived. "Ain't that wonderful; you and Bessie taking such good care of Nettie," she said between quick dabs at her tear-stained cheeks. I took her straight upstairs for the reunion with her sister.

Over the next several years, our family gladly took charge of Mama's care. Despite her bad knees and failing health, Aunt Carrie Mae caught two buses to Woodcrest once a week to comb Mama's hair. Her younger brother, my Uncle Willie, who had recently retired, visited Mama daily. Comforted by the knowledge that loved ones were with her while we worked, Bessie and I visited evenings and weekends. On Sundays, I happily scooped into plastic containers well-seasoned pureed butternut squash, chicken, spinach and potatoes that Bessie prepared because my mother could no longer chew her food.

For most of her years at Woodcrest, Mama was wheelchair-bound with greatly diminished speech, but her dancing eyes always made my heart sing. Time and again, I entered her room and asked playfully, "Do you love me?"

"Got to!" she'd answer in an emphatic gurgle.

"Why?" I'd beg for more.

"Cause you my son," she would let loose a hearty are-you-joking-me kind of laugh.

"You love me better than you love Carol?

"No."

" Frances?"

"No."

"Gloria?"

"No."

"Ruthie?"

"Ruth L.," she'd correct me.

"Okay, Ruth L., but do you love me better than you love your daughters?" I'd list them all again.

With each name, I'd get a resounding, "Can't! I got to love her more 'cause she's a girl." Mama knew much about pitfalls for women. In her own way she was telling me that my sisters encountered challenges that men don't have to face.

I'd whine a pretend jealousy, "Mama, how could you love them more? What about me?"

With a warm radiance she would declare, "You my heart," and mend my wounded soul. Her answer always made me pause and think: *She cannot love my sisters without a heart and I am that heart.* I'd soak up the deep expression of love then resume teasing.

"You love me more than you love Joseph, don't you?"

One afternoon she startled me, "Joseph dead. Mama dead too." Joseph had been dead for years and Granny had died back in 1984, but somehow Mama knew. Maybe Aunt Carrie Mae and Uncle Willie had been updating her about the family during their visits.

With little variation in content, we repeated playful dialogues and Mama continued to surprise me. Like most people, I underestimated her intelligence because she had mental problems but she quickly set me straight when I asked:

"How many fingers am I holding up, Mama?"

"Two."

"How many now?"

"Three."

"What's two plus two?"

"Four"

"Four plus four?

"Eight."

"Eight plus..."

"Sixteen! I finished the eighth grade!" she snapped, her garbled speech pattern knitted into clarity by anger. I never misjudged her intelligence again.

As Mama's speech worsened I relied more and more on Bessie to interpret what she said. The two of them communicated long past my ability to understand what she wanted or needed. In retrospect, I am convinced that their sustained relationship was due to the special capacity that women have for detail and to a depth of intuition that most men lack. Where womanly gifts ended, bountiful patience and compassion took over. If Bessie did not understand my mother, she swiftly shifted to a simpler but equally interesting topic and spared Mama the aggravation of trying to communicate what could not be understood. She also read the Bible to her and, though my wife is no singer, she soothed my mother as she softly hummed Mama's favorite hymn, "What a Friend We Have in Jesus."

The scars of separation will never disappear, but together, Mama and I snatched victory from our circumstances. She released a lifetime of pent-up emotions that filled the void and smothered the flames that tortured me. In a two-way exchange, I ceased being a motherless child and she gained power through tender expressions. Mama's speech was gone, but her eyes danced the language of love.

Once she declared her love I was no longer lost and neither was Frances. Embracing brilliant bouquets of flowers, my sister would spend hours of solitude at our mother's bedside. Lifting her sweet voice in song to Mama, Frances finally came home.

My mother lived to be eighty-four. In 1998, she died the day before her birthday and sealed October as the single most important month in my life. It's the month that both my mother and I were born. It's also the month my sister, Carol, and I were taken from our family and placed in a children's shelter. Happily, it's the month that Mama returned to be with me at Woodcrest Nursing Home. Sadly, October is the month she slipped away forever.

I planned a funeral that celebrated Mama's legacy of love. In death she was transformed to the regal beauty of her youth. Her black skin was without wrinkles, her hair—only slightly gray at the temples—was swept into a crown on the top of her head and her face was serene. We saluted our queen. RiShana played a beautiful rendition of "Wind Beneath My Wings" on her flute, followed by musical homage from Vera Moore, my 108th Street friend who had become a noted singer despite my boyhood pranks.

After the funeral Gloria, Carol, Frances, Ruthie and Kenny gathered at my house in Laurelton along with cousins Gereline, Elijah, Elizabeth, Harriet and Lorraine. My Uncles Jimmy and Willie, and Aunts Carrie Mae, Reather and Agnes were present too. The dining room table was loaded with fried chicken, potato salad, macaroni and cheese, smothered cabbage, collard greens and cornbread that the three aunts had prepared.

My sisters, cousins and I were children again. Seated at the dining room table, on the living room sofa, in occasional chairs, on radiator covers and on the stairs leading to the second floor, we stuffed ourselves with Aunt Carrie Mae's macaroni and cheese; annihilated Aunt Reather's butter pound cakes; and, gobbled down as much of Aunt Agnes' legendary sweet potato pies as we could hold before getting to the real action. With Gloria as the ringleader, we crammed Tupperware containers with leftovers.

We had secured our stashes in various corners of the house and settled into lazy conversation in the living room, when Aunt Agnes interrupted, "A whole sweet potato pie disappeared and it better show up back on that table!" The anger of our usually quiet and mild-mannered aunt sent a murmur around the room. "You know where the pie is?" "I haven't seen the pie." "Who got the pie?" In a second we were up and searching and that pie reappeared in no time.

Nobody saw her put it back, but Gloria whispered to me with a wink, "Whew! That was hot potatoes. I coughed that pie up; I don't want Aunt Agnes poking around and discovering what else I packed."

We had a big laugh and a much-needed sweet memory dropped into a very difficult day.

Mama took eternal flight and I sprouted wings in 1998. Beyond the knowledge that she loved me, I had learned important lessons about tenacity. Her response to hymns and scriptures taught me that survival depends on holding tight to faith at the height of life's storms. Her resilience declared that catastrophe need not end in collapse. Most of all I experienced with my own mother the joy MamMaw had described many years ago as "satisfaction and peace that flow from the very soul." I discovered small reasons to celebrate life because glorious years with Mama had buffed away charred areas of my soul and left a pure flame. A fire for service to others burned as never before.

Fight Jimmy Blake! "Fight is that brother's first name," MamMaw described my drive for social justice. Leave him alone she said to Bessie.

I could see why my wife wanted me to slow down. She had stopped working in 2001 and wanted us to spend time traveling together. I had promised to retire, but the pull of community and professional projects were too powerful. It was ironic; Bessie went to bed angry over what she dubbed my "cause of the day" while her mother cheered me on.

Late night conversations with MamMaw fueled many a journey to justice while Bessie sat home alone. Our children were all grown. Kanari and her husband, Charles, lived in New Jersey and both were educators. Shango was an assistant principal living in the Bronx with his wife, Ericka, and our five beautiful grandchildren: Ameer, Bilal, Nadirah, Na'im and Najah. RiShana and Takbir resided in Queens. Both had busy professionals lives—she as a college professor and he as a manager for Goodwill Industries' Workforce One.

Don't get me wrong, I received plenty of support from Bessie. Sometimes she volunteered enthusiastically and others times she was a reluctant political wife. On one occasion she cringed as she cruised through Laurelton while I sat in the back seat of the car blasting from my bullhorn: "Vote Blake! He gets the job done!" When we finished circling the community, I asked her to drop me at the Long Island Railroad Station. As a punishment, she drove slowly to the train nodding at neighbors who had Is-she-chauffeuring-Professor-Blake? looks on their faces. I was so embarrassed. I ducked down out of sight.

Though Bessie made frequent sacrifices in her role as political wife, the absolute worst fiasco occurred back in 1989 when I broke my promise to renew our marriage vows. That year, our twenty-fifth wedding anniversary fell on the first day to circulate petitions to qualify for the ballot as Democratic District Leader. Bessie had planned a ceremony deep in the woods of East Texas where her friends and relatives would gather in the family church to witness the wedding they had missed when we married in New York. Instead of fulfilling her dream, she spent a hot muggy morning climbing up and down stoops collecting signatures for my petitions.

By the afternoon, she was screaming into the phone: "I've been jilted! But, it's alright! I'll help him with this election! Then, I'm out of here!" Because MamMaw was thirteen hundred miles away, Bessie usually disciplined herself and refused to worry her mother with our marital disputes. However, her emotions were running raw when she made the rare angry call to Louisiana.

MamMaw listened patiently to the irate complaint then calmly asked, "How long did you say you been married?"

"Twenty-five years!" Bessie wailed.

"Ummm, twenty-five years, that is a long time."

"Yes, it is!"

"Twenty-five years," MamMaw repeated and after a considered pause added, "Why renew your vows? It seems to me they stuck the first time."

The simple logic of the response calmed Bessie instantly. Once again, Mam-Maw had smoothed a rough spot in my marriage.

Bessie's forgiving nature is one of the many traits I treasure about her. She forgave the anniversary slip-up and again allowed a soft landing for one of my many blunders. With scripture and by example, MamMaw had taught her to be gracious and show unmerited favor. In the spirit of godly love, my wife simply emptied her heart of malice and had mercy on me for jilting her. "Forgiveness," she said, "is not entirely for you; it's for me too. When I forgive, I don't have to carry the burden of anger. I am free to be myself—not the person someone else has twisted me into."

In applying Bible principles to daily living, Bessie has maintained the warm, caring, southern dignity that was revealed when I first met her. To this day, when I think home, I think Bessie. She continues to fulfill my deepest yearning for comfort and security. She understands my desires more than any other person on the planet.

Despite the bungled anniversary and her desire to ease into retirement, in my 2001 bid for the City Council, Bessie was by my side. For my campaign, she wrote speeches and press releases; designed placards and brochures; committed family finances to my cause; and, chauffeured me to numerous meetings, protests, courthouses, polling places as well as to various homes for "chat-and-chews." Her contributions bolstered me as a shoo-in frontrunner before the New York City elections became one of the smaller casualties of the 9-11 terror attack. During that tragic period when the city rocked with fear and grief, supposedly "secure" voting machines were left unattended for two weeks. When the elections were rescheduled, I was mysteriously trailing in the count.

Thankfully, the support of my biological and Woodycrest families soothed the pain of loss at the polls. Ruthie and Frances had made financial contributions. They had also showed up at the campaign headquarters to stuff envelopes alongside Miss Kellman, one of the social workers from Woodycrest, and Ernie Solis, a true brother to me. It had been gratifying to watch my two families blend together.

In addition to creating wonderful personal memories, the failed City Council bid sowed seeds of political success. Civic coalitions developed during my run for the City Council netted small but sweet victories. In 2002, I defeated the Queens County Democratic organization's candidate for Male District Leader. Over the course of my two year term, I expanded cross-community ties and helped establish and maintain the Harriet Tubman Regular Democratic Club. Among its stalwart supporters were Attorneys Fearonce (Ron) La Lande and Sidney Holmes (old buddies from Corona-East Elmhurst), Kim and Andrew Frances of the Concerned Citizens of Laurelton, Donald Whitehead of One Hundred Black Men of Queens, Ruth and Jim Wilkerson of The Eagles track team for youth, Etta Brown and Vashti Niles of Calvary Baptist Church; and, working feverishly from the Million Man/Woman March Coordinating Council were Sisters Nzingha Abina, Rosina Pou, Kathleen Boyce-Rollock, Pat Charles, Julet Borton, Clementine Robinson, and Vivian Stewart along with Brothers Richard Murphy, Joseph Jones and Dave Reeves. With the guidance of Audrey Bynoe, my BMCC colleague who had served as manager of my City Council campaign, our Democratic club offered workshops that outlined the nuts and bolts of election procedures in the hope of broadening participation in the political process.

In 2004, I ran for re-election but lost my position as District Leader. I took joy, however, in the victories of candidates supported by The Harriet Tubman Democratic Club.

With yet another election cycle behind me, Bessie focused again on my bloated schedule. "You got ten trains running; one of them is bound to crash," she referred to several projects at my job, to my political activities, and to the community programs that I ran. My head understood her annoyance, but a justice mission burned in my heart. I returned again and again to MamMaw for encouragement.

"You're doing a good work, Brother Blake" she consoled me in tranquil tones, except for the night spontaneous excitement broke loose in her voice: "Ooooo! People are going to read about you and everybody's going to understand that God has His hands on you!" Thirty-three years earlier, when MamMaw had foretold my coverage in the news, suddenly reporters and cameras from print and electronic media had sought me out for comments on topics about which I had only a casual knowledge. Before long they were featuring my community work on their programs and in their papers.

Back in October, 2000 *Newsday* ran a full page story under the headline, "His Is a Growing Family of Love." The article resulted from an honor bestowed by Representative Gregory Meeks who nominated me when asked by the Congressional Black Caucus to identify a family from his district to be acknowledged at the commemoration of the fifth anniversary of the Million Man March. Press coverage followed that inspired Bessie to write my life story. Perhaps MamMaw was speaking about this book when she again exclaimed in 2004, "Brother Blake, people are going to read about you!"

"No weapon that is formed against you is going to prosper, Brother Blake. God is working in your life," MamMaw soothed me with words of wisdom. I had developed the habit of calling Louisiana every night to talk her to sleep. She was seventy-six and tended to get restless at bedtime. "Is this the Sandman?" she would greet and I'd jumped right into a blow by blow account of my day.

"I confronted the President of the College today. I told him he needs to be removed. He's supposed to be helping students but he needs help himself. All I'm trying to do is reinstate an orientation requirement that helps students to understand college rules and regulations and prevents more of them from dropping out of school. For some misguided reason the president has ignored the Faculty Council, the Curriculum Committee, and research results that show the harm done to students who are the first in their families to go to college. He doggedly refuses to give credits for the orientation course like many schools with similar populations. Now, he's mounting a campaign to get rid of me."

With MamMaw's encouragement I continued to agitate for a required credit-bearing course that had a track record of positive results and against an ineffective non-credit Freshmen Year Experience Workshop where student attendance was voluntary.

I presented my case to over a hundred members of the Faculty Council where the president presided. He took his seat at the long table in the front of the room, reviewed the minutes of the last meeting and discussed old business. As soon as he called for new business, I jumped to my feet, "Mr. President, the College is engaged in a deception. It is morally reprehensible to tell students they are required to take the Freshmen Year Experience Workshop when that is not the case."

"Professor Blake, you're out of order," he shouted.

"This administration is out of order!" I turned my back on him and addressed the faculty. "What kind of message are we giving students when we tell them a lie about their academic program?"

Behind me, the president banged his hand against the tabletop, "Take your seat Professor Blake!"

"I'm not finished! This scandal will be brought to public light. We can't tell students that they are required to attend these workshops when it's not the truth."

"Sit down, Professor Blake!"

I ignored him. "If we show students that the College values the content of the workshops by awarding credit, they will attend and we won't have to lie."

"Quiet! Quiet!" the president raged in utter frustration before storming out of the room and slamming the door behind him. The faculty was stunned. All eyes were glued to the closed door. Seconds seemed to drift into minutes before the door slowly cracked. The president, with fury etched on his face, stepped out of the storage closet he had charged into and dashed across the room through the exit.

Within days, I received a letter accusing me of insubordination. I called MamMaw. "Brother Blake, don't grow weary in well doing," she prompted me to continue my effort to help students. As always, she prayed for me too.

The next Faculty Council session, I was back at it. I took a highly visible front row seat wearing a makeshift muzzle over my mouth. Actually, it was a dusk mask but it had the desired effect. Snickers went around the room. The president tried to ignore me and address the faculty but restrained chuckles broke into open laughter when I began to struggle to rip the mask from my face and free myself from the censorship imposed at the previous meeting.

My dramatization was not lost on faculty—the upholders of academic freedom and freedom of speech. At the end of the meeting scores of them signed a petition stating that I had not been insubordinate but had acted with the greatest advocacy and eloquence on behalf of my department and in the interest of students.

On hearing my report, MamMaw let out a mighty praise. "That's just what Jesus did," she exclaimed and told me how Jesus stood up to the Scribes and Pharisees, the scholars and self-righteous rulers of His day. "Oh, Brother Blake, you have a heart like His."

Today, I still fight for the little guy. More than forty years at BMCC and I continue to look beyond economic status, race, gender or other superficial disguises and see need. Daily, young people enter my office collapsing.

"I can't do this. I'm dropping out of school." The student sat across from my desk clasping her hands. "My instructor says we're going to be working with abused children. I can't do that. I've been in so many foster homes and when I was returned to my mother at the age of nine my uncle raped me. Now, I'm finally at peace with what happened. I don't want to relive all that pain. Besides, I don't even have a first name. On my birth certificate, it says 'Female Marino' (not the actual name of the student). I'm tired of having to explain to people that I was taken from my mother at birth. Ummmm," she moaned. "I'll just be a hooker on the streets."

"Stop it!" I commanded. "I'm not going to let you sit here and have a pity party! You haven't said one thing that's good about your life. You are enrolled in college; you kept your baby daughter and you're raising her. You're not on drugs; you are here. You are a survivor." She quieted down. "Now, about your name, have you tried to find out what your first name is so you can change your birth certificate?"

"Find out?   No. I don't know how to do that."

"Where were you born?"

"Monticello."

"Well, let's start with the child services agency in Monticello; every city has one.   Then, we'll look up court records for the year you were born.   A court order placed you in foster care.   Let's get to work, my sister."   She gave me a quizzical look. "I call you 'sister'," I told her, "because I grew up in different homes too."

Her eyes widened, "You?   Professor Blake?"

"Yes.   Me."

Female Marino and I booted up the computer and began the search for her identity.   She left my office with clues on how to research her name and a determination to stay in school.

I got up to go out for lunch and enjoy the crisp coolness of the early spring day.   When I opened my door, the shell of a human being stood before me.   He was soiled, stinking and twitching.   "You were right..." he started but staggered.   I grabbed him by the shoulder and guided him into a chair in my office.

With a person in his shape, I never mince words.   I gave it to him straight: "Brother, I see death in your face. In fact, it's all over you.   How long have you been putting that poison in your system?"

"For a while," he mumbled.   "Crack got me down. I'm trying to stop.   My life is slipping away.   I'm sleeping in the streets.   I haven't had a bath in... I don't know."   He twitched again.   "I just came by to see you 'cause when I was here you always told me things to help me.   I feel embarrassed to be in your office."

"You came to see me because you want to live. You're fighting.   You...

"I want to live," he cut me off, "but I don't know if I can make it. I just don't know." The twitching turned to trembling.

I leaned over my desk right into his face, "Chump!" I shouted. Look at me! You made it here because God brought you here. He wants you to live but you got to fight."

His lips curled into a twisted smile, "Ain't no chump, man," he half whispered and stopped shaking.

I laid it out for him. "You got to get off the streets because the streets will kill you. Go to a shelter. I don't care how bad it might be in there; you have to get off the streets." He nodded. "Afterwards, we have to talk about getting you back into school." A trace of excitement crossed his face. "But, two things you have to do right now! First, get off the streets and get yourself a bath. Second, stop using that poison."

I swung around to my computer and pulled up his transcript. He was in academic trouble but it could be resolved. "Here's the deal," I told him, "I'm going to work like hell to get you back in school but you have two weeks to get in a shelter and get that stuff out of your system. Come back, let me know you've done your part and I'll do my part."

He muttered as if talking to himself, "I'ma do it. I'm serious. I'ma do it."

Holding his gaze with a stern look, I summed up, "Brother, words plus actions equal results. If you do what you say, you'll be choosing life. If you don't, you're choosing death. It's that simple. God wants you to live; that's why He brought you here." I took him to the cafeteria and bought him some food.

Two days later, he was back at my door. I was with another student so I made it quick, "Hey Tony (again an assumed name), are you where you're supposed to be?"

"No, not yet," he answered shakily.

I stepped into the hallway and pulled him to the side, "Man, I told you don't come here until you have some results! The devil is kicking your tail and you want to rehearse what we already know. Until you get some courage to step up to that devil, don't come back." I walked off like I was angry but out of the corner of my eye I saw him stumble away. I whispered a prayer for his strength. I knew he had to move beyond just hearing and become a doer of the words he and I had shared.

By summer, Tony had stopped shaking. His face had life in it. "I'm in a men's shelter and I haven't had anything since I saw you," he beamed. "I'm finished with that stuff. I'm doing it, Professor Blake."

I got up from my desk and hugged him. "Brother you look like brand new money. Oooh, the devil is angry."

"Yeah, that devil keeps coming back and I say 'Get on outta here; ain't nothing here for you.'"

"He can't get a piece of you?"

"Naaaaw."

"Now, the next time he comes up to you, here's what you do, take that devil, throw him under your feet and stomp him. With each step squash him. The devil only has the power you give him. He's a bully and you know how a bully is, brother. A bully preys on the weak. There use to be this fellow on my block who took everybody's money but when he came to me I looked him straight in the eyes and didn't blink. That chump had to keep it moving and find somebody weak. That's the way the devil is; he can't deal with strength."

"That's deep," grunted Tony.

"You know what?" I continued. "When I see the devil, I'm so confident in God's power, I ball up my fist and yell, 'Take this sucker!' and he flees." We both burst out laughing and I knew that Tony would be okay.

Richard, a member of the EORO (Each One Reach One) mentoring program, entered my office just as Tony was leaving. I introduced them and in the exchange I reinforced the EORO (pronounced EeeRow) message of giving back.

EORO was started Fall 2006 as one of the positive results of reaching out to a group of BMCC students who were doing well academically, despite multiple hardships. I had enlisted the assistance of my colleague, Audrey Bynoe, in forming the Honor Society of Black Student Scholars. We helped the Student Government Association to organize a banquet that celebrated individual student achievement and, at the same time, highlighted successful role models for other Black students—especially males like Tony.

An alarming decline in Black male college enrollment had caused City University of New York to start a Black Male Initiative. Though BMCC had not been funded for a program, I urged students at the Scholars' banquet: "Don't wait. Each of you can do something to reverse this appalling trend. You don't have to wait for funding. Sitting here in this room is the cream of the academic crop. I'm proud of you but I would be remiss if I didn't remind you that responsibility comes with accomplishment. You don't have to wait to graduate to make a difference. Each one of you can reach back and help one of your brothers to succeed in college. Be a mentor. You have the knowledge and you are an example of what's possible. Don't let another brother have a revolving door experience: admitted to college today, dismissed tomorrow."

Inspired by those words, three student government leaders—Curtis Brown, Horace Henry, and Michelle Pierre—requested and received student government funding to start a Black Male Initiative at BMCC.

Michelle also recruited honor scholars as volunteers and kept track of administrative paperwork and details necessary to launch the EORO peer-mentoring program.

In the process of getting the program off the ground, I was reminded why life is formed in secret. Plants incubate as seeds in the earth and human beings in the darkness of the womb because there is a human tendency to pick apart new creations before they are fully formed. In the case of EORO, critics in the BMCC administration attempted to abort the program as it was taking shape. They said I cared only about Black students.

"That's your interest," one self-serving administrator nodded at the oil on canvas hanging behind my desk that proclaimed in bold letters "Apartheid is wrong!" She didn't know that a White student had painted it after being inspired to examine the environments of exclusion that he and his peers of all ethnic backgrounds were creating. Disgusted by their behavior, I had taken students to task: "You separate yourselves according to race. Here in the cafeteria, you have clusters of Latinos, Indians, Asians, Caucasians and Blacks. Then, it gets ridiculous because each group sub-divides at tables based on whether you are Italian or Jewish, Chinese or Korean, Puerto Rican or Dominican, Black American or Caribbean. When I went to school in the South there was forced legal apartheid, but here at BMCC, you choose to separate yourselves. Apartheid is wrong no matter how it's formed." I had ended my comments with the call, "Apartheid" and the students responded with a resounding, "is wrong!"

Of course, the remark about my exclusive devotion to Black students was false. Students and staff were well aware of my history with diverse groups. Over the years I had served as advisor to a variety of student clubs and to the Student Government Association whether the leadership was Asian, Caribbean, Latino, African or

African American. Black, White or green, it didn't matter. I had organized a Black-Jewish dialogue between Yeshiva University and BMCC students; advocated for handicap students; facilitated the integration of Eastern European and Russian students into the life of the college. I had a well-established record of helping anybody with a problem.

The administrator who complained of my exclusive commitment to Black students was aware of my many multi-cultural undertakings and she definitely knew of the Tolerance and Diversity Committee. The goal of the committee was to defuse racial tensions stemming from an alleged attack by drunken White students and other patrons of a local bar on Black members of the basketball team as they headed to a nearby subway station.

Instead of helping with efforts to bring students together, the disgruntled administrator circulated malicious remarks suggesting any program coming out of our multi-ethnic, multi-racial committee of faculty and students would be "pro-Black." Despite this obvious attempt at sabotage, the committee held effective forums on race relations; assembled a successful cross-cultural expo; and, hung more than sixty national flags that waved in the main lobby proudly announcing the many ethnic groups represented in the college community.

Bessie, my greatest debater and best critic, thought the cultural exchange series was wonderful, but as she had done with the VIP program, she forced me to look beyond the terms used to the goals sought. "Jimmy," she said, "I don't like the use of the phrase 'tolerance and diversity.' It points to cultural and racial differences in a way that suggests that diversity is to be tolerated rather than embraced."

She was right. During the 1960s civil rights movement, the term tolerance was adopted as a compromise. There were those who appealed to the decency of all human beings and believed we could be swayed to do right regardless of race; and those who said you can't change people's hearts but you can legislate their behavior. Martin Luther King, Jr. employed Bible principles: love thy neighbor as thyself. The courts enforced laws to achieve a certain level of civil behavior, and the idea, "tolerance," was popularized. Fifty years later, we are still tolerating one another. Tolerance implies putting up with someone or something that is irritating. Strain is inherent in the word.

I agreed with Bessie. It all boils down to "Love thy neighbor as thyself." If we embrace diversity in a spirit of love maybe we won't keep falling short of the goal of racial harmony. Our committee wanted to foster respect for cultural differences that were represented in the college community. The phrase "Harmony in Diversity" or "Embracing Diversity" would have implied acceptance, respect, appreciation and partnership among people of different backgrounds. I thought about changing the title of the program, but there was no time to build committee consensus.

I must also admit that I had been ready to confront the complaining administrator, but reflections on harmony cooled me out. Divisive ploys aimed at me, but really intended to advance my colleague's career, did not cause me to lose my focus. The University had identified Black males as the neediest group of students, and I had not shied away from my brothers because a few self-serving individuals pointed accusing fingers.

I steered Michelle around administrative land mines, and with printouts from the registrar, Greg Wist, I matched twenty probationary students with twenty Black male honor students. EORO was born. The venture took its first wobbly steps with the support of committed professionals such as Ardie DeWalt, Mike Giammarella,

Frank Elmi, Irma Fernandez, Isabel Cummings, Ed Bostick, Beryl Duncan-Wilson, Adrienne Faison, Emily Anderson, Frederick Reese, Vinton Melbourne and, of course, Audrey Bynoe, co-advisor to the Student Government Association.

Impressed by the results of EORO, in the spring of 2007, the University funded a Black Male Initiative at B.M.C.C. To celebrate our accomplishments, twenty young Black men (mentors and mentees) got dressed in suits and ties and broke bread together at the Baton Rouge restaurant in Harlem.

"Whoa!" "You brothers look good!" Men on 145th and 7th lit up with pride and slid their wine bottles behind their backs as we exited the subway. The students poked their chests out and Keon exclaimed, "Professor Blake, it feels good to be a Black man!" At dinner, Phillip Berry— former BMCC student and Vice Chair of the City University Board of Trustees addressed the group. He spoke of his achievements as a business man and told students to strengthen their knowledge of self. At the same time, he admonished them to expand their boundaries by getting to know other cultures and languages.

Riding on the success of its first year, by the fall of 2008, EORO was in high gear. When Tony returned to his studies, in addition to regular visits to my office, he was supported in his social adjustment and academic endeavors by young scholars who chose every semester to heed the call to give back to fellow students.

EORO mentors were from various religious persuasions, but all were guided by the spiritual principle that we are the same in the sight of God who has no favorites. They realized that their good academic standing could be overturned in just one semester of difficult circumstances. With a lack of arrogance and a genuine humility they helped their fellow students.

I have often heard people say, "God helps those who help themselves" and that might be true but I have discovered that God also helps those who help others. Matter of fact, the scripture says that it is more blessed to give than to receive.

I can't count the number of student mentors who seek me out to say that they get more from the mentoring experience than the students they are helping. They describe their volunteer work in EORO as the singular most rewarding experience of college life.

God's grace and mercy have dramatically altered my life. It does not matter that I started from a place of disadvantage. With faith and determination, I have soared beyond what I thought possible. In 2007, my friend Ron La Lande, then president of the Macon B. Allen Black Bar Association, invited me to be the keynote speaker at a special commemoration of African American History Month. Though my beginnings were in children's homes where courtroom judges placed me, I addressed a lofty group of lawyers and judges—decked out in black robes in the chambers of Chief Justice Leach of the Jamaica Supreme Court. A few days afterwards, Justice Leech wrote to me: "Our court employees and the jurors in attendance, like myself, were captivated by your remarks. Clearly you had a story to tell and made us feel as though we were there." His words signified to me that I had conquered the forces that marshaled me into Jamaica Family Court and the shelter as a frightened boy. This is not to say that I am completely transformed, but I have made small changes that make a big difference in the quality of my life as well as in the lives of others.

For the whole of my life, helping others has been my saving grace. I really should not be here but people who need help excite me to action. People who are bored puzzle me. There is too much pain in the world to sit idly asking, "What can I do?" Act! Do something! Hold the system accountable for its wrongs. If you make a mistake, make it trying to do the right thing. That's how I still battle abuse, injustice, and inequality wherever I find it. I try to squeeze enough oil from my pain to heal others. In the process, I am gradually learning that there is emptiness in my life that only God can fill.

Back in college my favorite instrument in the chemistry lab was the Bunsen burner because its flames broke down solid objects that no chemical could dissolve. Today, when I encounter hardness in administrators, drug dealers, and corrupt systems, like a Bunsen burner I release fire. For a long time I thought I was igniting the flame but I now know without a doubt that God is the power fueling my actions. That is why I advise people in crisis to pray. Prayer causes us to confront human frailties. When we pray, we recognize that God is the Powerful One. With this realization, we stop berating our failures and inflating our successes and we gain a greater understanding of the shortcomings of others.

With all my imperfections, God flows through me. Often I forget this truth, but The Almighty has a way of getting my attention. He appears in my dreams because my guard is always up when I am awake. After millions of misty-eyed stories, Bessie yawns and shakes her head, "No," when I wake up chirping, "I had a dream last night." But, I hope you will hear me out because I am burning to tell someone about this dream:

> *God treads over the landscape carrying a huge globe. I trot behind Him trying to help hold up the world. God looks over his shoulder at me, "The burden is mine not yours," He says. I let go but in a few steps I'm back trying to help Him. God repeats, "The burden is mine not yours." I quickly take my hand away. The third time He glances over His shoulder, my palm is pressed firmly against the*

globe. God lets go and the weight of the world flattens me like a cartoon character.

I awake with a smile. Again, God shows me that He is the fire; I am merely one of His Bunsen burners. Thanks to His Grace, the fire burning inside of me is released in my work with others. I have learned to put my trust in the Creator rather than the created and He uses me to bring hope to the hopeless. I stand with dignity in the middle of storms because I don't fear men. I fear God.

I still believe that words plus actions equal results but my mantra, the phrase I chant to myself is: "Trust in the Lord and do good." I encourage all who come to me for counseling to have faith that they will get through the pain and turmoil of their circumstances, and in the meantime, help somebody. That's what I do. As long as there are voices in the dark, I will be on my post.

Oh, before I go, allow me to share a brief poetic and pictorial history of my family.

My son Takbir—now married to his beautiful wife, Fritza, and the father of two sons, Noah James and Matthew Joseph—sums up my story in a Father's Day tribute:

> *I've seen many things:*
> *My mother spread her wings*
> *And plunged into my heart.*
> *That's how my journey started.*
>
> *Naked eyes roved down*
> *Paths that looked unbearable.*
> *Ripped from family,*
> *Abandoned in homes,*

A young man burning to belong,
I kept strong.

Sick mother, oppressed father,
Distant siblings:
Physically separated,
But spiritually linked.

Now, I'm older, wiser,
Realize the only reason
I survived the cold
Is because You, God,
Lit a fire in my soul.

For those who like to picture-read, here is brief glimpse of my life:

1950s:

Mama, Nettie Toomer Blake,
picnics at Pilgrim State Hospital
with daughter, Ruth.

Daddy, Joseph Blake, Sr.

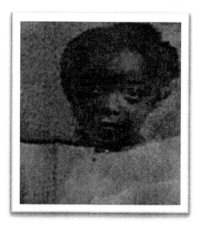

Gloria's 5th grade-school
photo at P.S. 143 Q

Granny, Essie Toomer

(l-r): Aunt Constance, son,
Butch and Uncle Lawrance
Toomer

(l-r): Wilbur, Aunt Reather
and Geraline Toomer

Sister, Carol (front row, 2nd from left) graduates Hillcrest Jr. High.

Woodycrest orphanage, 936 Woodycrest Avenue, Bronx, NY.

Plate currently installed in front of the Woodycrest building denotes its history.

1960s:

I graduate high school in 1960 and meet Bessie Waites in 1963.

Bessie and I marry in 1964.

Daddy, me (center) and brother Joseph (right) in 1965

(l-r) Cousin, Lydia Toomer, sisters, Frances, and Ruthie pose with me at 1964 World Fair.

My Buddy, Sam Greene

1970s:

Blake family, 1970

Blake children, 1977

**My brother, Joseph and
nephew, Eddie**

My brother, Kenneth

Seated is Gloria's husband, Tyrone; standing, (l-r)
are my sisters, Ruth and Gloria, and me.

Bessie and I entertain North Carolina Central University friends,
(l-r) William Mitchel, Warren Harris and Harold Fowler.

Along with faculty and students, I protest at President's Office for a Black Studies Department at BMCC, and then...

was led (above) to police vans (below).

1980s:

"Blake Gets The Job Done"

The above poster depicts some of my community projects.
Clockwise from top left: I serves as community liaison with local
police precinct; work with civic organizations to address drainage
and other problems of blight; coordinate youth pride and
community clean up days; and, as president of the local Chamber
of Commerce, I work with local merchants.

1990s:

With my aunt,
Carrie Mae Toomer Blake

With Rosa Parks in D. C.

Left, I am pictured with co-chair, Sister Abena Nzingha, of the
Million Man/Woman March of Queens. Above right, my grandson,
Ameer, and I at the annual *Fathers With Their Families March*
initiated on the first anniversary of the Million Man March.

Above left: I pose with Bishop Desmond Tutu and Sister Dorothy Ann Kelly, President of the College of New Rochelle, after a panel discussion on apartheid. Above right: Bessie, Gordon Parks and I chat with students at the opening of a gallery she established in his name.

Gil Noble, host of ABC's *Like It Is*, poses with me after taping a segment about my life.

New millenium, 2000s:

Above left: In 2001, I declare   my candicacy for the New York City Council with the support of Councilwoman Juanita Watkins (to my left), Queens Borough President Helen Marshall (to my right), and my grandchildren (clockwise) Nadirah, Ameer, Na'im in my arms, and Bilal.

I campaign with New York Senatorial Canditate Hillary Clinton.

A growing family of love...

With my mother-in-law, Evang.
Tommie Waites, Christmas 2004

I meet cousin Wessie Williams
in 2008 and discover   a new
branch of my family.

My cousin, Bill McQuarry of *Positively Black*, and I serve as co-chairs of
the annual dinner dance of the Million Man/Woman March of Queens.
Above left, we pose with honored guests. Above right, Bessie's and my
grandchildren pose in our living room. Front center: Na'im and Najah;
back row (l-r), Ameer holding Noah, Nadirah, and Bilal holding Matthew.

About the Author

Photo by Ruth Blake Groneveldt

God's Bad Boy is Dr. Bessie W. Blake's second book. Her first book, *Speak to the Mountain,* received a USA Book News national Best Book Award in 2007.

About Lit Lore

Lit is that which is guided or conducted by light. It means to be illuminated or ignited. Lore is experience, wisdom, tradition and knowledge about a subject. In keeping with its root meanings, **Lit Lore** is a literary press that publishes non-fiction and fiction that cultivates deeper understandings of diverse human conditions.